P9-AGH-991

Construction
Forms & Contracts

by Craig Savage & Karen Jones-Mitchell

Includes inside the back cover:
3½" computer disk with all 125 forms, in *WordPerfect, Word for Windows, Lotus, Excel* and *ASCII* formats to customize for your own use.

Craftsman Book Company
6058 Corte del Cedro / P.O. Box 6500 / Carlsbad / CA 92018

Looking for other
construction reference manuals?

Craftsman has the books to fill your needs. Call toll-free **1-800-829-8123** or
write to Craftsman Book Company, P.O. Box 6500, Carlsbad, CA 92018 for
a **FREE CATALOG** of books, estimating manuals and computer software.

Library of Congress Cataloging-in-Publication Data
Savage, Craig 1947-
     Construction forms & contracts / by Craig Savage & Karen Jones-Mitchell
        p.   cm.
     ISBN 0-934041-85-7
     1. Construction contracts--United States--Forms. I. Jones
-Mitchell, Karen. II. Title. III. Title: Construction forms and contracts.
KF902.A3S28   1994
343.73'07869'00269--dc20   94-19326
[347.303786900269]   CIP

Contents (by category)

■ Field Forms

■ General Office Forms

■ Installation Instructions   333

■ Applications Directory   341

■ Contractor's BBS   421

■ Index   428

Contents (by form & file name)

Construction Forms & Contracts

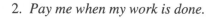

Give a contractor three wishes and you'll probably get three requests:

1. *Just leave me alone and let me do my work.*

2. *Pay me when my work is done.*

3. *Save me from all this paperwork!*

Between us, we've got 40 years as contractors under our belts. We know how you feel. And we agree, especially with the third request. Paperwork never built anything. In fact, paperwork keeps you from building. It inflates your overhead, drains away the valuable time of key people and increases the complexity of what's way too complex already.

So, you ask, why would any construction contractor want *Construction Forms & Contracts*? That's easy. We'll explain.

Think about it for a minute. Exactly why do you hate paperwork?

When we ask that question at seminars and trade shows, we get all the obvious answers. There are probably as many good reasons to hate paperwork as there are construction contractors. But nearly all come down to one point:

It's a waste of time.

So why do it? Glance at the top of this page again. Read the first two requests on every contractor's wish list: Remember "Let me build!" and "Pay me on time!" That's why you do paperwork. You're never going to get either wish until the paperwork is done.

This book addresses Wish 1 and Wish 2 by simplifying and systematizing Wish 3. That's our point in a nutshell. You'll have more time for productive work and get paid sooner if paperwork stops being a burden and becomes a breeze. That's the purpose of this book.

If you don't believe that paperwork can be simplified, keep reading. You're in for some surprises.

True enough, this is a book of forms. Nearly every contract and form you're going to need is here ready for reproduction on your copy machine. We've developed these 125 forms for our own company and have used them for many years. They're good. They're complete. They're going to save you time day after day. By themselves, they're worth the price of the book.

But that's just the beginning if you have:

▼ A computer, and

▼ A printer.

With that combination and the disk inside the back cover of this book, you're going to be a paperwork wizard. With any of the modern spreadsheet or word processing programs, you can open these forms on your screen and customize them to fit your needs exactly:

▼ Change the column headings or row widths.

▼ Add your company name and address.

▼ Delete what doesn't suit your operation.

▼ Add whatever you feel is missing.

If you know how to use any of the popular word processing or spreadsheet programs, you'll have no trouble using the forms disk in the envelope in the back of this book. Beginning on page 333 you'll find instructions for loading and using the forms with any of the popular word processing or spreadsheet programs. Even if you don't have a word processing or spreadsheet program, you'll be able to open these forms, make changes on the screen, then print the revised form on your printer.

What's the Advantage to You?

Just like a nail gun automates nailing, this disk is going to automate your paperwork.

Your time will be the biggest saving. But you'll save money, too. The cost of duplicating forms yourself is peanuts compared to the cost of custom-designed forms purchased from a forms vendor. Expect savings of at least several hundred dollars a year.

In short, your company is going to have the most professional, easiest to use, most complete set of accounting, estimating, contracting and field reporting forms available anywhere.

Why You Need Good Forms

Most construction tradesmen learn by watching others. For example, apprentice carpenters learn to set a nail before driving it. But for many, it takes a good whack on the thumb to bring the lesson home. Painful mistakes can be the best teachers.

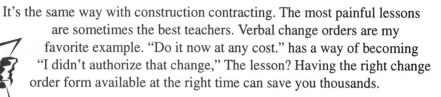

It's the same way with construction contracting. The most painful lessons are sometimes the best teachers. Verbal change orders are my favorite example. "Do it now at any cost." has a way of becoming "I didn't authorize that change," The lesson? Having the right change order form available at the right time can save you thousands.

Here's another example. Until your first workers' compensation audit, you probably didn't understand the importance of good payroll records. Afterwards, you'll never forget. Another painful lesson learned: Find and use good time cards and payroll ledgers.

We could go on and on. But we're sure you're getting the point. Most mistakes in the construction contracting business teach the same lesson: Either use good forms and keep good records or get out of the business.

Why Care About Forms?

We can think of at least five great reasons to use the forms in this book. Test yourself. See how many of these reasons make sense to you:

1. Good forms protect your company.

For example, collecting for extra work is a sore point with most of the construction contractors we know. Make it your policy that no extra work is started without a signed change order. A signed work order leaves no wiggle room when it comes time to get paid.

Consider making a written purchase order part of your procurement process. That should eliminate bills that exceed the quoted cost.

2. Good forms give your business a professional image.

A good paint job makes your finished product look great. Good forms, embellished with your company logo, give your business a sharper image and a real competitive advantage. They put you in the major leagues with construction professionals who know the importance of making the best possible presentation.

Some contractors can make a living writing estimates on the back of business cards and scratching out bills on napkins. But you're never going to make it that way with professional business people. It just isn't done. The people you want as clients are accustomed to professional business practice. That means you have to use good quality forms.

Clients who get an estimate, a proposal, a change order and progress billings on forms created in the same style know that you've got your act together. Good professional forms imply a real permanence to your business. Your company is more than a pickup truck and an answering machine. It's a quality, professional operation.

Few clients will ever see your office. But nearly all will see the contracting, estimating or accounting forms you use. Many will judge your competence (at least initially) by the quality of the paperwork you provide. Don't disappoint them.

3. *Good forms, used properly, create order where there had been construction chaos.*

Forms reduce errors and oversights. They force you to list, schedule, record, deduct, add, and follow procedures and checklists. That creates consistency and accountability. It extends your direct control to everyone in your company. No creativity is required. Just follow instructions on the form and everything will fall into place. Forms make automatic what might otherwise require regular supervision.

4. *Forms create a paper trail showing what happened and when.*

Your forms create a permanent record that's available weeks, months or even years after the fact. That makes it harder for others to shift blame or legal responsibility onto your shoulders. The higher the value of the work you do and the greater your work volume, the more important good records will become.

5. *Finally, good forms level the playing field.*

The contract form you use does make a difference. We've seen "standard" contracts so one-sided that no builder could make a dime. There's no reason why every dispute has to be resolved in favor of an owner. Don't get suckered into signing contracts like that. Offer to provide your own contract forms — the forms in this book. They're fair and reasonable.

125 Essential Forms

The forms you find here are those most commonly needed in a construction office. For your convenience, we've divided them into five major categories:

1. Accounting

2. Contracts

3. Estimating

4. Field

5. General Office

Each form is accompanied by a description of how the form should be filled out and used. We feel that this description is just as important as the form itself.

Not every form will be precisely right for every company. In some cases, we've provided several forms that serve the same general purpose. You'll have to decide which form fits your operation the best. For example, there are four time cards. Read the summary that accompanies each time card to determine which one of the four is best for your operation.

Some forms may not apply to your business at all. Others may not be appropriate at this time. Don't feel like you need to use a form just because it's here.

The balance between too much paperwork and too little is a matter of personal preference. Our inclination is to use too many forms rather than too few. If the living room is painted the wrong color and the kitchen is flat instead of gloss, you've got a fight on your hands. That's too late to have a client initial a color schedule for the paint contractor. It's much cheaper and easier to give the right form to a client and then pass that form to your paint subcontractor. Take that little step. Put your form to work. Lock down the colors and textures and save yourself the grief.

Construction Forms on Paper

If you don't have a computer, make form copies with any copy machine. Just slap the form you need down on the copier and copy away. Most forms intended for use out of your office have a place for your company name, address and phone number. Before running off any copies, paste your business card in the place reserved for your name and address.

A thick business card can create a shadow line around the card on each copy. If that happens, copy your business card onto thinner paper and paste that copy on the master. If you still get a shadow line, reduce the copier's contrast adjustment slightly. If that doesn't eliminate the problem, try painting white-out fluid around the edges of the pasted-on piece. Eventually you'll get usable results.

Some of the forms can be partially filled out before they're copied. Enter information that stays constant from job to job before you do any duplication.

The forms in this book should reproduce reasonably well on any good copier. Experiment with the contrast control and alignment to get best results.

Print quality will be better if you cut the form out of this book and give it to an instant printer for duplication. Be sure to add your business name and company logo to the form. Or select a printer who will set type for your company name and address at no cost.

Those forms most likely to be filled out with a typewriter have spacing that works correctly with the standard carriage return on most typewriters. Forms intended for use in the field (such as checklists and time cards) have larger spaces between lines. There's enough room for writing with a carpenter's pencil or keel marker. Fax forms have been stylized for easy reading once they're transmitted.

Once you've made copies of several forms, organization will be important. We suggest dedicating one file drawer for storage of blank forms. Put one manila folder in this drawer for each form you plan to use. Label these file folders with the form name and put the folders in alphabetical order. Storage in a file drawer keeps these forms readily available at all times.

Construction Forms on Disk

If your company is one of the growing majority that have joined the computer revolution, the disk in the envelope inside the back cover will be more valuable than the tree that had to be destroyed to put this sheaf of paper in your hand.

Each of the forms in this book is on the disk — in five formats. Why put each form on disk five times? Easy. Because the nerds who write computer programs haven't adopted a uniform method of storing graphics on disk. To be reasonably sure that you can use these forms, our publisher created five versions of each form. The version you use depends on the word processing or spreadsheet program you prefer. Here are the five versions you can select from:

▼ **Excel** if you use Excel 4 or Excel 5 or Quattro Pro for Windows or Claris Works for Windows.

▼ **Word for Windows** if you use Word for Windows 2 or Word 6.

▼ **WordPerfect** if you use WordPerfect 5.1 or 5.2 for DOS, WordPerfect for Windows, AmiPro 3 for Windows or WordPerfect for OS/2.

▼ **Lotus 1-2-3** if you use Lotus 1-2-3 for Windows or DOS.

▼ **ASCII** if you use WordStar 2000 or if you don't have any of the programs listed above.

You can reproduce these forms (on your printer) just the way they look in the book. Even better, you can customize each form so it meets your needs exactly. Cut out what you don't need and paste in what's required to make the form perfect for your company. The more capable your word processing or spreadsheet program, the more you can do.

You should have no trouble redesigning any of these forms to fit your style of doing business. Try importing your company's logo or letterhead and pasting it on several of the forms — creating instant stationery that's available whenever you need it.

Having the forms on computer means that you can print small quantities when only small quantities are needed. The savings in printing and storage costs will be substantial. When your address or phone number changes, modify the form in a minute or two, not after using up the last of that 5000 print run. And if you want to look like a remodel company to some clients and a custom home builder to others, it's a cinch to change the form and print a few dozen copies of each form type.

Each of the forms is stored on disk as a single file. But you may prefer merging several forms into one larger file that prints as a single document. That's handy when the same forms are needed every time you start a new job. If you have one of the more capable word processing or spreadsheet programs, consider merging the forms on your hard disk in the order you'll need them:

▼ Preliminary Job Survey first

▼ Proposals next

▼ Billings, etc.

▼ Finally, the client questionnaire that's sent at the end of the job

Using a combination of computerized custom forms and copied standard forms will probably be most efficient. For example, create a customized master time card with your favorite word processing or spreadsheet program. Print one copy with your laser or ink jet printer. Then run off lots more with any copy machine.

You'll print one-of-a-kind forms (such as contracts) only when needed and specifically for a particular job. The same will probably be true for invoices and progress billings.

A Word of Caution

We're not lawyers. We're construction contractors. The forms in this book haven't been reviewed for legal content and may not comply with laws in all states. Your best source of advice on the law will always be legal counsel familiar with the law in the communities where you do business.

Need a Mac Disk?

A *Construction Forms & Contracts* disk is also available for the Macintosh computer. Send your check for $15 to Craftsman Book Company, 6058 Corte del Cedro, Carlsbad, CA 92009. Or you can order on your credit card by calling 619-438-7828.

Accounting Forms

Purchase Order

File Name on Disk: PURCHASE

Accounting in construction is often done on a cash basis. But any contractor who wants to know where the business stands at any time needs to use an accrual accounting system. The Purchase Order (PO) is an essential form for accrual accounting because it records the purchase when it happens, not when the invoice is received.

When you buy the windows for a job, you owe the money when you place the order, not when you get around to paying the bill. That's how accrual accounting works. When you owe the money, you record the obligation. The purchase order is the first link in that chain.

Purchase orders are also labor and material control documents. Suppliers can be notified not to accept a material order without an accompanying PO number. Subs can be informed to begin work only after they receive a purchase order. No PO authorization, no work.

The PO also can be matched against the invoice when materials are delivered. Be sure the price quoted on the PO is the same as the price that appears on the invoice. Some accounting systems make you issue a change order when the PO doesn't match the invoice.

Finally, the PO is a tool for job costing. The POs generated for a job accurately reflect the job cost. Use them to enter the "actual" costs in any job cost sheet.

How to Use This Form

You issue the PO to the company providing the material or service. There's space for the date, PO number, and if you use them, a requisition number. The "ship to" address can be the job site or your warehouse.

The next section has spaces to describe who is making the order, when the expected shipping date is, how it is to be shipped and the FOB point. (FOB stands for free on board.) From that point to the point of installation, you will be responsible for freight charges and damage.

Terms describes how payments will be made and when they are due.

The last and largest section describes the material ordered: *Quantity ordered, Quantity received, Stock no./description, Unit price,* and *Total.*

You'll probably need to provide copies of the PO for the department making the purchase, the accounting department, and the warehouse, yard or job site where delivery is expected.

Purchase Order

Construction Company
Address
City, State, ZIP
Phone Number

Date: _____

PO number: _____

Vendor: _____

Project name: _____

Requisition number _____

Ship to:

_____

_____

_____

_____

Ordered by	Ship date	Ship via	FOB point	Terms	

Quantity ordered	Quantity received	Stock number and description	Unit price	Total

1. Please send_____copies of your invoice.
2. Order to be entered in accordance with price, delivery, and specification shown above.
3. Notify us immediately if you are unable to ship as specified.

Authorized Signature: _____

Fax Purchase Order

File Name on Disk: FAXEDPO

The Fax Purchase Order is nearly identical to the standard purchase order. The primary difference is that the fax PO includes several items that should appear on a fax, like the number of pages. Use a fax to get the purchase order confirmed immediately.

How to Use This Form

This fax version is filled out just like the regular version. You issue it to the company providing the material or service. There's a line for the date, and if you're using them, a requisition number. The "ship to" address can be the job site or your warehouse.

The next section has spaces to describe who is making the requisition, the expected shipping date, how it is to be shipped and the FOB point. If you're not going to pay for shipping, the FOB point should be the job address or your supply yard. *Terms* describe how payment will be made.

The last and largest section is for material descriptions: the quantity ordered, quantity received, stock number and description, the unit price and the extension total.

Depending on how you're using the purchase order, you'll need copies for the department making the purchase, the accounting department, and the warehouse, yard or job site.

Fax Purchase Order

Construction Company
Address
City, State, ZIP
Phone Number

Date: _____

Owner: _____

Contractor: _____

Project name: _____

Requisition number: _____

Vendor:

_____

_____

_____

Ship to:

_____

_____

_____

Requisition by	When ship	Ship via	FOB point	Terms

Quantity ordered	Quantity received	Stock number and description	Unit price	Total

1. Please send_____copies of your invoice.
2. Order to be entered in accordance with price, delivery, and specification shown above.
3. Notify us immediately if you are unable to ship as specified.

Signature: _____

Total number of pages including this page_____.
If you do not receive all pages, please contact us.

Progress Billing, Time and Materials

File Name on Disk: PROBIL1

We've included two types of progress billing forms. Use this version to bill time and materials contracts. However, if you typically work and bill on a lump sum contract basis, go on to the second progress billing form.

How to Use This Form

This is a rather complicated form. It can be completed by hand, of course. But using a computer with a spreadsheet program will save time and prevent most clerical errors.

Start with the *Contract item (task description)* and the *Budget amount*. In most cases, both pieces of data come from either an estimate or an itemized proposal that you filled out earlier. If you're using a computer, filling out a progress billing form is a snap. You simply cut and paste (or link) the information straight from the estimate or proposal.

If the original budget amount either increases or decreases, enter the new amount in the *Revised budget* column.

The first time you use the Progress Billing, the *Previous billing* column will be empty (since you haven't billed anything yet). Fill it in for the second and all subsequent billings with a running total of all the previous billings. (If you're using a computer, you can link the two cells together so the *Previous billing* sum is automatically brought forward to the appropriate cell in the current form.)

The *Balance to finish* column tracks the amount due when the work's complete. Calculate it by adding *Previous billing* for each item to *This billing* and subtracting the total from *Budget amount* (or *Revised budget* if it's filled in).

The *% complete* column is calculated as a percentage of the *Budget amount*. Add the costs from *Previous billing* and *This billing* and divide by the *Budget amount*.

The bottom section of this Progress Billing form starts with a *Subtotals* row. In most cases, the figure in the *Budget amount* column remains constant – while the *Revised budget* column shows how and if changes affect the budget. Incidentally, it's good accounting practice to double-check your work by "cross footing" the subtotals row. Add together *Previous billing, This billing*, and *Balance to finish*. The result should equal either the *Budget amount* or the *Revised budget*. The next three rows, *Contingency, Overhead & supervision* and *Profit*, are calculated from the subtotal amounts. The *Total contract costs*, the bottom row, is the sum of the subtotal and the three add-on percentages.

Progress Billing

Construction Company
Address
City, State, ZIP
Phone Number

Invoice number: _____

Date: _____

Owner: _____

Address: _____

City, State, ZIP: _____

Job name: _____

Item no.	Contract item (task description)	Budget amount	Revised budget	Previous billing	This billing	Balance to finish	% complete
1							
2							
3							
4							
5							
6							
7							
8							
9							
10							
11							

Subtotals: _____

Contingency _____ %: _____

Overhead & supervision _____ %: _____

Profit _____ %: _____

Total contract costs: _____

Progress Billing, Lump Sum Contract

File Name on Disk: PROBIL2

Use this billing form for lump sum contracts. This progress billing form is based on the allocation of draws specified in the contract. For instance, if your contract calls for half payment on completion of a certain task, then you use this form to bill your client for 50 percent of the total amount.

Both progress billing forms feature the same columns. However, this version ends with a simple *Totals* row. If you need to list and calculate any add-on percentages, for such things as contingency, overhead and supervision, and profit, you should use the first progress billing form.

How to Use This Form

You'll save time and prevent errors by using a computer and spreadsheet program to complete this form. Fill in the columns beginning with *Contract item (task description)* through to *% complete* the same way as in the first progress billing form.

This form includes both *Budget amount* and *Revised budget* columns. Use the *Revised budget* column to track changes in the budget. Use the *Previous billing* section to track and acknowledge any previous billings. The *Balance to finish* column shows you at a glance the amount due at the completion of the work. Finally, there's a *% complete* column.

Calculate the values for the last row, *Totals,* for each category or column. In most cases, *Budget amount* remains constant – *Revised budget* shows how and if any changes affected the budget. It's good accounting practice to double-check your work by "cross footing" the *Totals* row. Simply add together *Previous billing, This billing*, and *Balance to finish*. The result should be equal either to the *Budget amount* or the *Revised budget*.

Progress Billing

Construction Company

Address

City, State, ZIP

Phone Number

Date: _____

Owner: _____

Contractor: _____

Project number: _____

Project name: _____

Item no.	Contract item (task description)	Budget amount	Revised budget	Previous billing	This billing	Balance to finish	% complete
1							
2							
3							
4							
5							
6							
7							
8							
9							
10							
11							
12							
13							
14							
15							
16							
17							
18							
19							
20							
21							
22							
23							
	Totals:						

Time and Materials Billing Sheet

File Name on Disk: T&MBILL

This billing sheet is excellent for subcontractors, especially plumbers and electricians. However, nearly any contractor or home repair specialist working on a time and material basis can make good use of this form.

How to Use This Form

Filling out this form is a straightforward task. Since the form is very general, the first column, *Quantity (Qty.)*, serves for both material and labor. In the *Description* column, explain exactly what's being billed. To bill for labor, enter the hours in the *Qty.* column, then write "Hours" in the *Description* column. In the *Price* column, enter the hourly rate. Then multiply that figure by the quantity to find the *Amount*.

Follow the same procedure to bill for materials. In the *Quantity* column note the units installed for each material. Then enter the *Description*, its *Price*, and finally the *Amount* (quantity times price).

Finally, total the *Amount* column to find the *Total amount*.

Here's a word of advice: The more detailed you make the billing, the fewer objections you'll hear from most clients. The added detail will also help when you analyze labor and material costs on that job. For instance, suppose you've been estimating the time to install a recessed light at 45 minutes. You note from billing sheets that the actual installation time is closer to 30 minutes. Make that change in your Cost Book. The next time you bid a job with recessed lighting, use the more accurate price to gain a competitive edge.

Time and Materials Billing Sheet

Construction Company
Address
City, State, ZIP
Phone Number

Invoice number: _____

Date: _____

Owner: _____

Address: _____

City, State, ZIP: _____

Job number/name: _____

Qty.	Description	Price	Amount

Total amount: _____

Percentage Complete Invoice

File Name on Disk: PERCOMP

Use this invoice when your contract provides for payment in stages based on the work completed. List each work category and estimate the percentage complete. Work categories can be based on either Construction Specification Institute (CSI) divisions or bid items listed on your estimate. In either case, add overhead and profit as a percentage of the bill.

Estimating the percentage complete isn't an exact science. But the Job Progress Chart should provide some basis for your estimates. We prefer to have the progress chart filled out on site by the foreman or superintendent. That person then forwards the form to the office where it's used to prepare this invoice.

How to Use This Form

When you've listed all the job categories under *Description*, fill in the *Budget amount* for each, including net changes. You can copy this information directly from the estimate (or copy and paste from the estimate if you're using a computer).

If this is the second or subsequent billing, show the sum of any *Previous billing* amounts for each item. Then calculate the *% complete (this bill)*. Multiply that percentage by the *Budget amount* to find the *Total bill*. The *% complete (to date)* is the sum of all the previous percentages of completion.

At the bottom of the invoice, add all the items under *Total bill* to find the *Subtotal this invoice*. If overhead and profit are already in your total bid prices, the subtotal will also be the total. So simply transfer that number to *Total invoice*. If you do add overhead and profit to your bid items, then fill in a percentage amount for each and multiply by the subtotal to figure each component. Finally, add the overhead, profit and subtotal together to arrive at the *Total invoice*.

Percentage Complete Invoice

Construction Company
Address
City, State, ZIP
Phone Number

Date: _____

Project name: _____

Owner: _____

Invoice number: _____

Description: _____

	Description	Budget amount	Previous billings	% complete (this bill)	% complete (to date)	Total bill
1						
2						
3						
4						
5						
6						
7						
8						
9						
10						
11						
12						
13						
14						
15						
16						
17						
18						
19						
20						

Subtotal this invoice: _____

Overhead____% : _____

Profit____% : _____

Total invoice: _____

Job Invoice

File Name on Disk: JOBINV

This invoice has a complete listing of cost divisions in a format that's perfect for small jobs, especially jobs that can be completed in a single billing. The divisions let you account separately for material, labor, and subcontractor costs. If you use a supervision category, write it in under *Labor classification*.

This is the best invoice for contractors who like to present their clients with an itemized bill showing overhead and profit as a percentage of costs. It's as straightforward and businesslike as a form can get. It makes clear that you work for a percentage of the cost of construction plus profit.

Job Invoice

Construction Company
Address
City, State, ZIP
Phone Number

Date: _____

Owner: _____

Contractor: _____

Project name: _____

Name: _____

Address: _____

City, State, Zip: _____

Quantity	Materials	Unit price	Amount
	Total materials		

Hours	Labor classification	Rate	Amount
	Total labor		

Trade	Subcontractor	Item	Amount
	Total subcontract		

Subtotal: labor, materials and subcontracts	
_____% overhead	
_____% profit	
Total amount	

Contractor's Invoice, Pages 1 and 2

File Name on Disk: CONTINV1

This is a three-page form. Pages one and two are shown first. The last page is a different format and follows the first two pages. The disk name for the second part of this form is CONTINV2.

This form includes all the information needed to apply for payment under AIA document G702 and includes a certificate that the contractor's duties have been performed.

This type of invoice may be required on larger jobs where an architect is following job progress. It tracks change orders in a summary section and provides a complete change order audit trail. Retainage is also calculated. A contractor's certification and an architect's verification signature make it a legal and binding document.

How to Use This Form

This form will probably be required if an architect or project manager is acting as the owner's representative. The representative certifies that it's correct and sends it along to the owner. This form is fairly complicated, but you must deal with it if you're working with architects. Notice that the form assumes that billings will be monthly. If bills aren't sent monthly, you'll have to make some modifications to the form.

Page 1

Complete the *Change order summary* (near the top of the document) with the history of the change orders approved by the owner. First, fill in previous change orders, then any new change orders approved since the last billing. Notice that change orders adding to the contract price and change orders deducting from the contract price are put in different columns. The additions and the deductions are totaled separately in the boxes labeled *Subtotal change orders approved this month*.

Information under *Approved this month* includes change order numbers, the dates they were approved, and whether the change resulted in an addition or a deduction to the price.

Total change orders to date is the sum of all the change orders, still separated into additions and deductions. You'll enter these totals in the next month's invoice on the line for change orders approved in previous months.

The next portion of the invoice creates an audit trail for all project billing. Line 1, *Original contract sum*, is the initial total contract price.

Line 2, *Net change by change orders*, is found by subtracting total deductions from total additions to find change orders to date.

To complete line 3, *Contract sum to date*, add lines 1 and 2.

Line 4, *Total completed and stored to date* is the sum of all labor and materials installed plus any paid-for inventory delivered and on site. This allows you to charge for materials bought and stored on site but not yet installed. These amounts are determined on the summary sheet (see the following form which is also titled Contractor's Invoice).

Line 5 is *Retainage*. A tradition unique to the construction business is the withholding of a percentage of the contract amount (usually 5 to 10 percent) for a prescribed amount of time (usually 30 days) after completion of a project. Compute retainage by multiplying the retainage percentage by the amount of the completed work and by the amount of the stored materials, both of which are computed on page three of the form. Add the two amounts to find *Total retainage*.

For line 6, subtract *Total retainage* (line 5) from *Total completed and stored to date* (line 4) to find *Total earned less retainage*.

Line 7, *Less previous invoices for payment*, comes from line 6 on the last month's invoice.

Line 8, *Current payment due* is the difference between line 6 and line 7.

Calculate line 8, *Balance to finish*, by subtracting line 6 from line 3.

Page 2 (Signatures and verification)

The contractor should sign and date the document in front of a notary public (if required by the architect) before submitting the document to the architect for approval.

Contractor's Invoice

Construction Company
Address
City, State, ZIP
Phone Number

Date: _____
Owner: _____
Address: _____
City, State, ZIP: _____

Project name: _____
Architect: _____

Invoice number: _____
Architect's project no: _____

Change order summary		
	Additions	Deductions
Change orders approved in previous months:		

Change orders approved this month				
Number	Date	Description	Additions	Deductions
Subtotal of change orders approved this month:				
Total of change orders to date:				

1. Original contract sum _____

2. Net change by change orders (total additions less deductions above) _____

3. Contract sum to date (line 1+2) _____

4. Total completed and stored to date _____

5. Retainage:

    a. ____% of completed work _____

    b. ____% of stored material _____

    Total retainage _____

6. Total earned less retainage (line 4 less total of line 5) _____

7. Less previous invoices for payment (line 6 from prior invoice) _____

8. Current payment due _____

9. Balance to finish, plus retainage (line 3 less line 6) _____

Contractor's Invoice (Continued)

Contractor certifies that to the best of his or her knowledge the work covered by this invoice has been completed in accordance with the Contract Documents.

Contractor: _____

By: _____   Date: _____

State of _____   County of _____

Subscribed and sworn to before me this month and day: _____   of year _____

Notary Public: _____

My Commission expires: _____

Architect's Verification of Invoice

In accordance with the Contract Documents and based on on-site observations, the Architect certifies to the Owner that to the best of the Architect's knowledge, the work has progressed as indicated, the quality of the work is in accordance with the Contract Documents, and the Contractor is entitled to payment of the amount approved below.

Amount approved: _____

(Attach explanation if amount differs from the amount applied for)

Architect:

By: _____   Date: _____

File Name on Disk: CONTINV2

This is page three of a three-page form. See the prior form for pages one and two. This page provides detailed information about figures that are summarized on page one. Column A is the item number. The *Description of work* is the task or item. You can copy this from the proposal or estimate. Do likewise with the *Scheduled value*, which is the contract amount of each item.

How to Use This Form

Work completed is divided into two parts, *From previous application* and *This period*. *From previous application* is a running total that includes the sum of all the previous work completed. It's calculated by adding columns D and E on the previous summary.

Materials presently stored records the dollar amount of materials bought, paid for, and stored on the site, but not yet used in the work completed.

Total completed & stored to date is the sum of the *Work completed* and the *Materials presently stored*.

Balance to finish is the difference between the *Scheduled value* and the *Total completed*.

Retainage is figured by multiplying the *Retainage %* amount by the *Total completed*.

Contractor's Invoice

Construction Company
Address
City, State, ZIP
Phone Number

Application number: _____
Application date: _____
Invoice period: _____

A	B	C	D	E	F	G	H	I
			Work completed					
Item no.	Description of work	Scheduled value	From previous application (D + E)	This period	Materials presently stored (not D or E)	Total completed & stored to date (D + E + F)	% (G/C)	Balance to finish (C - G)	Retainage
Totals									

Statement of Contract

File Name on Disk: STATCONT

This Statement of Contract presents a complete job history on one statement. It contains the original contract amount, the net change orders to date, the adjusted contract amount, a change order record for current change orders, and an invoice record for current invoices.

You can use this form by itself or with the Contractor's Invoice or any of the invoices provided in this book.

The form provides a complete audit trail which leads your client through the complex billing maze. It works best with unit cost estimates, and allows you to bill as work progresses on each task or item.

How to Use This Form

This form is filled out each month or each billing period. It's handy to have prior statements available, since each statement builds on the last.

The top portion of the statement contains the *Original contract amount* from the contact or proposal. The *Net change orders to date* is the sum of all the change orders to date, not including the change orders for this statement. The *Adjusted contract amount* is the difference between the original contract amount and the net change orders to date.

Next, fill in the *Change order record*. It should show all the changes for the current billing period. Then enter the *Change #, Date* and *In reference to*, as well as the amount of *Decrease* or *Increase* caused by the changes. At the bottom of the section, total the decreases and increases and calculate a net change.

The invoice section records all the invoices for the billing period. It's set up so you can do partial billings for any task. First, fill in the *Invoice no.* and a *Description* of the task, including its original cost (from the itemized contract or proposal). Then add the *Amount this invoice,* backed up with a copy of the invoice. If there was a previous invoice for the same item, fill in the amount (from the prior Statement of Contract).

Finally, compute the *Balance to complete* by adding the previous invoice to this invoice and subtracting it from the amount of the original task.

Statement of Contract

Construction Company
Address
City, State, ZIP
Phone Number

Date: _____

Owner: _____

Contractor: _____

Project number: _____

Original contract amount	Net change orders to date	Adjusted contract amount

Change order record

Change #	Date	In reference to	Decrease	Increase
		Total:		
		Net change:		

Invoice number	Description	Amount this invoice	Previous invoices	Balance to complete	Percent to complete
	Totals:				

Total billed to date: _____

Less total retainage to date: _____

Plus amount this invoice: _____

Less _____ % retainage: _____

Pay this amount: _____

Thank You

■ Statement

File Name on Disk: STATMENT

The purpose of the Statement is to reconcile charges, payments and credits all on one form. You may want to send a statement like this monthly, even if all invoices have been paid at the end of the billing period. That helps keep everyone's records straight. But the usual reason for sending monthly statements is to prod clients to pay on delinquent accounts.

Invoices are different from statements. An invoice is an itemized bill for specific work or materials. Statements are summaries of all transactions for a period, usually a month. The statement will show the date and description of all unpaid invoices and a summary of all activity (invoices, payments and credits) for the month.

Keeping job accounts current is a tedious task when done by hand. Computerized accounting systems make the job much simpler. Your local computer store will offer several accounts receivable packages at prices that start under $250. Any of these software packages should be able to store all the accounts receivable information you need.

If you're doing the accounting by hand, the statement history can be found on the Project Account Summary.

Statement

Construction Company
Address
City, State, ZIP
Phone Number

Date: _____

Owner: _____

Contractor: _____

Project number: _____

Project name: _____

Date	Description	Invoice	Payments or credit	Balance
			Balance forward>	

Contract Statement

File Name on Disk: CONTSTAT

Like the contractor's invoice, this form requests payment from the owner for a portion of a lump sum contract. A little less formal than other forms, it doesn't track complete change order histories. Include supporting pages (like the Change Order Log) if more detail is needed.

How to Use This Form

The form is divided into three main parts: *Change order record*, *Statement of contract*, and *Billing history*.

The *Change order record* has four parts. *Number of change orders to date*, *Change order increase* and *Change order decrease* summarize the changes to date. Subtract the decreases from the increases and enter the result on the *Net change* line. This tracks the net effect on the contract of all the changes to date. A positive number increases the contract price, while a negative number decreases it.

The *Statement of contract* section has the *Original contract amount* (taken off the estimate, proposal or contract). Add to that (or subtract if it's a negative number) the *Net change orders* to date. The sum is the *Adjusted contract amount*, the most current total project cost.

The first line in the *Billing history* section is the *Adjusted contract amount billed to date*. Of course, on the first statement this is zero. On subsequent billings, it's a running total of all the previous billings. Take this figure from the Job Account Summary if you're keeping one. There's also a running total of all the retainage to date. Subtract it from *Adjusted contract amount billed to date* to arrive at *Total adjusted contract less retainage*.

For *Current invoice amount*, attach an itemized invoice (like the Progress Billing or Time and Materials Billing Sheet). Figure retainage on the *Current invoice amount* and enter it on the line where indicated. Subtract it from the *Current invoice amount* to arrive at the *Current invoice amount less retainage*.

Finally, calculate *Pay this amount*. Simply add *Total adjusted contract less retainage* to *Current invoice amount less retainage*.

Contract Statement

Date: _____

Construction Company
Address
City, State, ZIP
Phone Number

Owner: _____

Address: _____

City, State, ZIP: _____

Project name: _____

Change order record:

Number of change orders to date _____

Change order increase _____

Change order decrease _____

Net change _____

Statement of contract:

Original contract amount _____

Net change orders (see above) _____

Adjusted contract amount _____

Billing history:

Adjusted contract $ billed to date _____

Less _____% retainage _____

Total adjusted contract less retainage _____

Current invoice amount:

Less _____% retainage _____

Current invoice amount less retainage _____

Pay this amount | _____ |

Certified By:

The undersigned certifies that to the best of his/her knowledge the work covered by this statement has been completed in accordance with the contract documents, that previous invoices were issued and the current payment shown is now due.

_____   _____
Date   Signature

Thank You

Past Due Notice

File Name on Disk: PASTDUE

In any service business, the final payment is always the most difficult to pry loose from a client. Remember, contractors aren't bankers. You're entitled to payment when due and should insist on getting paid on time. This Past Due Notice will help you reach that goal.

One of a contractor's hardest jobs is matching the cash flowing into the business with cash flowing out. Any move that accelerates receivables (money owed you) is welcome. Prompt billing, followed by an immediate reminder when the payment is late, will help inform clients that you're serious.

We recommend adding a handwritten note to personalize this request. Your signature will help get the client's attention. The space for the customer's reply makes it harder for them to ignore the notice. It also gives them a place to vent their grievances, if some dispute is holding up payment.

Past Due Notice

Construction Company
Address
City, State, ZIP
Phone Number

Date: _____

To: _____

Attention: _____

Street address: _____

City, State, ZIP: _____

Project name: _____

This is a reminder that you have a balance that remains unpaid. If you've simply overlooked your payment please mail it today. If payment has been made it would help us if you would provide the information requested below so we can accurately credit your account.

Invoice number: _____

Invoice date: _____

Total amount due: _____

Reply

Check has already been sent on _____, check number: _____.

Additional information:

_____

_____

_____

_____

_____

_____

_____

_____

_____

_____

_____

_____

Signature: _____   Date: _____

Hourly Labor Rates

File Name on Disk: HOURRATE

Use this form to calculate and record the total hourly labor costs for each craft classification. List the base hourly rate, fringe benefits, taxes and insurance to get an accurate hourly labor cost for each classification. Your labor burden includes all taxes and insurance that must be paid on the hourly wage. Monitor this labor burden percentage to spot trends in your overhead costs. Many contractors find that their labor burden is about 33 percent of labor costs. You have to know the exact hourly labor cost to bill accurately on time and material contracts.

This sheet is usually prepared by the accounting or payroll department. Estimators should use this data when computing labor costs. You can use a separate copy of this form for wage rate classification.

How to Use This Form

The form is filled out whenever there's a change in pay scale, taxes, insurance, or other benefits. At the very least, you'll have to revise this form at the start of each year when new payroll tax tables arrive. Filling out the form is simple enough. Under *Base labor rate, Hourly rate* means the base wage paid the employee. If you pay $20 an hour to your lead finish carpenter, that's the base labor rate.

Vacation pay, figured as an hourly cost, goes on the next line. Suppose a 40-hour-a-week employee with a $20 hourly wage gets one week of paid vacation annually: One week (40 hours) times $20 per hour is $800. Then divide $800 by 2080 hours per year to find a vacation cost of 38.5 cents per hour.

The *Total base labor rate* is the sum of the hourly rate and the hourly vacation pay. For our hypothetical lead finish carpenter, that's $20.39 after rounding up the vacation pay.

The FICA, federal and state unemployment, workers' compensation and general liability are all based on a percentage of wages. In most cases, multiply the total base labor rate times the appropriate percentage to get the burden per hour. If workers' comp for carpenters earning $20 a hour is $24 per hundred, multiply 24 percent times $20 to find $4.80 per hour as your workers' comp burden.

Benefits can include pension fund contributions, medical insurance and many other categories. Figure each of these on a cost-per-hour basis and add them to the total. Again, divide the yearly benefit by 2080 hours to find the hourly cost.

Combine the *Total base labor rate* and *Total labor burden* to find the *Total hourly labor cost* for each craft category.

Figure the burden as a percentage of the base labor rate by dividing the total labor burden by the total base labor rate. For example, divide a $6.00 labor burden by a total base labor rate of $20 per hour. The labor burden for that classification is 30 percent.

Hourly Labor Rates

Construction Company
Address
City, State, ZIP
Phone Number

Classification: _____

Period from: _____

Through: _____

		Straight time	**Time & one-half**	**Double time**
Base labor rate:				
Hourly rate		$ _____	$ _____	$ _____
Vacation pay		$ _____	$ _____	$ _____
Total base labor rate:		$ _____	$ _____	$ _____
Labor burden:				
Payroll taxes & insurance:				
FICA	_____ %	$ _____	$ _____	$ _____
Federal unemployment	_____ %	$ _____	$ _____	$ _____
State unemployment	_____ %	$ _____	$ _____	$ _____
Workers' compensation	_____ %	$ _____	$ _____	$ _____
General liability	_____ %	$ _____	$ _____	$ _____
Benefits:				
Medical insurance	$ _____ /hr	$ _____	$ _____	$ _____
Other	$ _____ /hr	$ _____	$ _____	$ _____
Total labor burden:		$ _____	$ _____	$ _____
Total hourly labor cost:		$ _____	$ _____	$ _____
As a percentage of wage:		_____ %	_____ %	_____ %

Cash Paid Out

Think of this form as a receipt for your petty cash box. It provides an explanation for any cash paid out. You can also use it to explain a check given to an employee as reimbursement for any type of cash payment.

Insist that employees fill out this form any time they dip into the petty cash box. It records who the payment is to, what it's for, and what job it is applied against.

Occasionally, cash is the only acceptable payment. When a check is written for cash, use this sheet to explain the reason.

Cash Paid Out

Construction Company
Address
City, State, ZIP
Phone Number

Date: _____

Owner: _____

Contractor: _____

Project number: _____

Project name: _____

Date paid: _____   Check #: _____   Amount: _____

Paid to: _____

_____

_____

Job: _____

_____

_____

_____

Explanation: _____

_____

_____

_____

_____

_____

_____

_____

Project Account Summary

File Name on Disk: PROJACCT

This summary tracks bills and payments, including any changes to the contract. It shows, at a glance, the status of a client's payment performance and contract history.

How to Use This Form

Fill out this form every time a bill is sent out or a payment is received for each job (assuming there will be more than two billings). Enter the date and a description of the item, such as an invoice number.

There are two columns to record the *Contract amount* and *Change orders* billed on that invoice. The *Net contract* is the sum of the *Contract amount* and the *Change orders*. Fill out the *Payment Record* (*Date* and *Amount*) when a payment is received, and put the check number in the *Item* column.

When you record change orders or extras, transfer the information to this job ledger.

Project Account Summary

Construction Company
Address
City, State, ZIP
Phone Number

Date: _____

Owner: _____

Project number: _____

Project name: _____

Date	Item	Contract amount	Change orders	Net contract	Payment record	
					Date	Amount

■ Payroll Employee Summary

File Name on Disk: PAYSUM

This summary records weekly payroll information for each employee. Each form covers two quarters of the year for a single employee. This summary will make it easy to comply with audit requirements of your workers' comp insurance carrier.

How to Use This Form

Fill in this form with the date and employee name, address, and social security number when any new employee is hired. At each pay period, fill in a new row.

The *Period ending* column defines the work period – whether you pay weekly, every other week, or monthly. Next, you fill in the hours worked during the pay period and the rate per hour.

In the *Regular* column, fill in the number of regular hours worked during the period. Use the OT column for overtime hours. *Total earnings* is the sum of the hourly rate times the regular hours, plus the overtime rate (usually time and a half) times the overtime hours.

Deductions from earnings include FICA, federal and state taxes, and state disability insurance. These amounts come from the tax tables or are percentages of total earnings. You'll get these amounts when you figure payroll, or from your payroll service (which, by the way, is a good solution to the common payroll headache).

Net paid is the total earnings minus the deductions from earnings. And, of course, *Check #* is the number on the check stub.

Payroll Employee Summary

Construction Company
Address
City, State, ZIP
Phone Number

Date: _____
Employee: _____
Address: _____
City, State, ZIP: _____
Social Security Number: _____

Period ending	Hrs	Rate per hr	Regular	OT	Total earnings	Deductions from earnings				Net paid	Check number
						FICA	Federal	State	SDI		
Total for quarter											
Year to date											
Total for quarter											
Year to date											

Overhead Calculations

File Name on Disk: OVERHEAD

At the bottom of most estimates and many proposals, you'll see one line for profit and another for overhead. For either to have any meaning, your overhead must be a real number. Adding a 5 percent profit to an overhead figure is meaningless if you're guessing at the overhead. This sheet helps take the guesswork out of the overhead figure and provides a foundation from which to build that elusive profit margin.

How to Use This Form

Your overhead expense includes all costs of running a business from day to day. These costs can't be applied to a specific job. If an item can be singled out as a job-related cost, it doesn't belong here.

The first items to fill in are the *Gross income this year* and *Gross income last year*. This should include all the construction-related income of the company for the year. If you can't arrive at a whole year's income, use any time period that's available – the longer the better. Remember that any guess is better than no guess. As time goes on, averaging will turn the guess into reality.

Next, fill in the totals for each of the categories. First fill in the yearly total for last year and this year, then divide by 12 to arrive at the average monthly amount for each year. (If you have only three months' history, divide by 3.) Do that for every category and total the columns at the bottom of the form. We have provided space for two years' worth of data so you can compare your overhead costs from year to year.

Finally, divide the total overhead amount for this year by the gross income for the same period to arrive at the percentage of overhead to gross. This is the figure you'll use when doing an estimate. As an example, if your overhead figures out to be 20 percent of gross income (not uncommon in the construction business), then your bids must include 20 percent markup to cover overhead.

Then use this figure on all jobs you bid. It's the minimum amount needed to cover your business operations. Use the percentage calculated until some other figure seems more accurate. This overhead percentage is set in stone. But you can still lower bid prices by increasing productivity.

Labor burden for trades working on site should not be included in your overhead percentage. Each cost estimate you submit should include both wages and *burden* for every trade working on that site. The same holds true for liability insurance where it's a percentage of labor costs.

Overhead Calculations

Construction Company
Address
City, State, ZIP
Phone Number

Date: _____

Gross income this year: _____

Gross income last year: _____

	Last year	This year	Last year month average	This year month average
Owner's salary				
Office personnel wages				
Employer's payroll tax expense (on above)				
Office rent				
Utilities				
Office supplies				
Telephone, including business at home				
Mobile phone/pagers				
Advertising, all types				
Legal, accounting and professional fees				
Licenses and dues				
Office equipment, lease and rental				
Computer hardware and software				
Insurance, liability and auto				
Medical insurance				
Travel, hotels & meals				
Truck expense, gas, oil, maint./repairs				
Associations and publications				
Education and seminars				
Business entertainment				
Business meals				
Bad debts, ___%				
Small tools and equipment				
Depreciation				
Other: _____				
Total:				
Overhead %: Total overhead/gross income:	%	%	%	%

Equipment Ledger Sheet

File Name on Disk: EQUPLEDG

This form records use and expense of more expensive company-owned equipment. It's also the source of current ownership and operating costs that are used to estimate equipment expense.

How to Use This Form

For each piece of equipment, fill in the *Date acquired, Equipment number*, and *Initial cost*. The *Estimated use per year* for most equipment is 2000 hours. But use your experience to make a more accurate estimate if possible. Estimated life is usually five years for depreciation purposes and estimated salvage value is normally assumed to be zero at the end of the five years.

Use the formula $A = C (n+1) / 2n$ to figure *Average annual investment* (where C is the original cost, and *n* is the number of useful years of the machine).

Calculate annual depreciation by dividing the purchase price by the useful life in years.

You'll use the Daily Equipment Report to fill in the columns headed *Charge* and *Operating hours. Cumulative hours* are found by adding each year's operating hours to the previous years' cumulative hours. Of course, the *Cumulative hours* column will be blank for the first year. Find *Cost per hour* by dividing the operating hours by the yearly total. After the first year, find the *Cost per hour* by dividing the *Cumulative hours* by the yearly charge. This form allows you to figure hourly costs for each item (insurance, tires, fuel, etc.) and compare them on a yearly basis.

This sheet is very useful when deciding if a piece of equipment is worth keeping. Has it passed its useful life? Compare operating costs to rental costs. Would it be better to rent than own?

Equipment Ledger Sheet

Construction Company
Address
City, State, ZIP
Phone Number

Date: _____

Equipment number: _____

Description: _____

Date acquired: _____

Initial cost: _____

Estimated life: _____

Estimated use per year: _____

Estimated salvage: _____

Average annual investment: _____

Annual depreciation: _____

Year	Item	Charge	Operating hours	Cumulative hours	Cost per hour
1st year	Depreciation				
	Interest, taxes, insurance				
	Fuel, oil, lube				
	Repairs, parts				
	Tires				
	Operating labor				
	Total				
2nd year	Depreciation				
	Interest, taxes, insurance				
	Fuel, oil, lube				
	Repairs, parts				
	Tires				
	Operating labor				
	Total				
3rd year	Depreciation				
	Interest, taxes, insurance				
	Fuel, oil, lube				
	Repairs, parts				
	Tires				
	Operating labor				
	Total				

Expense and Travel Report

File Name on Disk: EXPENSE

Use this form when the company pays for construction crews to travel to and stay near a job site. It's a comprehensive form, organized on a daily basis, and designed to be filled out quickly by each employee.

In the construction business it's not uncommon for construction crews to travel long distances to complete their work. Accumulate on this form all the expenses accrued on jobs away from home, including traveling to and from the job. Each employee should fill out the form each day and turn it in weekly (by fax if necessary) with the time cards and other job information.

How to Use This Form

The employee starts by filling in the date for each day of the week. Employees driving their own cars to the job site will fill in the *Starting* and *Ending mileage*, and subtract the starting from the ending to find the *Mileage/day*. The *Reimburse/mile* line is for the amount per mile paid to the employee. The other items are self-explanatory. Just make sure all employees understand that they're required to provide receipts for all expenses except mileage.

Expense and Travel Report

Construction Company
Address
City, State, ZIP
Phone Number

Date: _____

Employee: _____

Period from: _____

To: _____

	Sun	Mon	Tue	Wed	Thur	Fri	Sat	Total	Details of expense items
Date:									
Starting mileage									
Ending mileage									
Mileage/day									
Reimburse/mile									
Air/ground fare									
Auto rental									
Parking									
Tolls									
Lodging									
Telephone									
Meals									

Signature: _____ Date: _____ Approved: _____

Final Payment Release

File Name on Disk: FINALPAY

This document is required under California law and is common in many other states. It's used to release "any mechanic's lien, stop notice, or bond right" before release of payment. Be sure to compare this with the approved version in your state before using this form.

There are two forms of release, the Conditional Waiver and Release Upon Final Payment and the Unconditional Waiver and Release Upon Final Payment. We've combined the conditional and unconditional versions onto one handy sheet. Use the conditional version for partial or progress payments, where more work is to be done. Use the unconditional waiver when the job is substantially complete and you have been "paid in full for all labor, services, equipment or material . . ."

How to Use This Form

Normally, the waivers are filled out and submitted with an invoice or request for payment. If the job isn't finished and a partial draw or payment is requested, use the conditional waiver. The form states that once a check from the undersigned (client) has been "properly endorsed and has been paid by the bank" the document becomes effective. In other words, once you cash the check, the waiver goes into effect.

When the job is substantially finished, fill out the unconditional waiver and return it to the client after final payment. Both forms have a space for "disputed" claims which allow both parties, the contractor and owner, to note the cost of extra work not covered by the waiver.

As the notice on the bottom of the unconditional waiver says, "This document waives rights unconditionally and states that you have been paid for giving up those rights." Keep in mind that once you've signed this unconditional waiver and given it to the customer, you *cannot* go back and ask for payment for something. If he says he'll pay you as soon as his wife comes home with the checkbook, and you give him the signed waiver, he can decide not to pay you after all. *And there's not a thing you can do about it*. Unless you have the cash in hand and know the check is good, use the conditional release form.

Final Payment Release

Construction Company   Date: _____

Address   Owner: _____

City, State, ZIP   Project number: _____

Phone Number   Project name: _____

Conditional Waiver and Release Upon Final Payment

Upon receipt by the undersigned of a check from _____ in the sum
Maker of check

of $ _____ payable to _____ and when the check has been
Amount of check   Payee or payees of check

properly endorsed and has been paid by the bank upon which it is drawn, this document shall become effective
to release any mechanic's lien, stop notice, or bond right the undersigned has on the job of

_____ located at _____
Owner   Job description

This release covers the final payment to the undersigned for all labor, services, equipment or material furnished
on the job, except for disputed claims for additional work in the amount of $ _____

Before any recipient of this document relies on it, the party should verify evidence of payment to the
undersigned. I/We certify that all labor and/or laborers have been paid in full to the below referred date.

_____   _____
Dated   Company name

By: _____
Signature

Unconditional Waiver and Release Upon Final Payment

The undersigned has been paid in full for all labor, services, equipment or material furnished to

_____ on the job of _____ located at _____
Your customer   Owner   Job description

and does hereby waive and release any right to a mechanic's lien, stop notice, or any right against a

labor and material bond on the job, except for disputed claims for extra work in the amount of $ _____

I/We certify that all labor and/or laborers have been paid in full to the below referred date.

_____   _____
Dated   Company name

By: _____
Signature

Notice to persons signing this waiver: This document waives rights unconditionally and states that you have been paid for giving up those rights. This document is enforceable against you if you sign it, even if you have not been paid. If you have not been paid, use a conditional release form.

Time and Material Log

File Name on Disk: T&MLOG

This form is used to log actual labor, material, and equipment used on a specific task or project. It's usually filled in by a foreman or superintendent when payment will be for time and materials. Use it on T&M jobs when the client wants a daily record of expenses incurred or when the job requires some unusual type of work. When a subcontractor's work is deficient and work needs to be done to correct it, this sheet records all the effort needed to make corrections. Finally, you can use it to track or "cost" a specific construction task.

How to Use This Form

This form has space for all the labor, materials, equipment, notes and signatures needed to record work performed. Make sure it's filled out as completely as possible. The foreman or super who fills it out shouldn't show any prices. Pricing is done in the office by the accounting department.

A line is provided for the signature of the person who fills out the report. This might be important if later there's a dispute between subcontractor and contractor.

Time and Material Log

Construction Company
Address
City, State, ZIP
Phone Number

Date: _____

Owner: _____

Contractor: _____

Project number: _____

Project name: _____

Description of work performed:

_____

_____

Labor

Name	Trade	Classification	Straight time	Overtime

Material   Equipment

Description	Quantity	Unit	Description	Quantity	Unit

Comments: _____

_____

Signed: _____ **Date:** _____

Accounting Adjustments

File Name on Disk: ACCTADJ

This is a reminder sheet that creates a paper trail for adjustments in your accounting system. It helps you remember, months or years later, why and how you made an accounting adjustment.

When your accounting system forces you to create a debit or credit, use this form to put it – and the reason for it – down on paper. For instance, if you're using a computerized accounting system that forces you to make a new entry to correct a mistaken entry, this form records the reason for the correction.

This form is also very useful when you make any adjustment to an account balance. In the construction business, negotiation at the end of the job is as common as it is at the beginning. When you take that inevitable cut to make the clients feel they've been fairly treated, you credit the client's account and record the reason on this form. If the adjustment is for materials or a subcontracted portion of the job, fill in the supplier or subcontractor on the *Vendor name* line.

Accounting Adjustments

Construction Company
Address
City, State, ZIP
Phone Number

Date: _____
Owner: _____
Contractor: _____
Project number: _____
Project name: _____

Customer: _____

Vendor name: _____

Account no.	Account name	Amount	
		Debit	Credit
	Totals		

Explanation:
_____
_____
_____
_____

Profit and Loss Statement

File Name on Disk: PROF&LOS

The Profit and Loss Statement (also known as the Income Statement) shows whether or not, during a specified time period, a business achieved its primary objective of making a profit. Essentially, the Profit and Loss Statement is a listing of all the revenue earned during a defined period and all the expenses incurred in earning that revenue. Then subtract expenses from revenue. A positive number is a profit; a negative number is a loss.

This Profit and Loss Statement is specifically designed for the small- to medium-sized contractor. When filled out properly, it gives you a picture of how your business did over a specific period of time – usually a month or a year.

Customize this form by adding or deleting categories. Many accountants would suggest that you start out with a list of expenses longer than on the form. But we've elected to begin with a small, manageable list. Add or create categories as you need them. The larger the list, the more chance you have of misplacing information.

The list of categories on the Profit and Loss Statement should be the same as the chart of accounts in your accounting system. The chart of accounts should closely match categories you record on IRS Schedule C (job costs are costs of goods sold on Schedule C). If the categories are the same, it's an easy matter to transfer totals from your Profit and Loss Statement to Schedule C.

How to Use This Form

Collecting all the company revenue and expenses on one sheet isn't an easy job. So you'll have to spend some time completing this form. You'll probably have to scramble and scratch, add and subtract, to find all the amounts — unless, of course, your books are kept by an accounting software package. All accounting systems use a chart of accounts (whether called that or something else). So this list will be the starting point when you begin entering data in the computer.

Revenue (Income)

Revenue should include all the money earned by the business in the time period specified. We've divided it into four broad construction categories. You might want to use more or fewer categories, depending on the type of work you do. The more categories, the more likely the confusion as to what goes where. But tracking every type of income gives you the most accurate information. Only you know what's right for your company.

Total revenue is the sum of all the individual revenue categories. Make sure it accounts for every penny of construction-related income you've received in the time period covered by the statement.

Job costs (expenses)

Job costs include any expenses that can be directly attributed to a specific project or job. The cost of labor and the burden attached to labor, materials, subcontractors, equipment rentals, fees and permits are all job costs because you can assign them to a specific job. When liability insurance and bonds are based on a particular job, they are also job costs.

Total job costs are the sum of all the job costs during a given time period.

Overhead expenses

Overhead expenses include all costs that can't be allocated to some particular job. Dividing the overhead into several categories will give a detailed picture of company expenses. The whole reason you divide up these expenses, other than to satisfy the IRS, is to get a handle on where you're spending money.

For instance, if you know that advertising costs are averaging 5 percent of gross, you have a basis for deciding that 5 percent isn't enough. Maybe 7 percent would be better. If you'll need to trim 2 percent from some area to provide 2 percent more for advertising, the overhead categories give you a place to begin trimming.

Here are a few words of warning: Too much detail can make it impossible to see the forest for the trees. Too little detail makes it impossible to see where the blood is coming from as you bleed to death. Remember, this list is just a good starting point. Modify it to suit the way you do business.

Advertising should include all the costs of marketing such as phone book ads, newspaper ads, printing, flyers, home shows, and the cost of any effort used to promote your business.

Entertainment and business meals are costs you incur furthering your company's marketing effort. If you take a client to lunch, write down the name, time and place, save the receipt, and record the expense as a business expense.

Dues and publications and books like this one are the costs of staying current in your business. As such, they are legitimate overhead expenses.

Officers' salaries are what you pay to officers such as the owner, partner, vice president, or anyone whose salary can't be charged to a particular job.

Administrative wages are labor costs paid to anyone (except officers) doing work that can't be charged to a particular job. Under some time and materials contracts, you can earmark office time spent on a specific job and "cost" part of the office wages to that job. Wherever possible, apply wages to a specific job. This results in more accurate job costs – which promotes more realistic future bidding.

Overhead labor burden includes workers' compensation, FICA, FUTA, and state taxes paid on office personnel.

Office and shop rent are obvious costs. Telephone and mobile phone can't be job costed unless there's a site phone, so they're considered overhead expense. Utilities include electricity, gas, and water for the office. Utilities at the job site should be costed to the job. Business license and fees cover all the miscellaneous costs and charges that towns, counties, and states tack on to your cost of doing business.

Office supplies include pencils and paper, tape, fax paper, and toner, but can also include the software you need to run the forms on the Construction Forms & Contracts disk.

Legal and accounting expenses include payroll services, bookkeeping services and the attorney's fees when lawsuits make contractors wonder why they're in the building business. Bad debts are the sum of all the money you have decided won't ever be paid to you. Basically, you're subtracting the bad debts from your profit margin.

Bank charges are the cost of checking accounts, escrow fees, dispersal accounts, and any other service charges you may run up against. Job-specific fees, of course, should be costed to the job.

Business vehicle expenses include gas, oil and repairs, license, registration and insurance.

Small tools are usually tools that can't be depreciated, so they're "expensed" in the year they're purchased. A safe rule of thumb is that any tool under $300 can be expensed. More expensive tools should be depreciated over several years.

Depreciation is a way spreading the cost of equipment, vehicles and buildings over the useful life of that equipment, vehicle or building. For example, suppose you spend $4,500 on a new computer and printer and expect to use that equipment for four years. Suppose also that the equipment will be worth $500 at the end of four years. You've purchased $4,000 worth of "usefulness" which you'll use at a rate of $1,000 each year for four years. In that case, you'll depreciate $1,000 in each of the four years.

Of course, you would prefer to expense the new computer and printer immediately. That would reduces your taxable income by $4,500 in the year of purchase. Unfortunately, the tax law doesn't allow that. True, you've spend the money. But government needs to keep tax revenue high and growing. So government is going to treat a portion of that $4,500 as though it were profit this year. You'll pay taxes as though $3,000 of that $4,500 were profit this year. But don't worry. After four years, you'll get the money back, because by then, the computer and printer will be depreciated down to the $500 residual value.

Tax law has allowed several ways to figure depreciation, including the straight line method, declining balance method, and the sum of the digits methods. Each has its benefits. Consult an accountant before picking a method.

Total overhead expenses are simply the sum of all the overhead expenses. Since most estimates are a total of material, labor, overhead and profit, tracking overhead expenses carefully can help your bottom line. Profits are more predictable and reliable when your estimates reflect the true cost of doing business.

Net income or (loss) is the difference between what you earn (revenue) and what you spend (expense). With good record-keeping practices and hard work, you should be able to keep totals in the income rather than the loss column.

Profit and Loss Statement

	From _____ to _____	%	Year to date _____	%
Revenue				
Residential remodel income	_____		_____	
Commercial rehabilitation	_____		_____	
Residential development	_____		_____	
Other income	_____		_____	
Total revenue	_____		_____	
Job costs				
Direct labor	_____		_____	
Direct labor burden	_____		_____	
Materials	_____		_____	
Subcontractors	_____		_____	
Equipment rentals	_____		_____	
Dump fees	_____		_____	
Permits	_____		_____	
Total job costs	_____		_____	
Overhead expenses				
Advertising	_____		_____	
Business meals	_____		_____	
Entertainment	_____		_____	
Dues & publications	_____		_____	
Officers' salaries	_____		_____	
Administrative wages	_____		_____	
Overhead labor burden	_____		_____	
Office & shop rent	_____		_____	
Telephone & mobile phone	_____		_____	
Utilities	_____		_____	
Business license & fees	_____		_____	
Office supplies	_____		_____	
Legal & accounting	_____		_____	
Bad debts	_____		_____	
Bank charges	_____		_____	
Gas, oil & repairs	_____		_____	
Vehicle lic., reg., & ins.	_____		_____	
Small tools	_____		_____	
Depreciation	_____		_____	
Total overhead expenses	_____		_____	
Net income or (loss):	_____		_____	

Contracts

Proposal

File Name on Disk: PROPOSE

Use this proposal on small jobs involving, at most, one or two items with just a few materials or a few subcontractors. A job like pouring a sidewalk, installing a sliding glass door or painting a room is perfect for this form.

This form is short and sweet. But don't underestimate what it does. When signed and dated, it's a legal, binding agreement.

Be very specific about what's included in the job and what's excluded, even if the task is clear and straightforward. Spell out what materials you're going to install. Then specifically exclude what *isn't* included in your price.

Set due dates for payment with the payment schedule line – weekly, biweekly, or whatever you agree on.

Proposal

Date: _____

Construction Company
Address
City, State, ZIP
Phone Number

To: _____

Of (company): _____

City, State, ZIP: _____

Good until: _____

Project name: _____

We propose to furnish all material and perform all labor necessary to complete the following:

_____

_____

_____

_____

_____

_____

_____

_____

_____

_____

_____

_____

We propose to furnish material and labor, complete in accordance with above specifications, for the sum of: _____ Dollars $ _____

Payments to be made as follows: _____

_____

Contractor's signature: _____

Acceptance of proposal The above price, specifications and conditions are satisfactory and are hereby accepted. You are authorized to do the work as specified. Payment will be made as outlined above.

Owner's signature: _____ Date: _____

Remodeling Proposal

File Name on Disk: REMPROP

This proposal is a written offer. By itself, the offer isn't a contract. Of course, it identifies the price and what's going to be done. But there's no contract until the offer is accepted completely by the owner. Anything less than complete acceptance is just a counteroffer. The offer is also your conditional promise: Once accepted unconditionally by the owner, you're bound to do the work at the price stated.

This form will help you get agreement on all the key points before work actually begins. That should keep you and your client out of most disputes as the job progresses.

If any form needs to be scrutinized for accuracy and completeness, it's a contract proposal – any proposal. A major discrepancy can turn a good deal into a financial disaster. Our advice: "Check twice, sign once."

How to Use This Form

After filling in the client and job information, complete the *Date of plans* and *Architect* lines. The plan date identifies the set of plans on which your proposal is based. That's important if several sets of plan revisions are in circulation. Don't get suckered into doing work that appeared on a plan set drawn after you bid the job.

The next two lines ask for approximate starting and completion dates. *Approximate* means *approximate*, nothing more and nothing less. But try to be realistic. Our experience is that clients expect you to show up at 7 A.M. on the morning of the *approximate* start date. That won't always happen and the contract isn't breached if you're a few days (or even weeks) late. But be courteous. Do your best to estimate the start date and give advance notice if you can't meet that date.

The *We hereby submit specifications and estimates* for section is the meat of this form. Here you must list what you propose to do. Except for the smallest of jobs, the space provided on one form probably isn't enough. Add more sheets as necessary so you don't feel compelled to abbreviate the work description. Write *As Described on Exhibit A* and attach a sheet titled *Exhibit A* if you need more space.

Be very careful about the words you use to describe the work. *Don't say*, *Tear off the existing roof and reroof with Certainteed Hallmark 340 lb., 30-year asphalt shingles.*

That's exactly wrong and will get you into trouble 90 percent of the time. Instead, describe the jobs as:

Remove and dispose of 18 squares of shingles.

Install 18 squares of Certainteed Hallmark 340 lb., 30-year asphalt shingles.

What's the difference? The difference is like night and day. The first description says the owner is going to get a new roof. The second says you're going to install 18 squares of shingles. Still don't see the difference? Here's the difference:

▼ 47 LF of eave drip

▼ 8 SF of chimney flashing

▼ 3 sheets of 4 x 8 roof sheathing

▼ 60 LF of 2 x 10 rafter

▼ three plumbing vent cones

▼ your profit on the job

▼ your reputation as a contractor

The first description says the owner is going to get a new roof. Until you tore off that old roof, there was no way of knowing how much flashing, sheathing and rafter material had to be replaced. Many owners (and some courts) would insist that your proposal was for reroofing, no matter what was required. If the sheathing is so rotten it won't hold a nail, that's your problem. You'll have to install new sheathing (and rafters and flashing) just to complete the roofing job you bid. That's just your tough luck, buster. Too bad!

Compare the words in the second proposal. You're going to remove 18 squares of shingles and install 18 squares of shingles. Nothing more and nothing less. If the job requires flashing, rafters, sheathing, or anything else, that's obviously not part of the agreement.

So, how do you find the right words that avoid these disputes? Here's our solution. Etch it into your memory. Don't ever forget this, the first commandment of construction contract drafting:

Don't describe the work. Just list the materials.

If it turns out that the job needs more materials, fine. You'll be happy to furnish and install whatever is needed. *At extra charge*, of course. That way, there's no dispute about what's in the contract. Eighteen squares of shingles means eighteen squares of shingles. There's no mention of flashing, rafters, sheathing or anything else.

To be completely honest, we like to identify in our contracts some of the common items that may be required but are not included in our price. That way, the owner understands the risk right from the beginning. If you know the job may require new sheathing, flashing or rafters, exclude that specifically: *No sheathing, rafters or flashing included.*

The contract also has space for *Alternates*. That's common in remodeling jobs because the work probably has to be done within a client's budget.

The last part of this section is for items not covered in the proposal. Every remodeler should consider this section carefully before submitting the proposal. If you can't match the existing 10-year-old wood flooring, *say so in the proposal*. Remember, plans show what needs to be done, not what can't be done! Put what can be done in your written proposal.

Give careful consideration to the payments section. Cash flow problems start and end on these lines. Try to consider all the likely variables, including supplier credit lines, sub-contract payment schedules, payroll deposits and late payments from suddenly hard-to-find clients. Add another page if you need more space to explain how the payments will be made.

Finally, get someone to check your numbers and specs before going anywhere near the *Contractor's signature* line.

Remodeling Proposal

Construction Company
Address
City, State, ZIP
Phone Number

Date: _____

Submitted to: _____

Of (company): _____

City, State, ZIP: _____

Good until: _____

Job: name/number: _____

Date of plans: _____

Architect: _____

Approximate start: _____

Approximate end: _____

We hereby submit specifications and estimates for:

_____

_____

_____

Alternates: _____

_____

This proposal does not include:

_____

_____

_____

We propose to furnish material and labor, complete in accordance with above specifications, for the sum of:

_____ Dollars $ _____

Payments to be made as follows: _____

_____

Contractor's signature: _____

Acceptance of proposal The above price, specifications and conditions are satisfactory and are hereby accepted. You are authorized to do the work as specified. Payment will be made as shown above.

Owner's signature: _____ Date: _____

Fixed Fee Itemized Proposal

File Name on Disk: FIXFEEPR

We've included two cost-plus-fee proposals. This is the first. The next one is titled Time and Material Itemized Proposal. The difference in these two forms is in the way markup is treated. Occasionally you'll find a client who believes that contractors working for a fixed fee aren't entitled to a profit on the job. For those folks we designed the Fixed Fee Itemized Proposal with an internal (hidden) markup. Your markup (including labor burden, contingency, overhead and profit) is figured into the cost of each item described. If the client deletes one or more items in the proposal, only the *Total estimate* line has to be refigured. Every itemized cost in the form includes a portion of your markup.

How to Use This Form

The Fixed Fee Itemized Proposal is simply three columns and a box at the bottom for the total. If you're using the Unit Estimate Sheet, the *Description* and *Notes* are already complete. Just transfer them (cut and paste with your computer) to this proposal. Do the same with the *Cost*. However, with this version of the proposal, be sure to add labor burden, contingency, overhead and profit into the itemized cost, since there's no place for markup at the bottom of the form.

Fixed Fee Itemized Proposal

Construction Company   Date: _____

Address   Owner: _____

City, State, ZIP   Telephone number: _____

Phone Number   Address: _____

City, State, Zip: _____

Description	Notes	Cost

Contractor will furnish all labor and materials to construct and complete, upon the project, in a good workmanlike manner, only the work described above.

Total estimate: _____

Time and Material Proposal

File Name on Disk: T&MPROP

Use this proposal to charge for materials by the unit and for time by the hour. A personnel billing rates table, which you fill in, defines the division of labor and identifies the hourly wage scale. Materials are reimbursed at cost plus the percentages indicated for overhead and profit. Use this form when most work is subcontracted and you'll be billing for other work by the hour.

How to Use This Form

All proposals should be filled out carefully. This form is no exception. Be especially careful to list items *not included*. Enter the description and hourly rate for each wage scale in the *Labor rates* section of the form. Don't forget to include your own job description. Remember, these figures are your billable rates. Make sure they include all taxes, fringe benefits and insurance. See the Hourly Labor Rates form for details on hourly labor costs.

Time and Material Proposal

Construction Company
Address
City, State, ZIP
Phone Number

Proposal date: _____

Submitted to: _____

Address: _____

City, State, ZIP: _____

Project name: _____

We propose to:

_____

_____

_____

_____

Not including: _____

_____

We propose to perform the above work on an hourly basis plus expenses as outlined below:

1. Labor rates: All time spent by personnel shall be compensated at the following rates:

Category	**Rate**
_____	_____
_____	_____
_____	_____
_____	_____
_____	_____

2. Materials: All materials furnished on this project shall be reimbursed at cost.
3. Overhead & profit: Weekly invoices shall include _____% overhead charge & _____% profit.
4. Invoices: All invoices shall be due immediately. Any invoices not paid within 10 days will be charged a late charge of 2% per month.

Acceptance: The above prices, specifications and conditions are satisfactory and are accepted. You are authorized to do the work as specified. Payments will be made using the rates above.

Owner: Contractor:

By: _____   By: _____

Date: _____   Date: _____

Time and Material Itemized Proposal

File Name on Disk: T&MITEM

This proposal shows your markup at the bottom of the form. Figures in the *Cost* column are estimated costs to perform the tasks described. Figure markup separately and display it at the bottom of the proposal. This proposal is good for bids based on time and materials if the client understands that you're entitled to a fair markup. Use this form on larger, more complex jobs with a long list of billing items.

How to Use This Form

The boxes at the bottom of the form deserve some explanation. First, calculate the *Subtotal*, which is the total of the direct costs. Then, fill in the percentages you use for *Contingency, Overhead & supervision*, and *Profit*. Multiply each of those percentages by the *Subtotal* and enter these figures in the boxes at the right. *Total estimate* is the sum of the figures in the boxes.

Time and Material Itemized Proposal

Construction Company   Date: _____

Address   Owner: _____

City, State, ZIP   Telephone: _____

Phone Number   Address: _____

                              City, State, ZIP: _____

Description	Notes	Cost

Contractor will furnish all labor and materials to construct and complete, upon the project, in a good workman-like manner, only the work described above.

Subtotal _____

Contingency _____ % _____

Overhead & supervision _____ % _____

Profit _____ % _____

Total estimate _____

■ Subcontract Agreement

File Name on Disk: SUBCONTA

Every general contractor (or *prime* contractor) needs a good standard form of agreement with subcontractors. Under this contract, the subcontractor agrees to do a portion of the work on a project in accord with the contract documents. While the agreement establishes no direct link between the owner and the subcontractor, the owner or architect may wish to approve the contractor's choice of subcontractor.

All provisions in the prime construction contract, including change procedures, warranty periods and quality controls, extend to this subcontract. But be sure that provisions unique to the work being subcontracted are clearly noted in this agreement.

How to Use This Form

This form includes space for the subcontractor's insurance information, including company name, policy number and amount of coverage. Most insurance carriers require that you get this information (and a certificate of insurance) from each subcontractor.

Subcontractor federal ID is for tax purposes. If the agreement is accepted, record the insurance information and the federal ID on your *Subcontractor Insurance Verification Log*.

After *Description of work*, list the contract documents, specifications and plans that define the work to be done.

The *Payment schedule* defines the flow of payments. The subcontractor should consider cash flow requirements before signing this portion of the agreement. It's common for the general contractor to withhold a percentage due each subcontractor until the general contractor is paid in full. This retainage, usually about 10 percent, may be the subcontractor's entire profit.

Start and completion days may be obvious. But be careful to give yourself enough time. Construction seldom takes less time than expected.

Subcontract Agreement

This agreement is between Contractor:

_____

_____

_____

_____

and Subcontractor:

_____

_____

_____

_____

Date: _____

Owner: _____

Project name: _____

Project address: _____

Insurance company & policy #: _____

Amount of insurance: _____

Subcontractor federal ID #: _____

Subcontractor license number: _____

Description of work to be performed:

_____

_____

_____

_____

_____

_____

_____

_____

_____

_____

Payment schedule: _____   due on or before _____

_____   due on or before _____

_____   due on or before _____

_____   due on or before _____

for the total price of $: _____

Work shall start on: _____   and shall be complete within _____ number of days.

Contractor's signature:

_____

Subcontractor's signature:

_____

Date: _____

Date: _____

Subcontract Policy

File Name on Disk: SUBPOLIC

This form is a general policy statement by the general contractor informing the subcontractor of what's expected. Remember that your work is only as good as the work of your least competent sub. If a subcontractor doesn't work out, it shouldn't be due to a lack of communication. This agreement makes very clear exactly what you expect from subs. You can use this form on nearly any type of subcontract work.

Feel free to change this policy agreement any way you wish. Just make sure to have each new subcontractor read the agreement and sign it.

Subcontract Policy

Construction Company	Date: _____
Address	Subcontractor: _____
City, State, ZIP	Address: _____
Phone Number	City, State, ZIP: _____

We welcome your association with our company. This agreement lists our subcontractor policies. Please sign and return one copy.

1. As a subcontractor of our company, you have become part of our team. We look to you to help our jobs run smoothly. If you anticipate a problem not addressed in our plans, or find any code violation or technical problem, please notify us promptly. Acceptance of all bids should be based on a job site visit. Any problem caused by conflicting conditions becomes your problem and your responsibility.

2. All your personnel on our job should support our company and speak well of it. You are an integral part of our marketing program. Both of our businesses stand to lose or gain by your job behavior.

3. Referrals: If any of our clients request work directly from you, such as extras or future work, you will need written permission to do the work. According to our original contract with the client, if any neighbor or passerby asks you to do a job, you must refer them to our office. Any subcontractor who takes such a job directly shall be in direct violation of this agreement.

4. Changes: All changes must be approved by our superintendent or our office. If time is a problem, you may proceed with our verbal approval, but you must follow up with a written change order. No prices may be given directly to the client.

5. Insurance: Our company carries a blanket insurance policy. If a copy of your general liability or workers' compensation coverage is not in our hands prior to any and all payouts, we shall deduct ___% from the amount due you for the general liability and ___% for the workers' compensation.

6. Job schedule: If for any reason you go to a job and additional work is needed before you can proceed, please call our office immediately. We can often solve the immediate problem and avoid such work stoppages in the future.

7. Client relations: Don't talk to the clients except to be cordial. Problems go to the contractor.

Contractor: _____   Subcontractor: _____

Prime Construction Contract

File Name on Disk: PRIMCONT

The basic purpose of every construction contract is to define the rights and obligations of the contractor and owner. On smaller jobs, the proposal becomes the contract when it's signed by the owner. But for larger, more complex jobs, you'll need a longer, more detailed and technical contract – like this one.

Depending on the scope and scale of the project, this form may constitute the entire contract. Or it may just be part of a package that includes the addenda, drawings, technical conditions, and perhaps some special conditions.

How to Use This Form

Filling out the form begins with the description of the work *(Contractor will furnish all labor and materials . . .)*. Usually this section includes references to the drawings and specifications. If the job is small, just a list of the items to be installed may be enough. If the job is larger, use the next section *(In accordance with the following contract documents . . .)* to identify other documents that describe what you're going to do – and not do!

Everything described on either the plans or the specifications becomes a part of your obligation. Double-check the plans and read every paragraph of the specifications before signing your name to a contract like this.

The payment schedule *(Installments to be made as follows:)* identifies when you're going to get paid. Here's our advice: Get as much as you can as fast as you can. After all, you're not a bank. Any contractor with a computer should have no trouble billing the work out weekly. Doing that should ensure weekly payments and avoid the cash shortages that plague many contractors.

Many lenders use a funding service to disburse construction money. These services act as escrow holders. They make sure the work is complete, labor releases are in order and suppliers have been paid before releasing any progress payments. Although these services work well, they put one more layer of paperwork between the you and your payments. So figure this additional hurdle into your cash flow projections. If a funding service will be used, fill in the service name under *Funds are to be disbursed by*.

On the *Work shall commence* line, insert the date you propose to start construction and the number of working days you estimate the job will take. Notice the term *working days*. That doesn't include holidays, weekends, weather days or other delays beyond your control.

Prime Construction Contract

This agreement is between (Contractor):

<table>
<tr><td>Construction Company</td><td>Date: _____</td></tr>
<tr><td>Address</td><td>Project name: _____</td></tr>
<tr><td>City, State, ZIP</td><td>Address: _____</td></tr>
<tr><td>Phone Number</td><td>_____</td></tr>
<tr><td></td><td>City, State, ZIP: _____</td></tr>
</table>

And (Owner):

Name: _____

Address: _____

City, State, ZIP: _____

Contractor will furnish all labor and materials to construct and complete the project described above in a good workmanlike manner: _____

_____

_____

In accordance with following contract documents: _____

_____

Owner agrees to pay Contractor the total sum of: _____

Installments to be made as follows: _____

_____

_____

Funds are to be disbursed by: _____

_____

Work shall commence: _____

and shall be complete within the following number of working days: _____

Owner signature: _____   Contractor: _____

Date signed: _____   Date signed: _____

Project Management Contract

File Name on Disk: PROJMAN

Today many owners want to act as their own general contractor, subcontracting all the actual construction work. Wise owners also understand that they lack the knowledge needed to manage a complex construction project. So they contract for management services from an experienced general contractor.

Success in this type of arrangement requires good communication between the owner and the manager. This contract tries to resolve in advance the most frequent conflicts that arise under management agreements. It spells out in detail the roles of both owner and project manager. The fee schedule is based on a percentage of the total cost of construction, with incentives for finishing early and under budget and penalties for finishing late.

How to Use This Form

This four-page form is divided into four main sections:

1) General project information

2) The project manager's roles and responsibilities

3) The owner's roles and responsibilities

4) The fee schedule

The general information section describes the project, dates the contract, and defines the parties involved.

The project manager's section is divided into two phases: pre-construction and construction. Both are lists of the project manager's duties. These lists are as comprehensive as we could make them. But if you have a computer, you'll probably want to make changes to fit the job you're planning.

Notice in the section on owner's duties that many tasks traditionally performed by the general contractor are now classified as the owner's responsibility. Again, you may want to make changes in this section.

Your fee is a percentage of the total cost, 10 percent in the sample document. Of course, you'll have to negotiate the actual fee. There's space to fill in the amount of the initial retainer and when it will be paid. The number of installments will depend on project duration. We've used 12 months in the sample contract. Change that to fit your job.

As an incentive to complete the job under budget, there's a 50-50 split of any unspent construction funds. The sample contract also provides that the full final draw will be paid if the certificate of occupancy is issued by a certain date. The penalty is 10 percent of the final draw for each 15 days that the certificate is delayed. Delays beyond the manager's control are excused. Be careful when filling out these dates – they're critical to your bonus!

Project Management Contract

Construction Company
Address
City, State, ZIP
Phone Number

Date: _____

Owner: _____

Project name: _____

Project number: _____

This agreement is made this _____ day of _____, 19____ by and between _____ _____, hereinafter called the Owners, whose address is _____, and _____, hereinafter called the Project Manager, Contractor's License No. _____, whose address is _____.

The parties above hereby agree as follows:

The Project Manager agrees to manage and see to completion in an excellent and substantial manner, the construction of a single family residence (herein called the "Project") for _____ _____ upon the real property located at _____.

The Project Manager's Roles and Responsibilities are to be as follows:

Pre-Construction Phase

1. Assist in finding a lender;

2. Obtain all necessary permits and handle all interface with the building department (general, grading, electrical, mechanical, plumbing, etc.);

3. Provide a complete materials takeoff (bill of materials) for lumber and framing hardware;

4. Coordinate the bidding process with at least three bids per each major craft;

5. Act as the clearing house for information to bidding subs;

6. Check up on the references of each subcontractor;

7. Assemble presentation to the lender;

8. Provide a detailed cost breakdown sheet for the lender;

9. Develop a critical path time line with completion of the living space targeted _____;

Project Management Contract (Continued)

10. Act as the contractor of record with the lender;

11. Recommend to the Owners the most qualified and reasonably priced subcontractor for each phase of construction based on the bids submitted;

12. Finalize the contract documents with each sub, making sure everything is "spelled out";

13. Develop a list of contract addenda covering areas of payment disbursement, safety, workers' compensation, cleanup, and craftsmanship standards.

Construction Phase

Goal: Make sure something progresses on the job site every working day in order to get the _____ _____ into their new home by _____.

The Project Manager will see to it that the Project is constructed and completed in strict conformance with the plans and specifications and that all laws, ordinances, rules, and regulations of the applicable governmental authorities are adhered to. Further, he agrees to:

1. Be the Owners' "eyes and ears in the field";

2. Meet with Owners on a regular basis to review progress;

3. Coordinate all utilities hookups;

4. Coordinate with the geologist and/or soils engineer;

5. Coordinate with the grader;

6. Supervise day-to-day construction, making sure the Project is built as intended by the Owners and the Designer as per plans;

7. Make sure neighbors' property is respected;

8. Ensure subs maintain the highest degree of craftsmanship;

9. Schedule subs and suppliers;

10. Review workers' comp. of each sub--Have a Certificate of Workers' Comp. sent to Project Manager by their carrier;

11. Coordinate incidental day labor;

12. Keep track of change orders;

13. Verify lumber and materials deliveries to make sure we get what we ordered;

14. Authorize payment of subs based upon ongoing review of their work;

Project Management Contract (Continued)

15. Obtain lien releases;

16. Provide on-site problem-solving with subs;

17. Coordinate with interior designer's installation;

18. Call for and handle inspections and interface with Building Department;

19. Make sure the job site is cleaned on a regular basis (Owners to provide manpower or funds for labor);

20. Insist that all workers maintain the highest safety standards;

21. Pass along to the Owners any discounts the Project Manager is entitled to as a General Contractor without charging any markups.

The Owner's Roles and Responsibilities are to be as follows:

1. Finalize negotiations with a lender and secure the construction loan;

2. Apply for and pay for the General Building Permit. All other permits are to be paid for and taken out by each respective subcontractor;

3. All construction expenses are to be borne by the Owners. The Project Manager is not to be held liable for any unpaid bills;

4. Sign all contracts with each subcontractor upon the recommendations of the Project Manager;

5. Clear through Project Manager any work or changes on the Project;

6. Maintain an account for incidental purchases (petty cash)--Project Manager will keep track of these expenses;

7. Provide a job site phone upon commencement of rough grading (cost included in the construction loan);

8. Provide a temporary construction field office available to the Project Manager upon commencement of rough grading (cost included in the construction loan);

9. Accept the liability for theft or destruction of building materials;

10. Provide ALL the appropriate insurances (public liability, course of construction, fire, theft, etc.);

11. Provide a chain-link fence around the Project area;

12. File Notice of Completion within 5 days of substantial completion of the Project.

Fee Schedule

In consideration for the above services rendered by the Project Manager, the Owners agree to pay the Project Manager a Base Fee of 10% of the cost of construction, based on the amount of the construction loan, plus, as an incentive to bring the Project in under budget, a Final Draw of 50% of any unused loan funds that exist

Project Management Contract (Continued)

when the Notice of Completion is filed by the Owners and all construction budgeted for in the construction loan is completed.

The Base Fee is to be computed based on the total hard construction costs approved in the construction loan, including permit costs, appliances and fixtures. Any soft costs included in the construction loan, such as design, engineering, interior design as well as furniture and drapery costs, are not to be considered in determining the Base Fee.

The Base Fee is to be broken down into installments as follows:

* An initial retainer of $_____ to be paid by _____, to cover the first month of pre-construction services.

* A monthly installment of 1/12th of the base fee to be paid on the 1st of each following month up to _____ _____ .

The final draw is to be paid within 15 days of filing the Notice of Completion, based on the following:

* As a mutually-beneficial incentive to finish the construction in a timely manner and to meet the completion goal stated above, the Project Manager shall receive the full 50% final draw as stipulated above if construction of the living space is completed to warrant a Certificate of Occupancy from the City by by _____ enabling the Owners to move in by _____ .

* If Certificate of Occupancy is not granted by _____, 10% shall be deducted from the Project Manager's final draw for each 15 calendar day increment beyond _____.

* If progress is delayed for any reason beyond the Project Manager's control, the time frame for computing the final draw shall be shifted beyond _____ by the amount of the delay. Examples of such delays include: unseasonably rainy weather, earthquakes, fire, work stoppages and unreasonable delays in city approvals (defined as requests that may delay rough grading beyond _____).

* Cost overruns, in any particular construction budget category or allowance, made by the Owners during construction that are a result of changes or upgrades not called out in the plans and specs, are not to be considered as part of any remaining construction funds for purposes of determining the final draw.

We hereby execute this Agreement in _____on _____.

Owner (s):   Project Manager:

_____   _____

_____

_____

Cost Plus Percentage Contract

File Name on Disk: COSTPLSP

Under this contract, the owner agrees to reimburse the contractor for the direct "cost of the work" plus a percentage of all costs incurred to cover overhead and profit. Use this contract on custom home building jobs when cost is secondary to quality or when the plans or specifications are inadequate. This form is also appropriate for jobs that have to be started before complete details are available. In any case, the owner should understand the risk. Costs are almost certain to be higher on jobs where the owner insists on design flexibility during construction.

Good communication between the owner and contractor is essential when working under a cost plus percentage contract. Watch change orders and cost summaries carefully to keep track of cost variances and trends. Keep very accurate and complete cost records. Any costs you can't document fully come out of your profit margin.

We feel that job cost accounting is part of the cost of the job and should be charged as "cost of the work." We suspect that you agree.

Cost Plus Percentage Contract

Construction Company
Address
City, State, ZIP
Phone Number

Date: _____

Owner: _____

Address: _____

City, State, ZIP: _____

Project name: _____

This agreement is made this _____ day of _____, 19_____

between _____, the owner, and _____

_____, the contractor. The owner and the contractor agree as set forth below:

1. The contractor accepts the relationship of trust and confidence established between his company and the owner by this agreement. He covenants with the owner to furnish his best skill and judgment in furthering the interest of the owner. He agrees to furnish efficient business administration and supervision and to use his best efforts to furnish at all times an adequate supply of workers and materials, and to perform the work in a most expeditious, economical and workmanlike manner.

2. The work to be performed under this contract shall commence _____.

The contractor shall use his best efforts to complete said work of improvement on or before _____

_____.

3. The owner agrees to reimburse the contractor for the direct "cost of the work" as defined in paragraph 6 below. Such reimbursement shall be in addition to the contractor's fee stipulated in paragraph 4.

4. In consideration of the performance of the contract, the owner agrees to pay the contractor as compensation for his services a contractor's fee as follows:

_____ % (percent) of all costs incurred over total project length paid as per paragraph 11.

5. The scope of the work shall consist of the "categories of work" described on the estimate attached hereto. The estimate is attached solely for the purpose of describing the category of work. The pricing on the estimate shall have no bearing on the cost of the work.

6. The term "cost of work" shall mean costs necessarily and reasonably incurred in the performance of the work and actually paid by the contractor, including all costs incurred due to changes and extras not listed on the attached estimate.

7. The contractor shall procure the necessary permits for the work of improvement. Owner shall pay the governmental fees and contractor's charges for said permits.

Cost Plus Percentage Contract (Continued)

8. All portions of the work that contractor's employees cannot perform directly shall be performed under subcontracts. Unless owner has agreed in advance all subcontracts shall be on a fixed price basis. The contractor shall secure the owner's consent before entering into any subcontracts.

9. The contractor shall keep full and detailed accounts as may be necessary for proper financial management under this agreement. The owner shall be afforded access to all the contractor's records, books, correspondence, instructions, drawings, receipts, vouchers, memoranda and similar data relating to this contract, and the contractor shall preserve all such records for a period of three years after the final payment.

10. The owner agrees to pay a twenty-five percent deposit upon obtaining permits or start of job, whichever occurs first.

11. The contractor shall, every two weeks during the course of work, deliver to the owner a statement showing in complete detail all costs incurred by his company in the execution of this contract for the preceding two week period. Accompanying said statement shall be a copy of all back-up documentation including material procurement invoices, payrolls for all the labor and all receipted bills for which payment is due. The owner shall review the statement and shall remit such amount within three days of the owner's receipt of the statement. The final payment, constituting the unpaid balance of the cost of the work and the final contractor's fee, shall be paid by the owner to the contractor when the work has been completed and the contract fully performed.

12. The contractor agrees to maintain workers' compensation and liability insurance throughout the course of the work.

13. The contractor hereby agrees to hold the owner harmless and to indemnify the owner against any and all claims which may arise during the course of the work as a consequence of the negligent acts or deliberate omissions of the contractor, its agents or employees.

This agreement is executed the day and year first written above.

_____   _____
Owner   Contractor

                                    _____
                                    License number

_____   _____
Date   Date

Cost Plus Fixed Fee Contract

File Name on Disk: COSTPLSF

We recommend using this contract if you expect your client may require several changes as the job progresses. You'll manage the project to the best of your ability for a fixed fee. This contract establishes an "open book" policy, so your business records are wide open to your client's scrutiny.

We've found that this type of agreement works well when the owner and contractor have a relationship based on trust and confidence. The owner must understand that you're doing the best you can at the best possible price. This contract guarantees you a fair return while allowing for any number of changes in the course of the job. One advantage is that much of the change order procedure is eliminated with this type of contract. The disadvantage is that the owner has no guarantee of the final project cost.

The owner should understand that the contractor's fee is based on plans and specs available when the contract is signed. If the scope of the job doubles, the contractor's fee has to increase proportionately. Paragraph 4 identifies the contractor's fee. For example, a $52,000 fee for a job expected to take a year might be $1,000 per week. If the job takes 60 weeks, the fee should increase to $60,000.

Cost Plus Fixed Fee Contract

Construction Company	Date: _____
Address	Owner: _____
City, State, ZIP	Address: _____
Phone Number	City, State, ZIP: _____
	Project name: _____

This agreement is made this _____ day of _____, 19_____

between _____, the owner, and _____

_____, the contractor. The owner and the contractor agree as set

forth below:

1. The contractor accepts the relationship of trust and confidence established between his company and the owner by this agreement. He covenants with the owner to furnish his best skill and judgment in furthering the interest of the owner. He agrees to furnish efficient business administration and supervision and to use his best efforts to furnish at all times an adequate supply of workers and materials, and to perform the work in a most expeditious, economical and workmanlike manner.

2. The work to be performed under this contract shall start on the date _____.

The contractor shall use his best efforts to complete said work of improvement on or before _____

_____.

3. The owner agrees to reimburse the contractor for the direct "cost of the work" as defined in paragraph 6 below. Such reimbursement shall be in addition to the contractor's fee stipulated in paragraph 4.

4. In consideration of the performance of the contract, the owner agrees to pay the contractor as compensation for his services a contractor's fee as follows:

   All costs incurred over total project length paid as per paragraph 11, plus a fixed fee of

_____ per _____.

5. The scope of the work shall consist of the "categories of work" described on the estimate attached hereto. The estimate is attached solely for the purpose of describing the category of work. The pricing on the estimate shall have no bearing on the cost of the work.

6. The term "cost of work" shall mean costs necessarily and reasonably incurred in the performance of the work and actually paid by the Contractor, including all costs incurred due to changes and extras not listed on the attached estimate.

7. The contractor shall procure the necessary permits for the work of improvement. Owner shall pay the governmental fees and contractor's charges for said permits.

Cost Plus Fixed Fee Contract (Continued)

8. All portions of the work that contractor's employees cannot perform directly shall be performed under subcontracts. Unless owner has agreed in advance all subcontracts shall be on a fixed price basis. The contractor shall secure the owner's consent before entering into any subcontracts.

9. The contractor shall keep full and detailed accounts as may be necessary for proper financial management under this agreement. The owner shall be afforded access to all the contractor's records, books, correspondence, instructions, drawings, receipts, vouchers, memoranda and similar data relating to this contract, and the contractor shall preserve all such records for a period of three years after the final payment.

10. The owner agrees to pay a twenty-five percent deposit upon obtaining permits or start of job, whichever occurs first.

11. The contractor shall, every two weeks during the course of work, deliver to the owner a statement showing in complete detail all costs incurred by his company in the execution of this contract for the preceding two week period. Accompanying said statement shall be a copy of all back-up documentation including material procurement invoices, payrolls for all the labor and all receipted bills for which payment is due. The owner shall review the statement and shall remit such amount within three days of the owner's receipt of the statement. The final payment, constituting the unpaid balance of the cost of the work and the final contractor's fee, shall be paid by the owner to the contractor when the work has been completed and the contract fully performed.

12. The contractor agrees to maintain workers' compensation and liability insurance in effect throughout the course of the work.

13. The contractor hereby agrees to hold the owner harmless and to indemnify the owner against any and all claims which may arise during the course of the work as a consequence of the negligent acts or deliberate omissions of the contractor, its agents or employees.

This agreement is executed the day and year first written above.

_____   _____
Owner   Contractor

                                           _____
                                           License number

_____   _____
Date   Date

Contract Transmittal

File Name on Disk: CONTTRAN

This cover letter should be included in the package of contract documents sent to each subcontractor. It includes a request for a current certificate of insurance. The letter should show the project name and cost category code numbers (if you use work codes for job costing).

Contract Transmittal

Construction Company
Address
City, State, ZIP
Phone Number

Date: _____

Owner: _____

Contractor: _____

Project number: _____

Project name: _____

_____

_____

_____

_____

Dear _____:

Enclosed please find two copies of our contract for the project referenced above.

Please sign both copies and return them to this office with your certificate of insurance. A countersigned copy will be forwarded to you upon our receipt of your signed copies.

Please note your project name and number for future reference. To expedite administration of the contract, please make reference to this project number in all your written correspondence to this office.

Thank you.

Sincerely,

_____

Enclosures

Change Order – Generic

File Name on Disk: CHANGORD

There are probably as many types of change orders as there are types of contracts. But they all do three important things: modify the original contract, and record changes in the contract price and project schedule.

Every change order is an addendum to the contract created after the original contract was signed. The architect, if there is one, usually initiates the change order. Of course, anyone on the job could be the first to notice that a change is required.

Most contracts allow the owner to make changes (at the owner's cost, of course). From your standpoint, change orders protect your financial interest. They're a routine part of the construction business.

This form is more generic than the change orders that follow. There's space for you to describe nearly any type of change in job scope, specifications, price or method of payment. This form lets you mold the change order to fit the underlying contract. Contractors and subcontractors alike can use this form. If you don't fill in any other space on the change order, at least describe the change and get the owner's signature. Otherwise, the owner is free to deny that any extra work was authorized.

How to Use This Form

Every change order describes work that wasn't covered in the original contract – and the change in the contract price. That's why you have to be so careful when describing the work required by a change order. The change order should also identify:

▼ The cost of the change (including your time spent negotiating and administering the change)

▼ A fair profit

▼ Any change in the job's schedule

Describing the work accurately is usually harder than it sounds. Changes are labor-intensive. Don't forget to include the cost of tear out, new plans, modifications of existing plans, resubmissions, resubmittals, rescheduling, and reappraisals. Every change order will boost your overhead and most will cause at least some delay in completion.

Use this change order form to educate your client on the high cost of changes. Your client's response may be very revealing: *How willing is that client to pay the cost of making extensive changes?* The earlier you demand strict change order compliance, the fewer requests you'll see.

This simple change order form provides plenty of space for filling in the description, the cost, and the schedule change (delay). Language can be tailored to your style of doing business, making it as brief or as detailed as you deem necessary. Even if you do business with a handshake (which we've done, but don't recommend), this form – filled out by you and simply signed by the owner – will preserve your working relationship and your legal right to get paid.

Change Order

Construction Company
Address
City, State, ZIP
Phone Number

Date: _____

Owner: _____

Project number: _____

Change order number: _____

Original contract date: _____

Change (add or delete) the following work to the original contract:

_____

_____

_____

_____

_____

_____

_____

_____

_____

_____

_____

_____

_____

_____

_____

_____

_____

_____

_____

_____

Change the original contract amount by: $ _____

Payment to be made as follows: _____

_____

We agree to furnish labor & materials complete in accordance with the above specifications at the price stated above.	Above additional work to be performed under the same conditions as specified in the original contract unless otherwise stipulated.
_____ _____ General Contractor Date	_____ _____ Owner Date

Note: This change order becomes part of the original contract.

Change Order – Running Total

File Name on Disk: CHANGEOR

This alternate change order form tracks the original contract price and the running total of the net changes, then calculates a new contract price based on the net changes. If you fill out this form completely each time there's a change, you'll always have an up-to-date running record of the job. That helps keep the current job price in the forefront of the client's mind – and yours.

By the way, many spreadsheet programs (such as Excel) let you link cells in one document to cells in another document. For example, the cell *Total original contract amount plus or minus net change orders* is the cell *The new contract amount including this change order* from the last change order.

How to Use This Form

If you don't fill in any other space, at least describe the change and get the owner's signature – for your own protection. Better by far, fill out the form completely. Describe the work accurately. The most important point is that the owner authorized the change and you have a signed paper to prove it. You can argue about the cost and the delay later.

This form is especially useful on larger or long-term jobs where changes are the norm rather than the exception. A change order is the only way to amend a lump sum contract.

Eight lines detail the history of the contract and its alterations:

1) The description of the change.

2) *The original contract sum.* This number will always stay the same.

3) The *Net amount of previous change orders* is simply the sum of all change orders previous to this one.

4) The next line adds the original contract amount and all the previous change orders.

5) *Total amount of this change order* is simply the cost to do the change. (This total should include all your costs to make a change plus your markup.)

6) *The new contract amount including this change order* is the sum of *The original contract sum*, the *Net amount of previous change orders*, and *Total amount of this change order.* This amount is the new total contract price.

7) *The contract time will be changed by* is an estimate of the increase or decrease in the actual amount of time the change will take.

8) *The date of completion as of the date of this change order* is the new completion date after adjusting for this change.

Change Order

Construction Company
Address
City, State, ZIP
Phone Number

Date: _____

Owner: _____

Contractor: _____

Project name: _____

Change order number: _____

Original contract date: _____

You are directed to make the following changes in this contract:

The original contract sum was: $ _____

Net amount of previous change orders: _____

Total original contract amount plus or minus net change orders: _____

Total amount of this change order: _____

The new contract amount including this change order will be: _____

The contract time will be changed by the following number of days: (   ) Days _____

The date of completion as of the date of this change order is: _____

Contractor:

_____
Company name

_____
Address

_____
City, State, Zip

_____
Date

_____
Signature

Owner:

_____
Name

_____
Address

_____
City, State, Zip

_____
Date

_____
Signature

Subcontractor Change Order

File Name on Disk: SUBCONTC

This form directs the subcontractor to make changes as specified by the contractor. The form is identical to the basic change order – except for the signature lines. This change is just between the contractor and the subcontractor. The owner isn't involved.

How to Use This Form

Normally this form is initiated by the contractor after receiving a change order from the owner. The contractor directs the subcontractor to make the changes specified. Be sure to describe the change completely and to refer to all the relevant plans, addenda, specs and notes.

1) Again, the description of the change is the first thing you fill out.

2) *The original contract sum* is the original amount of the subcontract.

3) The *Net amount of previous change orders* is a running total of all the change orders to date.

4) The next line totals the original contract sum and the net change orders.

5) *Total amount of this change order* fills the next line.

6) Calculate and fill in the new contract amount by adding this change order amount to the original contract amount plus the net amount of previous change orders.

7) The schedule delay (or speed up) is recorded next.

8) Calculate and fill in the date of completion.

Only the contractor and subcontractor sign this form since it's an addendum to their contract, not the contract with the owner.

Subcontractor Change Order

Construction Company
Address
City, State, ZIP
Phone Number

Date: _____
Owner: _____
Contractor: _____
Project name: _____
Change order number: _____
Original contract date: _____

You are directed to make the following changes in this contract:

The original contract sum was: $ _____

Net amount of previous change orders: _____

Total original contract amount plus or minus net change orders: _____

Total amount of this change order: _____

The new contract amount including this change order will be: _____

The contract time will be changed by: ( ) Days

The date of completion as of the date of this change order is: _____

Contractor:

_____
Company name

_____
Address

_____
City, State, ZIP

_____
By

_____
Date

Subcontractor:

_____
Company name

_____
Address

_____
City, State, ZIP

_____
By

_____
Date

Cash Change Order

File Name on Disk: CASHCHAN

This form is a good choice for remodelers and subcontractors who expect to be paid either in advance or on completion of the work.

This form is very simple and direct. You have to fill in only the *Description of change*, the cash price and the payment schedule. It gets the owner's attention without being rude. You're happy to do the work, but expect to be paid well for your effort.

Cash Change Order

Construction Company
Address
City, State, ZIP
Phone Number

Date: _____

Owner: _____

Project number: _____

Change order number: _____

Original contract date: _____

Description of change:

Contractor agrees to furnish and supply all labor and material necessary to do the work in a neat and workman-like manner

The owner(s) agree to pay the sum: _____

As follows:

Cash (today) _____

Cash (on completion) _____

Owner: **Contractor:**

_____   _____
Company name   Company name

_____   _____
Address   Address

_____   _____
City, State, ZIP   City, State, ZIP

_____   _____
By   By

_____   _____
Date   Date

Fax Change Order

File Name on Disk: FAXCHANG

Get quicker approval of change orders by faxing documents between owner, contractor and architect. You can waste days waiting for approval to go through the mail. In many cases you can get a signed change order back by fax in minutes instead of days. That allows the job to proceed without unnecessary delay.

How to Use This Form

This form is designed to be completed with minimum effort. After the obvious job data (name, number, etc.) is filled in, note who initiated the proposed change or addition in the *Requested by* space. This could be the contractor, architect or owner.

In the *Description* column, enter a description that's specific and detailed enough to differentiate it from any work in the original contract. Detail works in your favor here, making the point that the work is worth the added cost. It's important to note lost time, retooling, added procurement efforts and all the other extra effort a change creates for the contractor.

Next, list the *Materials*. Enter the total material cost and labor rate. Depending on your billing agreement, you may not have to fill in these spaces. The same is true for *Estimated total hours*. If the cost of changes is based on the time and material required, fill in your estimate of time and materials. Otherwise, fill in the line *Total change to contract*. Since all changes have some impact on the completion date, space is provided for your estimate of the change in the project schedule.

The signature line has a box which lets you request a mailed paper copy. But don't hesitate to begin work on a change when the faxed approval is received.

Fax Change Order

Construction Company
Address
City, State, ZIP
Phone Number

Date: _____

Company: _____

Attention: _____

Fax number: _____

Telephone number: _____

Project name: _____

☐ Change order   ☐ Deletion from contract

☐ Addition to contract

Requested by: _____

Description: _____

_____

_____

Materials: _____

_____

_____

_____

_____

_____

Total estimated materials cost: _____

Labor:

Estimated total hours: _____

Rate: _____

Total estimated labor cost: _____

Total change to contract: _____

Estimated effect on the project schedule: _____ days.

Client approval

☐ Please follow up with mailed hard copy   Signature: _____

Change Transmittal

File Name on Disk: CHANGETR

Send a customized copy of this letter with any change order you send to a subcontractor. Fill in the change order number before you send it. And don't forget to record the change order on the Change Order Log.

Change Transmittal

Construction Company   Date: _____
Address   Owner: _____
City, State, ZIP   Contractor: _____
Phone Number   Project number: _____
                                     Project name: _____

To:

_____

_____

_____

_____

Dear _____:

Enclosed please find two copies of our Change Order Number_____ for the project referenced above.

Please sign both copies and return them to this office. A countersigned copy will be forwarded to you upon receipt of your signed copies. Thank you.

Sincerely,

_____

Enclosures

Change Order Log

File Name on Disk: CHANGLOG

Chaos is going to be the result if you don't have some organized way of tracking the submission, approval and rejection of changes. This change order log fills the bill. Use a separate log to record the initiation and approval or rejection of change orders for each project. Record change orders by number and keep the status of each change current in the log.

How to Use This Form

Enter the change order number in the left column. Then enter the *Description* and dollar *Amount* of the change. In the *Schedule change* column, record the delay in days.

In the *Status* section of the log, check the *S*, *A*, or *R* column to indicated that the change order has been submitted, and then approved or rejected by the architect and owner.

Change Order Log

Construction Company
Address
City, State, ZIP
Phone Number

Date: _____

Owner: _____

Contract amount: _____

Project name: _____

Project number: _____

S = Submitted A = Approved R = Rejected

C.O. number	Description	Amount	Schedule change	S	A	R

Page _____ of _____

■ Warranty

File Name on Disk: WARRANT

Don't assume that your subs guarantee all their work. Ask and you may discover that many don't guarantee certain parts of their work – probably the part that needs repair.

This Warranty is a written promise by the subcontractor to the owner, confirming the quality of the work done. It certifies that the work meets specified requirements and will perform satisfactorily.

This Warranty also covers the cost of associated work which may be "damaged or displaced" due to work that's "defective in workmanship or materials." For example, if a drain line under the slab breaks, the cost of fixing the line may be peanuts compared to the cost of breaking out and replacing the slab.

Note that this form creates a warranty for everything installed or provided by the subcontractor. That's very broad. Your subs probably feel that manufacturers of the equipment they install are responsible for premature failures of their equipment. Maybe so. But this is clear: If the water heater starts to leak after six weeks, replacement shouldn't be at your expense.

Send a copy of this form to all subcontractors. Get them to return a signed copy before you make their final payments. (See the Project Closeout Letter.)

Each subcontractor should fill in the length of the warranty and starting date. Typical warranties run for a period of one year. If the warranty period will be longer or shorter, get an agreement with the subcontractor on that subject before making the final payment.

Warranty

Construction Company   Date: _____

Address   Owner: _____

City, State, ZIP   Contractor: _____

Phone Number   Project number: _____

      Project name: _____

We hereby guarantee to the above named Owner the   _____

_____

_____

which we have installed in the above-named project for _____ years use starting _____ .
We agree to repair or replace, to the satisfaction of the Owner, any or all such work that may prove defective in workmanship or materials within that period, ordinary wear and tear and unusual abuse or neglect excepted, together with any other work which may be damaged or displaced in so doing. If we fail to comply with the above-mentioned conditions within a reasonable time after being notified in writing, we collectively and separately do hereby authorize the Owner to proceed, have the defects repaired and made good at our expense, and we will pay the costs and charges, including reasonable attorney's fees, upon demand. This guarantee covers and includes any special terms, including time periods, specified for this work or materials in the plans, specifications and contract documents for this project.

Signature: _____

In the capacity of: _____

Date: _____

Type of business:

☐ Corporation

☐ Sole proprietorship

☐ Partnership

Notary stamp:

Estimating Forms

Plan Log

Form Name on Disk: PLANLOG

It's good practice to keep a tight control over plans. You don't want subs bidding from obsolete plan sets. Furthermore, sometimes the architect or owner makes the return of all plan sets a condition for recovery of your deposit. The Plan Log will help you keep track of plans as they move from office to subcontractor and back. This form also controls in and out dates and tracks addenda to the plan sheets.

How to Use This Form

Keep this form near the plan storage area. Make an entry on the form every time a set of plans leaves or returns. In the *Company* column, record the name of the company that's checking out the plans. And be sure to fill in the name of the *Contact person* and their *Phone number*. Having the phone numbers handy saves time when you have to make reminder calls to get the plans back.

Make an entry in the *Notes* column every time you receive revisions to any plan set. Before accepting an estimate, check to be sure the bid was based on the latest plans.

Plan Log

Company Name
Address
City, State, ZIP
Phone Number

Date: _____
Owner: _____
Contractor: _____
Project name: _____
Number: _____

Print #	Company	Contact person	No. of sets	Deposit ($)	Date out	Date in	Phone number	Notes

■ Bid Log

File Name on Disk: BIDLOG

Use the bid log as the collection point for information about bids submitted, bids requested and bids received on each of your projects. The Bid Log should also show the type of work being bid, who the bidder is, and the bid price. There's even a column for modifications when changes in the plans make it necessary to change the contract price.

If a bid is past due, you'll see that immediately on the Bid Log. You're alerted right away to contact the sub. If you don't have many subs bidding, this sheet can double as a plan log, showing who has each set of plans. Make an entry in your Bid Log every time you distribute plans and every time a plan set is returned by a subcontractor.

How to Use This Form

In most cases, the work schedule will determine the order of your requests for bids. Fill out the Bid Log ahead of time and then use it as a checklist when mailing or faxing requests for a bid. There's space to indicate the date you sent the bid package and when you sent any modified plans. The *Bid due* column pins down a due date for your sub's response so you can get your own bid in on time. Later on, it acts as a tickler so you can follow up on requests that are overdue.

When bids come back, usually with plans, you simply enter the date under *Bid received* and the amount under *Bid price*. There's also a *Comments* column, with space for a short note. If you need more room, use this space to refer to another document. For example, the comment might say "bid substitutions, see subcontract."

Bid Log

Construction Company
Address
City, State, ZIP
Phone Number

Date: _____

Project: _____

Project number: _____

Sheet number: _____ of _____

Type/ division	Bidder	Bid pkg. sent	Modification number/date	Bid due	Bid received	Bid price	Comments

Job Survey

Form Name on Disk: JOBSURV

This form is popular with remodeling and home improvement contractors. Use it to record the scope of the job on a preliminary walk-through with the owner. If there are no plans for the project, the information on this sheet is the basis for your estimate and proposal. If there are plans, use this sheet to supplement pieces missing from the construction puzzle.

How to Use This Form

Fill this form out during your first visit with the client at the job site. As the prospective client explains the scope of the job, fill in the numbered *Job descriptions* as quickly and as accurately as you can. This list becomes your checklist when compiling the estimate – so it can't be too detailed.

Be sure to record any problems you see at the site, including irregular work conditions, difficult logistics, or anything that might make the job easier or more difficult than usual. Also record what isn't included in the scope of the job, and keep the sheet stapled to your copy of the estimate. You'll be happy you have this information if there's a contractual disagreement later.

Make field drawings and sketches in the grid. A good scale to use for most projects is approximately ¼ inch to 1 foot. Information recorded here will help you do the material and labor take-off when compiling the estimate back at the office.

Use as many of these sheets as necessary to be sure you've collected all the important information when doing the site survey. Once you're back in the office, it's harder to recall all the details. Use this form to jog your memory when translating the survey items to a cost estimate.

Job Survey

Construction Company
Address
City, State, ZIP
Phone Number

Date: _____
Owner: _____
Owner phone number: _____
Project address _____
Project name: _____

Number	Job description
1	
2	
3	
4	
5	

■ Quantity Sheet

Form Name on Disk: QUANTITY

Most of us are familiar with the "napkin approach" to bidding and understand its inherent drawbacks: There's no way to review how you arrived at the estimate. When you've finished a job, it's nice to know why your cost estimate was $5,000 too low. Or why you ordered twice as much sheathing as you really needed. Or why you ran out of siding before you finished the north wall. To do that, you'll need to review your calculations. If you don't, expect to make the same mistakes again on the next job, and the next job, and the next job. That's an expensive way to learn estimating.

The most important part of every estimate is the quantity takeoff. This is often referred to as the *quantity survey*. You'll spend about 80 percent of your estimating time doing the quantity survey and the other 20 percent doing the pricing (finding the installed cost of each item).

Start your estimates with the Quantity Sheet. Remember that you're creating a permanent record that will be referred to many times. Remember also that someone is going to check your calculations before the bid is submitted. So show all your calculations. Work neatly and systematically. Let this Quantity Sheet help organize your take-off, reduce math errors, omissions, and duplications, and increase both the reliability and accuracy of your estimate.

Whether you do one-piece-at-a-time, stick by stick estimates, unit price estimates, assembly estimates, or a hybrid of all three, this sheet is where you start. It provides a convenient place for recording all the estimating facts you need and for doing the calculations required. But remember, no pricing takes place on the Quantity Sheet. That comes later, as we'll explain.

We've tried to make this sheet as generic as possible. We want you to be able to use it in a way that's suited to your own estimating style and the size of your project.

How to Use This Form

Begin by calculating the quantity of material needed for each part of the project. On a larger job, use a separate sheet for each division of the work. For example, all excavation work might be listed on one Quantity Sheet. If there are lots of footings, you can devote an entire sheet to footings. On small to medium-sized projects, you might put several materials on one sheet. For instance you might group concrete, steel, lumber and drywall on one sheet for a small room addition. The important thing is to allow yourself enough space to clearly show just how you arrived at each quantity.

The *Description* column names the item being estimated. *Unit* describes the unit you're working in. *Location* describes where the material will be used. The next columns under *Dimensions* describe the coverage area: *w* for width, *l* for length, and *h* for height. Then calculate *Quantity* from the dimensions. Here's an example of how you might fill out one line on the form if you were pouring a garage slab. *Description*: 3½" 5 sack slab, *Unit*: SF (for square feet), *Location*: garage, *Dimensions*, *w*: 5', *l*: 5', *h*: 3½", *Quantity*: 25SF (5'l x 5'h = 25SF). Repeat these same steps for each cost item in the project.

On larger projects, we recommend using a different sheet for each material. Use each row of the form to define a definite area. For a drywall take-off, use one line for each room. That makes it easier to come back later and check your answers.

An estimate for a small project with just a few items may not require a quantity sheet. You may be able to skip right to the Unit Estimate Sheet for both quantity take-off and pricing.

Quantity Sheet

Construction Company

Address

City, State, ZIP

Phone Number

Date: _____

Estimator: _____

Estimate number: _____

Building location: _____

Date on plans: _____

Description	Unit	Location	Dimensions			Quantity	Location	Dimensions			Quantity	Total quantity
			w	l	h			w	l	h		

Quotation

Form Name on Disk: QUOTE

This form is designed for quoting prices for materials such as custom millwork, doors or windows. But it's versatile enough to use for time and material quotes also.

How to Use This Form

FOB point, which stands for "free on board," describes who pays the freight charges. If you're not going to pay for shipping, you would put your shop or the job site as the FOB point. Title to the goods won't pass to you until you take delivery at the specified location. The seller pays the freight and is also responsible for resolving any freight-damage claims.

Terms describes how you wish to be paid if the quotation is accepted.

Use the blank line in the paragraph at the bottom of the form to set a time limit on the quote's validity. Doing so puts buyers on notice: they only have a limited amount of time to make their decision. A time limit also protects you from price fluctuations.

Quotation

Construction Company
Address
City, State, ZIP
Phone Number

Quotation date: _____

Quotation number: _____

Owner: _____

Project name: _____

Salesperson: _____

To:

_____

_____

_____

_____

Estimated shipping date	Shipped via	FOB point	Terms

Quantity	Description	Price	Amount

We are pleased to submit the above quotation for your consideration. Should you place an order, be assured it will receive our prompt attention. This quotation is valid for _____ days. Thereafter it is subject to change without notice.

By: _____   Accepted: _____   Date: _____

Thank you!

Telephone Quotation

Form Name on Disk: TELQUOTE

Try as you may to eliminate them, last minute quotations are a part of the bidding process. The Telephone Quotation form will help you nail down a bidder's quotation taken over the phone.

The power of this form lies in its accuracy and completeness. So, be careful when filling it out. Make sure you've completed every applicable space, including the sections labeled: *Tax included,* or *Add tax, FOB point,* and *Discount.*

How to Use This Form

The main body of the form includes spaces for *Item number, Description, Quantity, Unit, Unit price* and *Total.* The bottom part of the form has several lines for your notes about *Additions or deletions.* At the very bottom of the form spaces are set aside for you to fill in *Total adjustment* and *Adjusted total bid.*

Fill in this form while you're talking on the phone. Be sure to note the following: *Talked to* and *Time received.* There's one key requirement here, the people at both ends of the phone line must completely agree on exactly what has been said. That means that after you take down a telephone quote, you read it back word-for-word to the caller. Don't hang up until both of you agree fully on every point. If possible use the Fax Quote form instead of taking a phone quote. A fax quote is also safer from a legal standpoint, because you have a written quote and signature in hand.

Telephone Quotation

Construction Company
Address
City, State, ZIP
Phone Number

Date: _____

Owner: _____

Contractor: _____

Project number _____

Project name: _____

Type of work _____

Time received _____   Taken by _____

Talked to _____   Phone _____

State license number _____   Classification _____

Add. number _____   Minority _____   IRS number _____

Tax included _____   Add tax _____   FOB point _____

Bond included _____   Add bond _____   Discount _____

Item number	Description	Quantity	Unit	Unit price	Total
	Total bid				

Additions or deletions:

			Total adjustment		
			Adjusted total bid		

■ Fax Quotation

Form Name on Disk: FAXQUOTE

This is the best and fastest way to send and receive price quotations. Use this form rather than a phone quote, whenever possible. Except for the last few lines, this form looks like a quotation form you would send through the mail.

Note the section at the bottom of the form that allows you to set an expiration date for the quote. This protects you against price fluctuations and puts buyers on notice that they have only so long to make a decision. If you don't set an expiration date, the quote expires in "a reasonable time." That could put you in the middle of a dispute. To avoid arguments over the meaning of "reasonable," list your own expiration date.

To be completely certain of the legality of the quote, you can ask for confirmation by phone, fax, or mail.

Fax Quotation

Construction Company
Address
City, State, ZIP
Phone Number

Date: _____

Quotation number: _____

Contractor: _____

Project name: _____

Salesperson: _____

To:

_____

_____

_____

_____

Estimated shipping date	Shipped via	FOB point	Terms

Quantity	Description	Price	Amount

We are pleased to submit the above quotation for your consideration. Should you place an order, be assured it will receive our prompt attention. This quotation is valid for _____ days. Thereafter it is subject to change without notice.

By _____ Accepted _____ Date _____

Total number of pages including this page _____ .

If you do not receive all pages, please call us.

Please confirm receipt of this fax by

☐ Phone   ☐ Fax   ☐ Mail

Thank You

■ Bid Form

Form Name on Disk: BIDFORM

This handy form is perfect if your bid includes multiple alternates, substitutions, or exclusions. The form is set up to show itemized costs for each alternate. That makes it very useful when clients need to see alternate costs. Tile subcontractors, flooring subs – just about any subcontractor who regularly bids alternate prices – will like this form.

How to Use This Form

This unique bid form has three major sections. Each section has room for a description of the work to be done on the specific item, its *Bid price*, what the *Item includes* and what the *Item excludes, Alternate* items and even *Alternate price* for the alternate item. It also includes check boxes to clarify who is paying *Tax, Delivery* and *Installation* charges, and whether or not the alternate price is included in the bid price.

Bid Form

Construction Company
Address
City, State, ZIP
Phone Number

Date: _____
Project number: _____
Phone number: _____
Contact person: _____

Item Number _____

Bid price: _____

Includes: Tax ☐   Job site delivery ☐   Installation ☐

Item includes: _____
_____
_____

Item excludes: _____
_____
_____

Alternate: _____

Alternate price: _____ included in price above ☐   not included ☐

Item Number _____

Bid price: _____

Includes: Tax ☐   Job site delivery ☐   Installation ☐

Item includes: _____
_____
_____

Item excludes: _____
_____

Alternate: _____

Alternate price: _____ included in price above ☐   not included ☐

Item Number _____

Bid price: _____

Includes: Tax ☐   Job site delivery ☐   Installation ☐

Item includes: _____
_____
_____

Item excludes: _____
_____

Alternate: _____

Alternate price: _____ included in price above ☐   not included ☐

Letter - Bid Follow Up

Form Name on Disk: LETRFOLO

Most jobs are awarded to the lowest responsible bidder. It's common courtesy for the owner, architect or general contractor who solicited the bids to inform every bidder of the results – win or lose. However, more often than not, only the winner finds out who won. The losers are left to guess at the result, or make an embarrassing inquiry about the winning bid.

How to Use This Form

If you don't get a call from an owner about the bid results, send this follow up letter. It's both good business and a subtle reminder that courtesy deserves to be reciprocated. It should put just enough pressure on the owner, architect or general contractor to produce a response. It also serves as a reminder. Creating accurate bids is hard work. You expect the courtesy of a response for your effort, even if you don't win. The letter also shows that you would like to be kept on the bidders' list.

Letter — Bid Follow Up

Construction Company
Address
City, State, ZIP
Phone Number

Date: _____

Owner: _____

Contractor: _____

Project name: _____

Project number: _____

Dear: _____ :

On _____ our company submitted a bid for your _____

for the amount of $ _____ .

I am following up to inquire if you have made a decision on our bid.

We are planning new projects now and would like to include your job on our schedule. If you have any questions, or if I can clarify anything regarding our bid, please call me. I look forward to hearing from you.

Sincerely,

_____

■ CSI Estimator

Form Name on Disk: CSI-EST

The CSI Estimator lists over 400 items commonly found in residential and light commercial projects. It's based on the standard 16 division CSI (Construction Specification Index) numbering system.

No list of possible construction cost items could ever be complete. Construction is too complex and there are too many variables. But this list hits all the high spots. Use the list as a tickler to remind you of items you may have overlooked on a bid.

Many contractors use a list like this to do their estimates. Using a computer, it's easy to read down the list and delete all the items that don't apply to the job you're bidding. Then cut and paste the list into the Unit Cost Estimate Sheets to do the actual estimate, and into the Cost Book to update the prices listed there.

CSI Estimator

Task description	Materials				Labor				Sub bids	Task total
	Unit	Amt.	Cost	Total	Unit	Amt.	Cost	Total	Equip/rent	
General Conditions										
Fees										
Fee - City license										
Fee - Parks & recreation										
Fee - Plan check (general)										
Fee - School district										
Fee - Sewer assessment										
Fee - Miscellaneous										
Fee - Coastal development										
Fee - Dedication										
Fee - Environmental health										
Fee - Front end advances (utilities)										
Fee - Mitigation										
Fee - Parking										
Fee - Safety OSHA										
Fee - Traffic control										
Fee - Transportation corridor										
Fee - Utilities tie-in										
Fee - Water department (water meters)										
Fee - Water share rights										
Permits										
Permit - Building										
Permit - Demolition										
Permit - Grading										
Permit - Power pole (temporary)										
Permit - Public work										
Permit - Retaining or property line walls										
Permit - Miscellaneous										
Permit - Electric										
Permit - Encroachment										
Permit - Fire sprinklers										
Permit - Fireplace										
Permit - Mechanical										
Permit - Plumbing										

CSI Estimator (Continued)

Task description	Materials				Labor				Sub bids Equip\Rent	Task total
	Unit	Amt.	Cost	Total	Unit	Amt.	Cost	Total		
Permit - Sewer cap										
Permit - Street use/dumpster/etc.										
Temporary On Site										
Dumpster										
Electric meter & power billing										
Fence & gates										
Job shed or trailer										
Phone / fax line										
Power pole & equipment										
Rental equipment										
Job toilet										
Water billing										
Temp. miscellaneous										
Barricades										
Container storage										
Crane										
Dewatering										
Dust protection										
Progress photos										
Protection, finishes										
Protection, pedestrian (walk with cover)										
Protection, weather										
Security lighting										
Superintendent (full/part time)										
Carpenter										
Finish carpenter										
Semi-skilled labor										
Day labor										
Transportation										
Contractor's Insurance										
Builder's risk (fire & theft)										
Performance bond										
Public liability & completed operations										

CSI Estimator (Continued)

| Task descriptions | Materials | | | | Labor | | | Sub bids | Task total |
	Unit	Amt.	Cost	Total	Unit	Amt.	Cost	Labor	Equip\Rent	
Miscellaneous Conditions										
Architectural drawings										
Engineering consultants										
Bid procedure										
Blueprints & specifications										
Certified inspectors										
Perishable supplies billable to job										
Cleanup final subcontract										
General cond. miscellaneous										
As-built drawings										
General contractor consulting										
Operation & maintenance manuals										
Product warranties packages										
Sitework										
Demolition										
Concrete coring										
Cut & break & remove all concrete indicated										
Demolition, major										
Tree removal										
Asbestos removal										
Shoring costs										
Grading										
Backfill & compact										
Backhoe trench										
Footing soils remove										
Erosion control and drainage										
Grading rough										
Grading finish										
Import/export (allowance)										
Utilities to Building										
Fire hydrant										
Relocate/remove power pole										
Relocate/remove street light										
Cable TV service										
Electrical service										

CSI Estimator (Continued)

Task description	Materials				Labor				Sub bids Equip\Rent	Task total
	Unit	Amt.	Cost	Total	Unit	Amt.	Cost	Total		
Fire sprinkler service										
Gas service										
Telephone service										
Water service										
Laterals sewer										
Storm drainage										
Street signs										
Asphalt										
Patch										
Paving										
Slurry coat										
Striping & bumper										
Gates & Fences										
Fence (chain link, wood, glass)										
Gates (chain link, wood, glass)										
Wrought iron or metal										
Landscaping										
Backflow preventer										
Landscape lighting										
Planters, preformed										
Stepping stones										
Planting & irrigation										
Concrete										
Footings										
Gunite										
Offsite (sidewalk/curb/gutter/driveway)										
Onsite (swale/curb/sidewalk/etc.)										
Piles & caissons										
Precast products										
Retaining wall concrete (poured in place)										
Masonry										
Fencing or planters										

CSI Estimator (Continued)

Task description	Materials				Labor			Sub bids Equip\Rent	Task total
	Unit	Amt.	Cost	Total	Unit	Amt.	Cost	Total	
Retaining walls									
Trash enclosure									
Miscellaneous Sitework									
Soils engineering & inspections									
Civil engineering & survey									
Stucco walls/trash area/planter/etc.									
Painting gates/fence/bollards/other									
Bridge									
Docks & boat facilities									
Shoring & bulkheading									
Sitework miscellaneous									
Bollards									
Cap sewer									
Drainage systems									
Soil poisoning or treatment									
Vaults & vault doors									
Concrete									
Foundation (footings and slab)									
Concrete patch work									
Gypcrete, lightweight, etc.									
Lab testing concrete									
Prestress concrete construction									
Tilt-up construction									
Masonry									
Block foundation walls									
Glass block									
Lab testing masonry									
Masonry miscellaneous									
Masonry special finishes (cast conc. columns)									
Sandblasting									
Stonework									
Veneers									
Metal									
Metal - ornamental (handrails/railings/etc.)									
Registered inspector metal									

CSI Estimator (Continued)

Task descriptions	Materials				Labor					Sub bids Equip\Rent	Task total
	Unit	Amt.	Cost	Total	Unit	Amt.	Cost	Total			
Structural steel											
Steel miscellaneous											
Metal – equipment screens											
Metal – light gauge frame											
Metal siding											
Metal – shop drawings											
Metal – stairs/spiral/access ladders											
Metal – structural connections											
Structural steel specialties											
Carpentry											
Carpentry, rough & light hardware											
Light framing hardware											
Lumber, glue laminated beams											
Lumber, rough											
Lumber, truss or joist											
Lumber list (send out for builder's list)											
Carpentry, rough set exterior doors & windows											
Carpentry, finish											
Cabinets, millwork installed											
Architectural millwork											
Fireplace mantel											
Special railings											
Wood base & casing (material)											
Plastic, special fabrications											
Plastic laminates											
Lumber finish											
Lumber wood siding											
Wood siding, labor to install											
Storage shelving											
Moisture Protection											
Caulking & sealants											
Insulation/air infiltration											
Hot mop (tub & shower base)											
Roof accessories											
Roof patch											

CSI Estimator (Continued)

Task description	Materials				Labor				Sub bids Equip\Rent	Task total
	Unit	Amt.	Cost	Total	Unit	Amt.	Cost	Total		
Roofing										
Roofing metal fabrication										
Rain gutters										
Sheet metal standard										
Sheet metal special fabrication										
Skylights										
Waterproofing										
Weatherstripping										
Door, Window, Glass										
Doors										
Coil roll up door										
Garage door										
Powered operators garage door openers										
Security, iron type (rolling or overhead)										
Access doors										
Entry doors and frames										
Fire doors and frames (1, 2 hour)										
French doors and frames										
Metal doors and frames										
Specialty doors and frames										
Wood doors and frames										
Glass										
Glass bath enclosure										
Glass screen walls										
Glass special application										
Mirror										
Stained/beveled glass/etched										
Storefront glass										
Wardrobe (mirror, vinyl, other)										
Window glazing										
Windows aluminum										
Windows & French doors install										
Windows wood										

CSI Estimator (Continued)

Task description	Materials				Labor				Sub bids Equip-Rent	Task total
	Unit	Amt.	Cost	Total	Unit	Amt.	Cost	Total		
Hardware										
Finish (knobs, latches, closers)										
Installation of hardware (labor)										
Medicine cabinets										
Toilet and bath accessories										
Finish										
Decking										
Elastomeric, mer-kote, dexotex, other										
Hot mop										
Wood decking										
Drywall										
Metal stud framing										
Drywall & metal studs + hang, tape & texture										
Drywall - hang, tape & texture										
Drywall - special finish										
Flooring										
Carpet & pads										
Floor preparation (subfloor, float, other)										
Vinyl base										
Vinyl flooring										
Wood flooring										
Painting										
Paint - exterior only										
Paint - interior & exterior										
Paint - interior only										
Paint - special finishes										
Paperhanging										
Lath & Plaster										
Plaster - exterior only										
Plaster - interior & exterior										

CSI Estimator (Continued)

Task description	Materials				Labor				Sub bids Equip\Rent	Task total
	Unit	Amt.	Cost	Total	Unit	Amt.	Cost	Total		
Plaster - interior only										
Plaster - tile backing										
Tile										
Marble										
Stone										
Terrazzo										
Ceramic										
Special Finish										
Acoustical ceilings										
Acoustical treatments										
Marlite										
Top / simulated marble										
Top / Corian										
Top / unilav (top w/molded sink complete)										
Paneling										
Upholstered treatments										
Specialties										
Access floors and walls										
Awnings										
Chutes (laundry, trash, etc.)										
Directories										
Fireplace masonry										
Fireplace prefab metal										
Louvers & vents										
Luminous ceilings (wood frame)										
Pest control										
Postal facilities										
Screens										
Security grilles										
Signage & graphics										
Stairs construction (wood, metal, hidden)										
Toilet partitions										
Attic access stair										

CSI Estimator (Continued)

Task description	Materials				Labor			Sub bids Equip\Rent	Task total
	Unit	Amt.	Cost	Total	Unit	Amt.	Cost		
Shutters exterior									
Wardrobe & closet specialties									
Equipment									
Appliance (stove/hood/dishwsh/disp/micro)									
Appliance (washer & dryer)									
Central vacuum									
Safe or vault									
Equipment miscellaneous									
Furnishings									
Blinds, shades & shutters interior									
Drapery & curtain hardware									
Interior plants & planters									
Moveable partitions									
Furnishings miscellaneous									
Special Construction									
Jacuzzi & equipment shed or vault									
Pool or spa decking									
Swimming pool & equipment shed or vault									
Sauna & equipment									
Fountains or waterscape									
Tennis courts									
Wine storage room									
Conveying									
Dumbwaiter									
Elevators									
Wheelchair lift									
Mechanical									
HVAC									
Heating and air conditioning									
Fan special use									
Ducts for all ventilating fans									
Registers grilles & diffusers									
HVAC shop drawings									
Exhaust fan system									
Refrigeration									

CSI Estimator (Continued)

Task description	Materials				Labor				Sub bids Equip\Rent	Task total
	Unit	Amt.	Cost	Total	Unit	Amt.	Cost	Total		
Fire Equipment										
Fire sprinkler system										
F.S. shop drawings										
Alarm special application										
Halon system										
Hose cabinet ____ racks ____ reels ____ hose ____										
Extinguishers ____ & cabinets ____										
Plumbing										
General plumbing										
Fixture trim										
Fixtures Jacuzzi tub										
Fixtures plumbing										
Fixtures tub/shower (fiberglass)										
Plumbing shop drawings										
Cesspool/septic tank/pump										
Sump pump/sewer injector										
Wall heaters										
Solar system										
Electrical										
Electric general										
Exhaust fans interior (bath/kitchen/laundry)										
Shop drawings										
Lamps & bulbs										
Low voltage - alarm, burglar										
Low voltage - cable TV prewire										
Low voltage - communications (intercom syst.)										
Low voltage - emergency lights										
Low voltage - music system										
Low voltage - telephone prewire										
Low voltage - TV antenna										
Parking lot lighting										
Smoke detectors										
Door bell										

CSI Estimator (Continued)

Task description	Materials				Labor				Sub bids Equip\Rent	Task total
	Unit	Amt.	Cost	Total	Unit	Amt.	Cost	Total		
CSI Summary										
General Conditions										
Sitework										
Concrete										
Masonry										
Metal										
Carpentry										
Moisture Protection										
Doors Windows & Glass										
Finish										
Specialties										
Equipment										
Furnishings										
Special Construction										
Conveying										
Mechanical										
Electrical										

Contingency _____ %:

Profit _____ %:

Overhead _____ %:

Total: _____

■ Estimate Checklist

Form Name on Disk: ESTCHECK

This is a long reminder list, set up in the unit estimating format. Its main purpose is to act as a checklist for the person doing the quantity take-off and estimating. Check off each item to be sure nothing was omitted from your estimate.

Again, this list is far from complete. There are literally thousands of items in the average construction job. What your jobs include will depend on the types of work you do: remodeling, new construction, residential or commercial, heavy or light construction. But here's a tip for everyone. You'll make this list an even more valuable tool by adding anything you use on your jobs that we haven't included in the list already. Then copy and paste the additions into your cost book and your estimate.

Estimate Checklist

Task description	Materials				Labor				Sub bids/ Equip. rental	Task total	Notes/ allowances
	Unit	Amt.	Cost	Total	Unit	Amt.	Cost	Total			
Planning & initialization											
Building permits											
Construction heating											
Inspection fees											
Office trailer setup											
Plans											
Safety barriers											
Sewer connection fee											
Temporary power											
Water meter fees											
Other											
Site work											
Backfill & grading											
Basement excavation											
Earth imported/export											
Footings excavation											
Off site improvements											
Sewer lateral/waterline											
Site preparation											
Soil treatment											
Other											
Concrete											
Flatwork											
Footings											
Foundation											
Additives											
Area wells											
Bolts											
Chamfer strips											
Cold joint											

Estimate Checklist (Continued)

Task description	Materials				Labor				Sub bids/ Equip. rental	Task total	Notes/ allowances
	Unit	Amt.	Cost	Total	Unit	Amt.	Cost	Total			
Columns											
Drayage											
Expansion joint											
Form oil & cleaner											
Forms & whalers											
Forms, stakes, braces											
Poly/visqueen											
Rebar-1/2" @ ft.											
Rebar-3/8" @ ft.											
Rebar-5/8" @ ft.											
Rebar-7/8" @ ft.											
Rental equipment											
Straw/hay											
Ties & tie wire											
Waterproofing foundation											
Window & door bucks											
Wire mesh											
Other											
Rough lumber											
Studs 2 x 4											
Studs 2 x 6											
Trusses											
Fir 2 x 8 x 8											
Fir 2 x 8 x10											
Fir 2 x 8 x12											
Fir 2 x 8 x14											
Fir 2 x10 x10											
Fir 2 x10 x12											
Fir 2 x10 x14											
Fir 2 x12 x10											
Fir 2 x12 x12											
Fir 2 x12 x14											
Fir 2 x12 x _____											

Estimate Checklist (Continued)

Task description	Materials				Labor				Sub bids/ Equip. rental	Task total	Notes/ allowances
	Unit	Amt.	Cost	Total	Unit	Amt.	Cost	Total			
1 x 4 #2 Grade											
1 x 6 #2 Grade											
1 x 8 #2 Grade											
1 x 10 #2 Grade											
Post-4 x 4"											
Post-6 x 6"											
Glulam											
Plywood 3/8"											
Plywood 1/2"											
Plywood 5/8"											
Plywood 3/4"											
Plywood T & G 5/8"											
Plywood T & G 3/4"											
Fascia											
Soffit											
Frieze											
Caulking & sealants											
Builders adhesive											
Scaffolding											
Equipment rental											
Nails 16d box											
Nails 16d nail gun											
Nails 8d box											
Nails 8d nail gun											
Nails 16d duplex											
Nails 8d duplex											
Nails-finish (rough only)											
Bolts, washers, nuts											
Framing connectors											
Saddles											
Staples, air gun											
Other											
Roofing											
Built-up											

Estimate Checklist (Continued)

Task description	Materials				Labor				Sub bids/ Equip. rental	Task total	Notes/ allowances
	Unit	Amt.	Cost	Total	Unit	Amt.	Cost	Total			
Tile											
Shake											
Cedar											
Drying-in											
Felt-#15											
Felt-#30											
Ice & water shield											
Flashing & counter F.											
Drip edge											
Valley tin											
Roof jacks & vents											
Galv. roof nails-3/4"											
Galv. roof nails-1-1/2"											
Simplex nails											
Roofing cement											
Other											
Insulation											
Walls											
Ceiling											
Miscellaneous insulation											
Radiant barrier											
Vapor barrier											
Drywall											
Corner bead											
Drytite nails-@ lb.											
Hot mud											
J-Metal											
Knife blades											
Masking supplies											
Perfa-tape											
Quick-tape											
Topping-boxes											
Other											

Estimate Checklist (Continued)

Task description	Materials			Labor				Sub bids/ Equip. rental	Task total	Notes/ allowances
	Unit	Amt.	Cost	Total	Unit	Amt.	Cost	Total			
Finish carpentry											
Base molding											
Chair rail											
Crown molding											
Doors											
Door casing											
Front door											
3/0 exterior											
2/8 exterior											
Fire rated/self-closing											
3/0 Hollow Core interior											
2/8 H. C. interior											
2/6 H. C. interior											
2/4 H. C. interior											
2/0 H. C. interior											
Bi-fold 7'											
Bi-fold 6'											
Bi-fold 5'											
Bi-fold 4'											
By-pass 7'											
By-pass 6'											
By-pass 5'											
By-pass 4'											
Pocket 3/0											
Pocket 2/8											
Pocket 2/6											
Pocket 2/4											
Specialty doors											
Garage door											
Shelving 1 x12											
Shelving 1 x16											
1 x 4" pine											
1 x 6" pine											
1 x12" pine											

Estimate Checklist (Continued)

Task description	Materials				Labor				Sub bids/ Equip. rental	Task total	Notes/ allowances
	Unit	Amt.	Cost	Total	Unit	Amt.	Cost	Total			
3/4" Ply/pressed wood											
Shims											
Keyed locks											
Deadbolts											
Privacy locks											
Passage locks											
Other locks/latches											
Pulls & catches											
Door bumpers/stops											
Towel bars/rings											
Paper holders											
Soap dishes											
Closet rods											
Robe hooks											
Other bathroom hardw.											
Door viewer											
House numbers											
Mail box											
Garage door operator											
Thresholds											
Weatherstripping											
Screen doors											
Other											
Wall coverings											
Acoustical ceiling tile											
Ceramic tile											
Masking supplies											
Paint rollers/brushes											
Paint-alcohol sealer											
Paint-latex											
Paint-oil											
Paint-PVA											
Paneling (sheets)											

Estimate Checklist (Continued)

Task description	Materials				Labor			Sub bids/ Equip. rental	Task total	Notes/ allowances
	Unit	Amt.	Cost	Total	Unit	Amt.	Cost	Total		
Sandpaper, caulking, etc.										
Stain & varnish										
Textured paints										
Wainscot										
Wallpaper tools/glue										
Wallpaper/border (rolls)										
Other										
Floor covering										
Area rugs										
Asphalt/rubber tile										
Base (rubber)										
Carpet glue										
Carpet tool rental										
Carpets										
Ceramic tile										
Concrete sealer										
Cove										
Hardwoods/parquet										
Linoleum										
Linoleum glue										
Metal trim										
Nails & glue										
Other exterior carpets										
Other floor paint										
Padding										
Quarry tile										
Rock										
Roller & blades										
Seam filler										
Seam tape										
Staples										
Synthetic turf										
Tack strips										
Other										

Estimate Checklist (Continued)

Task description	Materials				Labor				Sub bids/ Equip. rental	Task total	Notes/ allowances
	Unit	Amt.	Cost	Total	Unit	Amt.	Cost	Total			
Glazing											
Windows											
Patio sliding door											
Stained glass											
Sandblast/etched glass											
Other glazing											
Specialty glass											
Mirrors											
Medicine cabinets											
Skylights											
Other											
Masonry											
Fireplace											
Fireplace face											
Veneer											
Masonry sidewalks/paths											
Fence											
Other											
Plumbing											
Rough											
Finish											
Jacuzzi - spa											
Shower stall											
Tub - enclosure											
Extra water heaters											
Fixture allowance											
Water softener											
Sprinkling sys./rough											
Other											
HVAC											
Furnace & distribution											
Attic vents											

Estimate Checklist (Continued)

Task description	Materials			Labor				Sub bids/ Equip. rental	Task total	Notes/ allowances
	Unit	Amt.	Cost	Total	Unit	Amt.	Cost	Total			
Bathroom vents											
Kitchen vent											
Other vents											
Evaporative cooler											
Air conditioning											
Special controls											
Area heater											
Wood-burning stove											
Fireplace - gas log											
Fireplace blower											
BBQ grill											
Humidifier											
Electronic air purifier											
Other											
Electrical											
Rough											
Finish											
Light fixture allowance											
Landscape light(s)											
Connect HVAC, etc.											
Doorbell/chime											
Security system											
TV/ stereo sys/antenna											
Intercom system											
Computer system											
Smoke/fire alarm sys											
Telephone installation											
Other											
Cabinets											
Kitchen cabinets											
Bath cabinets											
Linen closets											
Bookshelves											

Estimate Checklist (Continued)

Task description	Materials			Labor			Sub bids/ Equip. rental	Task total	Notes/ allowances
	Unit	Amt.	Cost	Total	Unit	Amt.	Cost	Total	
Pantry									
Clothes chute									
Garage - cabinets									
Garage - workbench									
Other									
Hard surfaces/counters									
Ceramic tile									
Corian									
Extra materials									
Plastic laminate bid									
Synthetic marble									
Other									
Appliances									
Countertop unit									
Dishwasher									
Disposal									
Freezer									
Microwave oven									
Range									
Range hood									
Refrigerator									
Separate oven(s)									
Trash compactor									
Under cabinet units									
Other									
Exterior wall coverings									
Gutter & downspout									
Rock									
Siding									
Stucco									
Other									

Estimate Checklist (Continued)

Task description	Materials				Labor				Sub bids/ Equip. rental	Task total	Notes/ allowances
	Unit	Amt.	Cost	Total	Unit	Amt.	Cost	Total			
Decorating											
Decorator fee											
Model home furnishing											
Other											
Landscaping											
Bark/gravel/rock											
Boxes /borders/ pots											
Flowers											
Fountain											
Grading											
Irrigating											
Shrubs											
Sod/ lawn											
Topsoil											
Trees											
Yard light											
Other											
Misc. & other structures											
Breezeway											
Decking											
Fence - block @ ft.											
Fence - chainlink @ ft.											
Fence - other											
Fence - prefab concrete											
Fence - wood @ ft.											
Final cleanup											
Gazebo											
Glass breakage allow.											
Greenhouse											
Interest incurred											
Lattice											
Ornamental iron											
Railing											

Estimate Checklist (Continued)

Task description	Materials				Labor				Sub bids/ Equip. rental	Task total	Notes/ allowances
	Unit	Amt.	Cost	Total	Unit	Amt.	Cost	Total			
Shed											
Signs											
Theft											
Vandalism											
Other ___											
Other ___											
Other ___											
Subtotals:											

Contingency _____ %

Overhead _____ %

Profit _____ %

Total estimate _____

■ Unit Estimate Sheet

Form Name on Disk: UNITEST and UNITEST&

Use this form to list estimated costs based on unit prices. It's closest to the paper estimating system that most contractors use, or used in the past. It's based on unit pricing. You enter the number of units, then the known cost per unit (square feet, board feet or cubic yards).

On small estimates, with just a few items, you might do all the quantity and cost calculations right on the Unit Estimate Sheet. If so, use the last lines to enter subtotals and totals. On more complex estimates, do all of your figuring on the Quantity Sheet. Then transfer a summary of the accumulated costs onto the Unit Estimate Sheet.

How to Use This Form

This form can be filled out either with a computer or by hand. Notice that major headings divide the form into *Task description, Materials, Labor, Sub bids/Equipment rental, Task total* and *Notes/allowances*.

The first column, *Task description*, is a list of all the tasks needed to complete the job. When filling out this portion, it's a good idea to refer to a checklist or tickler list of general construction tasks. That prevents overlooking items like construction cleanup or bonds. In fact, if your jobs usually include items such as association fees or plan fees, enter them permanently on the version of this form kept with your computer.

The first column in the *Materials* section *Unit* defines the units used to estimate each material. Use the unit that's most convenient. For example, if you're estimating the cost of framing a floor, use either square feet or board feet as the unit. The choice is yours. Use standard abbreviations, such as SF for square feet, LF for linear feet, CY for cubic yards, BF for board feet, etc.

The second *Materials* column is *Amt.*, for amount or how many units are needed to complete the task. This figure usually is taken from your quantity take-off sheet. However, if the task is simple or small, you might choose to do your take-off right on this estimate sheet.

Enter your unit cost in the next *Materials* column *Cost*. This figure might come from your cost book or from a supplier. Be sure the unit of measure is consistent for each item listed. The fourth, and last column in the *Materials* section is *Total*. This figure is the result of multiplying the *Amt.* column by the *Cost* column. If you're working with this form in a spreadsheet program, you can enter a formula that will automatically calculate the total.

You'll use the four columns in the *Labor* section in much the same way. Hr, Day, and Job are the sort of units that are most often used to measure labor. However, you can also use dimensional units, like square feet, if you know the labor time per square foot. In other words, if you know a carpenter can install 1,250 board feet of 2 x 10 joists in 8 hours, you can figure the cost per board foot and use that cost in this section. You could just as well convert the cost to square feet of joist coverage and use SF. Use the method you prefer – or use whatever cost you already have on record.

Obtain the value for this *Cost* column either from your cost book or some other guide. Then multiply the *Amt.* by the *Cost* to find the *Total*. For example, ten hours times $15 per hour is $150. Be sure to use complete labor costs (base rate + burden) when you're figuring unit labor costs.

Use the *Sub bids/Equipment rental* column to record a subcontractor's bid price or to list equipment rental costs. If you're subcontracting a phase of the project, just enter the sub's total price in this space.

To find the *Task total,* add together the *Materials, Total* and the *Labor, Total* and enter the result.

Near the bottom of the form you'll find the *Subtotals* row. That's followed by lines to add in various percentages for *Contingency,* and *Overhead & profit*. The *Contingency* is intended as a safeguard to cover the unforeseen. However, it works just as well as a way to disguise an estimate omission. The *Overhead & profit* line is next. Calculate overhead and profit as a percentage of your estimated cost. Then you enter profit again as a percentage of the total estimated cost. The final line, *Total estimate*, sums up the entire sheet. This figure includes all the subtotals and the added percentages.

You can use this Unit Estimate Sheet as part of a four-part computerized system. The other three parts are: the Cost Book, the Proposal, and the Progress Billing. These four forms are a "system" in the sense of being designed from the start to work together. You can set up your computer's database so that it will "look up" an item, group it with related items already in the same estimate, and then cut and paste the cost data into the estimate. All you do then, is fill in the material and labor quantities for the estimate. Once the estimate's complete, it's easy to copy and paste this same data into the itemized proposal and the billing sheet.

Unit Estimate Sheet

Construction Company
Address
City, State, ZIP
Phone Number

Date: _____
Owner: _____
Contractor: _____
Estimate number: _____
Project name: _____

Task description	Materials			Labor			Sub bids/ Equipment rental	Task total	Notes/ allowances
	Unit	Amt.	Cost	Total	Unit	Amt.	Cost	Total	

(Note: the Materials group contains Unit, Amt., Cost, Total; the Labor group contains Unit, Amt., Cost, Total.)

Task description	Materials Unit	Amt.	Cost	Total	Labor Unit	Amt.	Cost	Total	Sub bids/ Equipment rental	Task total	Notes/ allowances
Subtotals:											

Contingency _____ %
Overhead & profit _____ %
Total estimate _____

Unit Estimate Sheet (Additional)

Task description	Materials				Labor				Sub bids/ Equipment rental	Task total	Notes/ allowances
	Unit	Amt.	Cost	Total	Unit	Amt.	Cost	Total			

Estimate Recap Sheet

Form Name on Disk: ESTRECAP

Use this sheet to summarize labor, material and subcontract costs from your Quantity Takeoff sheets. For example, all the cost information on sidewalks (forms, concrete, finishing) might be listed on one line opposite "Sidewalks." All the gypsum wallboard might be listed on the line "Gypsum wallboard."

How to Use This Form

Use the *Task description* column to describe the work being done. Then list the item *Quantity* and the *Unit* it's measured in (such as Ea for each, or LF for linear feet) in the next two columns. If you're pricing a group of items with many mixed units (such as a plumbing or electrical system), you'll leave the quantity and unit boxes blank.

Record your total costs in the *Total material, Total labor*, and *Total sub bids/equipment rental* columns. Then use the *Unit cost* columns to break out your cost per unit. The last column of unit cost figures (on the far right side of the form) is especially important and useful. These figures are your installed cost per unit. All the costs for material, labor and equipment are included. This is the data you need to build a personalized cost book that's based on unit costs. However, remember to use consistent units, otherwise your unit costs are meaningless. For example, say your unit cost for sidewalks is per square foot of sidewalk. That means all the costs (concrete, as well as its forming, placing and finishing) must also be per square foot of sidewalk. It may seem awkward at first to convert all pricing to unit costs. But stick with it. These figures are the foundation for your personal cost book that will speed and simplify all of your cost estimates.

Estimate Recap Sheet

Construction Company
Address
City, State, ZIP
Phone Number

Date: _____
Owner: _____
Estimate number: _____
Project name: _____

Task description	Quantity	Unit	Total material	Unit cost	Total labor	Unit cost	Total sub bids/ equipment rental	Unit cost

■ Summary of Estimate

File Name on Disk: SUMESTIM

The Summary of Estimate is just that – a summary of the costs for each section of an estimate. Consider giving this summary to clients as a supplement to the proposal.

How to Use This Form

Fill out this sheet after you've completed the itemized estimate. It provides columns for *Classification, Total estimated material costs, Total estimated labor costs, Total sub-bids* (subcontractor bids) and *Total*. If there are equipment rental costs, list them in the *Total sub-bids* column.

A *Classification* includes whatever you want it to include – one item or the total for a group consisting of dozens of items. For instance, if there's only one kind of drywall in the project, the classification is identical to the item itself. On the other hand, if you're using concrete several places (footings, slab, sidewalks and planters, for example), the concrete classification could summarize all of the concrete items.

The data for filling in the next three columns: *Total estimated material costs, Total estimated labor costs,* and *Total sub-bids* comes from your Estimate Sheet. The last column, *Total* is simply the sum of the previous three columns.

Use the *Subtotals* row near the bottom of the form to list totals for each column.

If you include a *Contingency* in your bids, fill in the percentage on the next line, then multiply that percentage by the subtotal and enter the result in the box. Next, calculate your *Overhead* and *Profit* and fill in those boxes. For example, if your overhead is 10 percent of your gross costs, multiply 10 percent by the total cost.

Use the *Other* line for any other costs that are a percentage of the subtotal bid. For instance, if the cost of surety bonds will be a percentage of the bid, show that percentage on the *Other* line. Finally, you add it all up: *Subtotal, Contingency, Overhead, Profit,* and *Other*. Enter the result in the *Total* column on the *Amount of bid* line. This is the proverbial "bottom line."

Summary of Estimate

Construction Company
Address
City, State, ZIP
Phone Number

Date: _____

Estimator: _____

Owner: _____

Estimate number: _____

Project name: _____

	Classification	Total estimated material costs	Total estimated labor costs	Total sub-bids	Total
1					
2					
3					
4					
5					
6					
7					
8					
9					
10					
11					
12					
13					
14					
15					
16					
17					
18					
19					
	Subtotals:				
			Contingency: _____%		
			Overhead: _____%		
			Profit: _____%		
			Other: _____%		
			Amount of bid:		

■ FHA Cost Breakdown

Form Name on Disk: FHACOST

This form lists 46 construction classifications normally found in new residential or remodeling construction. From general conditions to blinds and shades, this form presents a professional-looking summary of your estimate. In all important aspects, it's virtually identical to FHA Form 2328.

This form groups certain items together into divisions. This grouping will seem logical to some and completely illogical to others. That's where working with this form on your computer gives you an advantage. With a computer, it's very simple for you to modify the form to suit your own logic and bidding style.

For example, you might bid metal flashings with roofing, not with miscellaneous metal. Or you might want to have screens, doors and windows broken out separately. (See the Unit Estimate Sheet.) But remember, what seems right to you may seem awkward to others. For example, many banks feel right at home using the FHA cost breakdown form just the way it is.

How to Use This Form

This sheet is filled out *after* you've completed the estimate. Start by filling in the blanks at the top right: *Date, Sponsor* (the lending institution), *Building ID* (an eight-digit assigned project number), *Project name* and *Location*. A separate form is needed for each structure type in the project.

The first two columns on the far left of the form are for identifying numbers. *L* stands for Line, and these are a simple series starting with 1 and ending with 53. *D* stands for Division. These numbers follow the standard FHA Division numbers developed from the cost accounting section of the uniform system.

We've already filled in the *Trade item* column for you. All you need to fill in are the *Cost* and *Trade description* columns. Some amount of shuffling will probably be needed to fit your estimate items into these preprinted categories. Use the space in the *Trade description* column to give a more detailed description of the item of work.

Under *Trade item*, numbers 1 through 31 are for the main structure. Line 32 is a structure subtotal. Costs for any *Accessory structures* such as shops, pump houses, and storage sheds go on Line 33. Then you add these costs to those for the main structure and enter that sum on Line 34.

If there is more than one structure, you need to do a summary form to cover the entire project. Use the part of this form that starts on line 34, with the total of all structure costs from the individual forms. Lines 35 through 40 respectively cover *Earthwork, Site utilities, Roads & walks, Site improvements, Lawns & planting,* and *Unusual site conditions.* On Line 41 you enter the *Total land improvements.* The figure you enter on Line 42 is the sum of Lines 34 and 41. On the summary copy of this form you'll also fill in the *General requirements*, Line 43, and the subtotal on Line 44.

On Line 45 enter the *Builder's overhead* and on Line 46 the *Builder's profit*. Enter costs for *Other fees* on Line 49 and *Bond premium* on Line 50. The amount you enter on Line 51 is the *Total for all improvements*. Line 52 is set aside for entering any portion of the *Builder's profit paid by means other than cash*. For example, if part of the builder's payment is made in the form of land or mortgages their value should be entered on Line 52. Line 53, *Total all improvements*, is the result of subtracting Line 52 from Line 51.

This form also includes three side boxes that you may need to fill in from time to time. Each side box has a *Description* column and an *Estimated cost* column. You would use the side box labeled *Non-residential and special exterior land improvements*, for example, if the project included a swimming pool. The other two side boxes are set aside for records of *Off site costs* and *Demolition* costs. Costs for the removal of existing structures, for instance, should be recorded in the *Demolition* side box.

FHA Cost Breakdown

Construction Company
Address
City, State, ZIP
Phone Number

Date: _____

Sponsor: _____

Building ID: _____

Project name: _____

Location: _____

L	D	Trade item	Cost	Trade description
1	3	Concrete		
2	4	Masonry		
3	5	Metals		
4	6	Rough carpentry		
5	6	Finish carpentry		
6	7	Waterproofing		
7	7	Insulation		
8	7	Roofing		
9	7	Sheet metal		
10	8	Doors		
11	8	Windows		
12	8	Glass		
13	9	Lath & plaster		
14	9	Drywall		
15	9	Tile work		
16	9	Acoustical		
17	9	Wood flooring		
18	9	Resilient flooring		
19	9	Painting & decorating		
20	10	Specialties		
21	11	Special equipment		
22	11	Cabinets		
23	11	Appliances		
24	12	Blinds & shades, artwork		
25	12	Carpets		
26	13	Special construction		
27	14	Elevators		
28	15	Plumbing & hot water		
29	15	Heat & ventilation		

FHA Cost Breakdown (Continued)

				Non residential & special exterior land improvement		Offsite costs (Not inc. in trade item breakdown)	
30	15	Air conditioning					
31	16	Electrical					
32		**Subtotal (structures)**					
33		Accessory structures					
34		**Total (lines 32 & 33)**					
35	2	Earthwork					
36	2	Site utilities					
37	2	Roads & walks					
38	2	Site improvements					
39	2	Lawns & planting					
40	2	Unusual site conditions		**Non residential & special exterior land improvement**		**Offsite costs** (Not inc. in trade item breakdown)	
41		**Total land improvements**					
42		**Total structure & land improvements**		Description	Estimated cost	Description	Estimated cost
43	1	General requirements					
44		**Subtotal (lines 41 and 42)**					
45		Builder's overhead					
46		Builder's profit		TOTAL: $ _____			
47		**Subtotal (lines 44 thru 46)**		**Other fees**		TOTAL: $ _____	
48						**Demolition** (Not inc. in trade item breakdown)	
49		**Other fees**					
50		Bond premium				Description	Estimated cost
51		**Total for all improvements**					
52		Builder's profit paid by means other than cash					
53		**Total all improvements (less #52)**		TOTAL: $ _____		TOTAL: $ _____	

Mortgagor: _____ By: _____ Date: _____

Contractor: _____ By: _____ Date: _____

FHA: _____ Date: _____
Processing Analyst

FHA: _____ Date: _____
Chief Underwriter

FHA: _____ Date: _____
Chief, Cost Branch or Cost Analyst

■ Cost Data Form

Form Name on Disk: COSTDATA

Accurate cost data is essential if you want to create accurate estimates. The most accurate cost information you'll ever find is the record of actual costs on your own jobs. There's no cost guide available that shows your costs on work done with your crews and under your supervision and using your equipment and doing it your way. Only you can collect information like that. If you're not doing it, your estimating results are going to be unpredictable at best. At least occasionally an estimate will become a disaster.

Every contractor should keep a book of current costs for the items the contractor bids most often. That's extremely valuable information at bid time. This Cost Data Form is the first step in creating your personal unit price book.

Cost data can be gleaned from many sources. Naturally, material costs are available from suppliers. Some suppliers have computer systems that let you access material costs and even buy materials with a modem. Subcontractors can help you with unit costs if you ask them. Commercial cost guides like the *National Construction Estimator* can also help. But none of this information should be anything more than a supplement to your own cost guide.

We recommend filling out the Cost Data Form during the estimating process. Use it to record the type of work, where the cost data came from, and information about the items being priced. Record any assumptions made during the estimating process so you know why each figure was used in the estimate.

Once it's complete, make one copy and then file the original in the job cost folder along with the estimate. The copy, meanwhile, goes into a three-ring binder. We'll call this your Cost Data Source Book. Use the data stored in this three-ring binder to update your cost book. The cost book is simply a list (either on paper or in a computer) of all the material and labor unit costs you regularly use in your estimates. This cost book should provide quick access to everything you know about pricing the types of work your company handles most often.

How to Use This Form

We've tried to make using this form as automatic as possible, since your estimator will be using it almost daily. We've simplified filling in the form to help save you time. For example, circling the source of information is faster and easier than writing it out each time you fill out this form.

As you do more bidding, you'll find that you fill out this form less and less often. That's because most of your cost items will already be listed in your cost book.

Task description describes the item being costed – a cubic foot of concrete or a square foot of shingle roof. Or it could be a single item like a bathtub, kitchen sink or permit fee.

Information obtained from this space is where you'll record the source of your cost information. Did it come from a telephone interview, a publication, or a subcontractor bid? Perhaps it's a combination of information from several sources. Circle the most appropriate source or fill in the line under *Other.*

In the *Take-off* section of the form we've used the same column headings, in the same order as you'll find them used in both the Cost Book form and the Unit Estimate Sheet. Our goal here was to make data easier to transfer from one sheet to another.

The estimating information in the take-off section should include any and all notes related to the cost of the item. Examples of some things you might want to note in this space include: optimum crew size, tooling requirements, or special tips and techniques that are important to the estimator. These notes also serve as a reminder to the job supervisor, who should review this form before starting the job. Fill in as many lines as needed to record these details. Paper is cheap, but an omitted detail can be very costly.

Cost Data Form

Construction Company
Address
City, State, ZIP
Phone Number

Date: _____
Owner: _____
Contractor: _____
Project number: _____
Project name: _____

Work description: _____

_____

_____

Information obtained from (circle one):

Estimate   Contractor   Publication   Other:

Subcontractor bid   As-built condition   Interview   _____

Take-off:

Task description	Material		Labor		Sub/equip. rental		Notes/ allowances
	Unit	Cost	Unit	Cost	Unit	Cost	

Cost Book

Form Name on Disk: COSTBOOK

Every article or book you read on estimating, and every estimating seminar you attend, will include a suggestion that you keep a book of current costs. This is your cost "bible." It should include cost estimates and actual costs for the work you handle regularly. Most of these costs will be from jobs you've completed. With an accurate and up-to-date cost book, it's easy to look up material and labor costs when compiling estimates for new jobs.

The layout of costs in your cost book should be the same as the cost layout in your Unit Estimate Sheet. That makes it easy to move information from the cost book to your estimates, especially if you're using a computer. Use the Cost Data Form to calculate and explain your current unit costs.

In the *Cost* columns under both *Materials* and *Labor* enter your cost per unit for each particular material or task. For example, under *Materials, Cost* for a 3½-inch concrete slab, you might record $1.55 and this cost would include not only the concrete but also the steel, sand and plastic for the slab as well. In the *Labor, Cost* column (for the same item) the figure $.60 might be entered. Combine these two costs to find the total unit or assembly cost. For example, the concrete slab's total unit cost is: $1.55 + $.60 = $2.15 per square foot of 3½-inch concrete slab.

For the *Unit* columns use whatever units are most convenient for you. For instance, you may consider the "unit" cost of plastic membrane used for curing concrete to be one roll of plastic. Maybe you decide to lump all labor and material cost for that roll together in a single figure, say $25 for the lot. Your entry in the cost book would simply be $25 for each roll, including both labor and material. In this case the entry in the unit columns is Ea meaning for each roll.

For more accuracy, you could just as easily divide the cost per roll ($25) by the number of square feet in the roll. If there are 1000 square feet in the roll, your unit cost would be $.025 per square foot.

How to Use This Form

In the first column, *No.*, record the number that identifies the item or task. You can either assign these numbers yourself or use the Construction Specification Index (CSI) format number. In the next column, *Task description,* record a description of the item or task. Next, comes the *Materials* column which is split into two parts: *Unit* and *Cost*. Record units of measurement using abbreviations, such as: SF for square feet, LF for linear feet, SY for square yards, CY for cubic yards, and Ea for each. It's up to you to decide which unit of measure to use. For instance, if you're recording costs for a 3½-inch slab, you might use either SF or SY for the units. Just remember to keep your units consistent.

Fill in the *Unit* and *Cost* columns in the *Labor* section in much the same way.

Keep your cost book up to date. Review and revise the figures regularly. There are some materials that you'll need to find current prices for each time you bid a job. The price of copper wire for instance can rise and or fall by a full ten percent within a single week. On the other hand, the labor costs for installing copper wire rarely change. As a result, those costs usually only need revision and review about once a year.

Subcontractors are a good source of information for your cost book. For instance, your electrician might tell you that his "rule of thumb" for adding an outlet is $75 if no home run is required and $125 if a home run to the panel is needed. Record costs like this both ways in your cost book. On your Cost Data Form, make a note about what's included in each figure. Does the $75 outlet cost include drywall repair, paint touchup and final cleanup? The figures in your cost book should make that clear.

If you like, enter both your own costs and costs from other sources in your cost book. But remember, your own costs are much more accurate for the work you do because they're based on the way you do business.

Cost Book

Construction Company
Address
City, State, ZIP
Phone Number

Date: _____

No.	Task description	Materials		Labor		Subs bid	Notes Allowances/alternates
		Unit	Cost	Unit	Cost		

Historical Project Cost Sheet

Form Name on Disk: HISTPROJ

Use the Historical Project Cost Sheet to record and analyze actual expenditures on a job. On large or long-term projects, unit costs can vary over time. This sheet can help keep those costs accurate.

This form will be extremely useful if you keep track of job costs. A good cost accounting system will record your actual costs and make it easy to retrieve those costs without too much effort. Most larger construction companies and subcontracting companies follow their actual costs very closely. Smaller companies can get a similar benefit by using the simpler Cost Book form to record costs.

How to Use This Form

Generally the accounting department is responsible for following actual job costs. So filling in the Historical Project Cost Sheet is an accounting function. When complete, it should be filed in a job folder along with a copy of the estimate, the hourly labor rates used on the job and the Cost Data Form for the job. The estimator will refer to this job folder to develop unit costs for the next estimate.

The first column is for *Work code*, which can be a name or perhaps a CSI division number. These codes should match the job cost codes in your computerized accounting system. Columns for *Description, Quantity* and *Unit/type* come next. The values you fill in for *Quantity* as well as *Material job cost, Total* and *Labor job cost, Total* all come from your job costing system. To find *Cost/unit* for either *Material* or *Labor,* divide the total by the units. Be sure to include your labor burden in the figure you enter in the *Total* column of the *Labor job cost* section. *Unit/type* refers to the unit you're using to cost the work. A concrete footing could be priced by the linear foot or the cubic yard. Framing can be priced by the board foot of lumber or the square foot of building.

Historical Project Cost Sheet

Construction Company
Address
City, State, ZIP
Phone Number

Date: _____
Project number: _____
Name: _____
Date started: _____
Date completed: _____

Work code	Description	Quantity	Unit/ type	Material job cost			Labor job cost		
				Total	Units	Cost/unit	Total	Units	Cost/unit

Field Forms

■ Job Information

....

Form Name on Disk: JOBINFO

Use this form as a collection point for information about a proposed construction project. Having all this information readily at hand will save time during your preliminary study of a project. Once you begin work on the job, this form will be useful to the superintendent in the field.

How to Use This Form

Regardless of the scope of the project, you'll always want to check for unusual conditions that could affect the project schedule or project cost. Use this list as a tickler to remind you of points to investigate when making the site visit and studying the plans and specs. Your efforts will be rewarded with more accurate estimates and fewer omissions.

We recommend having the project manager or site superintendent review the estimate documents with the estimator. The project manager or superintendent should check the quantity survey and labor estimate and consider any adverse conditions that present a potential for loss on the job.

Job Information

Construction Company
Address
City, State, ZIP
Phone Number

Bid date: _____

Bid time: _____

Project location: _____

Legal description: _____

Project name: _____

Projected budget: _____

Owner: _____

Billing address: _____

_____

_____

Project funding: _____

Contact person: _____

Telephone number: _____

Drawings/specifications:

Architect _____

Architect's phone number _____

_____complete   ____incomplete   ____ latest revision date

Schedule:

start date _____   duration _____

finish date _____

Site information:

good access	Yes ☐	No ☐	water available	Yes ☐	No ☐
on-site obstructions	Yes ☐	No ☐	power available	Yes ☐	No ☐
poor soils	Yes ☐	No ☐	telephone available	Yes ☐	No ☐
drainage problems	Yes ☐	No ☐	natural gas available	Yes ☐	No ☐
high security risk	Yes ☐	No ☐	office available	Yes ☐	No ☐
demolition needed	Yes ☐	No ☐	debris service available	Yes ☐	No ☐

comment: _____   miles from disposal area _____

_____   miles from home office _____

Job Information (Continued)

Building permit:

                    date filed: _____

                    issued on: _____

                    anticipated: _____

             cost by others: _____

                cost on bid: _____

Special requirements:

_____

_____

_____

_____

_____

Bond:

                    required _____

               not required _____

                    optional _____

Insurance:

                  typical ☐ yes ☐ no

             part of bid ☐ yes ☐ no

             special type: _____

                       _____

Miscellaneous:

_____

_____

_____

_____

_____

Signed: _____

Finish Schedule by Room

Form Name on Disk: FINISCHD

Use this multipurpose form to record all interior finish details. It lets you list, room-by-room, the trim, flooring and wall finish. There's also space for you to add comments about custom items in each room. The form will also be useful when making the material cost estimate takeoff, as an office checklist, as a client checklist, and as a field work list for subcontractors and superintendents.

How to Use This Form

This form should be completed by the cost estimator and perhaps checked by the designer or owner. In the vertical spaces at the top of the form, describe the material and finish for each surface. Then, across the rows, check off the floor type, trim types, wall finish and any other interior trim details for each room. There's room to note paint color and wallpaper styles in the blank columns.

Down the left column, list each *Room* in the project by either name or number. Across the top of the form, list all the finish materials to be used. For example, you might list:

Flooring (with types such as tile, oak, vinyl and carpet)
Paint (such as flat white, gloss white and eggshell)
Trim (such as wainscot, crown, casing and base)
Wallpaper (such as A-203 and D-308)

Then put a check mark in the column and row where each finish material will be used. For example, to show that the D-308 paper will be used in bedroom #2, put a check mark in the box where the bedroom #2 row intersects with the wallpaper D-308 column.

Be sure to record the latest plan *Revision number* or revision date in the upper right corner. Information in your finish schedule will change frequently. Be sure your form reflects the latest changes.

Finish Schedule by Room

Construction Company
Address
City, State, ZIP
Phone Number

Date: _____
Owner: _____
Revision number: _____   Date: _____
Sheet number: _____   of _____
Project name: _____
Project number: _____

Room	#	Flooring	Paint/color	Notes

Specialty Selection Sheet

Form Name on Disk: SPECSEL

Use this form to collect all those difficult-to-track details such as the style, color, size, and item number of the guest bathroom faucet. It's set up on a room-by-room basis. Of course, if the form is in a computer, you can sort the list any way you choose.

How to Use This Form

The form acts as a tickler, since many of the common items are already listed for you. There's also room to add your own items. Fill out this form with the help of your client. After you and the client check every item, have the client sign and date the list at the bottom.

Specialty Selection Sheet

Construction Company
Address
City, State, ZIP
Phone Number

Date: _____
Name: _____
Phone number: _____
Project name: _____
Project number: _____

Room	Description	Number	Color	Notes
Roofing				
Siding				
Kitchen	Cabinets			
	Countertop			
	Flooring			
	Appliances			
Bath 1	Fixtures			
	Countertop			
	Flooring			
Bath 2	Fixtures			
	Countertop			
	Flooring			
Laundry				
Carpet				

I agree to the selections made above and understand that if I wish to make any changes, the Builder has the right to deny the request or add a service charge to the cost of the project to cover any costs incurred in making the changes.

Client: _____

Signed: _____   Date: _____

Schedule Sheet

Form Name on Disk: SCHEDULE

This is a simple yet effective scheduling tool, designed mainly for the remodeler or contractor doing several small jobs concurrently.

Simply enter job names in the spaces at the top of each column. Then, as each phase is completed, put an X in the appropriate box. That makes it easy to scan down the columns and see where a job stands. Empty boxes mean something isn't finished. If you're using a computer, you'll probably want to modify the list of job phases to better fit your needs.

Schedule Sheet

Construction Company
Address
City, State, ZIP
Phone Number

Date: _____

Job name:												
1 Plans/permits												
2 Tearout/demo												
3 Excavation												
4 Concrete												
5 Masonry												
6 Floor/wall/roof framing												
7 Exterior trim, porch, deck												
8 Siding/stucco												
9 Doors, trim												
10 Windows, trim												
11 Plumbing												
12 Heat/cooling												
13 Electrical												
14 Insulation												
15 Interior wall covering												
16 Ceiling covering												
17 Interior trim												
18 Cabinets, appliances												
19 Tile, countertops												
20 Specialties												
21 Floor covering												
22 Paint, decorating												
23 Cleanup												

Job Progress Chart

Form Name on Disk: JOBPROG

This tightly-organized report graphs job progress while tracking actual and estimated start and completion dates. It also moves vital job schedule and percentage of completion information from the office to the job site and back again to the office. Your office staff should fill in the estimated portion. Your field staff should fill in actual start and completion dates. For small projects, use this form as both the project schedule *and* the progress chart.

How to Use This Form

Fill out this form at the start of a job and then at regular intervals as the job progresses. Have the estimator or job manager fill in the *Description* section of the form, using project divisions, tasks, items or any combination they wish to schedule. It's best to enter them as close to their naturally-occurring order as possible. That helps keep the chart more easily readable. Next, enter the estimated start date from either the estimate or the project schedule. On the initial form, leave the % column blank. That's filled in later in the field.

The *% comp.* graph is best filled out by the person most familiar with progress of the job, usually the site superintendent or engineer. Percent of completion can seldom be measured precisely. So it's best to leave this guess to the person responsible for work on the project.

When work starts on a particular item, record the date in the *Act. start* column. As work continues, enter the percentage of completion in the *% comp* column and on the graph portion. For example, when 10 percent of an item is completed, the lines next to that item are filled in. As more of the work is finished, the line is progressively filled in toward 100 percent. Under the line, record the current date.

The *% complete* columns are divided into 10 percent increments, but you can enter a 5 percent change by shading in only the first half of the column. For example, if half of the *30%* column is shaded in, the job is 25 percent complete. The bar graph that grows with the job is a snapshot of job progress. At a glance you can see the amount of work completed and the amount left to do.

Understand that this graph doesn't compare actual progress with estimated progress. So you can't tell, for instance, that drywall is 50 percent complete but should be 75 percent complete. This form gives you a picture of how much of the job is actually finished. It's up to you to forecast when work will be complete.

The good news, however, is that information on the graph flows back to the office. That's where you can compare actual completion with the schedule. That should show clearly how actual progress compares with the estimated completion schedule. At the end of each week, the site superintendent should send the completed form to the office and start a new one.

Use the information on this form to fill out the Percent Complete Invoice.

Job Progress Chart

Construction Company
Address
City, State, ZIP
Phone Number

Week ending: _____

Report number: _____

Sheet number: _____ of _____

Contractor: _____

Project name: _____

Project number: _____

No.	Description	Est. start	Act. start	% comp	10 %	20 %	30 %	40 %	50 %	60 %	70 %	80 %	90 %	100 %

Daily Construction Report

Form Name on Disk: DAILYCON

If you ever need to figure out what work was done on what date on a job, this form will be extremely valuable. Use this form to create a job history for each of your projects. You'll be surprised at how often you need this information to resolve subcontractor disputes or legal challenges, to clarify labor issues, or provide information your client requests months (or years) later. The information on this form will also help establish production rates.

Your site superintendent should fill out this report at the end of each day. Your super will be conscientious about filling out the form if he (or she) understands how important it is to create a job history on paper. Completing the form takes only a minute or two.

This report is divided into two major sections. One describes work of your crews. The other covers subcontracted work.

This form also serves as a source for labor and subcontractor production rate information. This is where the work code column *(Code)* comes in. Use the codes recommended in this book (C1 for rough carpentry, C10 for finish carpentry, F10 for forming, etc.) or assign your own labor codes. For example, you could use the Construction Specification Index (CSI code) to describe the task or material being installed.

Daily Construction Report

Construction Company
Address
City, State, ZIP
Phone Number

Date: _____
Owner: _____
Weather: _____
Project number: _____
Project name: _____

Task description	Code	Quantity	Remarks

Subcontract description	Code	Quantity	Remarks

Daily Work Sheet

Form Name on Disk: DAILYWOR

Use this form to record actual job costs. Categories include *Labor, Material used*, and *Overhead*. The form has room to record daily work conditions, weather, and has space for general remarks. For a simple job, you can use the form as a stand-alone job costing system — or you can use it to transfer job costs from the field to your accounting personnel for a more elaborate costing system.

This form is ideal for a construction company that does lots of small jobs with small crews moving from job to job. Since they usually keep their own time and buy their own materials, the job foreman or workers on the job should fill out the Daily Work Sheet. This form is also a good place to record extra work or extra materials needed that should be billed to the client on a time-and-material basis.

The labor section allows classification by trades. That's important information for payroll and workers' comp calculations.

How to Use This Form

Make it the responsibility of the job foreman (or whoever's closest to actual construction) to fill out this form. For every entry in the materials section, there should be an invoice that documents the purchase.

It's better if the accounting department enters trades in the labor classification columns. These classifications should describe the type of labor (carpentry, concrete, etc.). Then the employee checks off the boxes after doing the work. Back in the office, accounting can fill in the labor rates and calculate the total amount.

Daily Work Sheet

Construction Company
Address
City, State, ZIP
Phone Number

Change order number: _____
Date: _____
Owner: _____
Project name: _____
Location: _____

Labor		
Remarks	**Labor classification**	**Weather**
					Temperature	
					8 A.M.	
					1 P.M.	

Employee name	Description of work	Check classification				Hours	Rate	Amount

Labor burden _____

Total labor _____

Material used					
Quantity	**Item**	**Units**	**Amount**	**Total**	**Where purchased**

Total material _____

Total labor and material _____

Overhead expense _____

Total _____

Daily Material Report

Form Name on Disk: DAILYMAT

This report, filled out by the job foreman or superintendent, is intended to speed up the recording of materials delivered to and used daily at the job site. Use it in the office to monitor inventory of materials and as a daily record of material use.

How to Use This Form

If your job is large enough to have a temporary storage yard, make the yard attendant responsible for filling out the form. If the job is smaller, then the workers themselves or the superintendent should be responsible for filling out this form.

You'll use this report to record both the initial delivery of the material, and its use on the job. That means you'll enter each item on two different lines, when it's delivered and when it's used. As items arrive on the job, record the date and material description and circle the D, which stands for delivery. When the materials are requisitioned by the workers, circle the U (for used).

Under *Date*, identify the date the material was used or delivered. Use the *Description* column to describe the material. *Location used* tells where the material was installed and *Quantity received/used* describes how much material was received, then how much was taken.

In the office, transfer the information on this form to an inventory sheet for each type of material.

Daily Material Report

Construction Company
Address
City, State, ZIP
Phone Number

Date: _____

Building: _____

Location: _____

Project number: _____

Project name: _____

Date	Description	Circle delivered/used	Location used	Quantity received/used
		D / U		
		D / U		
		D / U		
		D / U		
		D / U		
		D / U		
		D / U		
		D / U		
		D / U		
		D / U		
		D / U		
		D / U		
		D / U		
		D / U		
		D / U		
		D / U		
		D / U		
		D / U		
		D / U		
		D / U		
		D / U		
		D / U		
		D / U		
		D / U		
		D / U		
		D / U		

Material Requisition

Form Name on Disk: MATLREQ

Your file of material requisitions for any job should show all the materials ordered, received, or back ordered for that job — including who did the ordering. All this information is essential if you need to call a supplier because a promised shipment hasn't arrived. There's also space on the form to enter material cost. That makes the form a source document for costs entered in your cost book.

How to Use This Form

Everyone in your organization who orders materials should know how to fill out this log. In most cases, it's filled out by the job superintendent. But anyone who's generally available when materials are ordered, received and stored can be responsible for recording material transactions.

When completed, put these forms in a file in date order. That way you have complete information on material orders readily at hand. That should eliminate nearly all confusion about when something was ordered and whether it has been delivered.

Material Requisition

Construction Company
Address
City, State, ZIP
Phone Number

Date: _____

Project name: _____

Project number: _____

Date	Description	Unit price	Quantity ordered	Cost ($)	Supplier contact	Date received	Back ordered

Daily Equipment Report

Form Name on Disk: DAILYEQ1

Whether you rent or own, the cost of heavy equipment is generally proportional to time the equipment is in use. Equipment time records are the starting point for figuring the cost of owning and operating your equipment.

This form will help you develop reliable costs for using major pieces of equipment. Record on the form the hours of equipment use, production quantities and descriptions of work.

Two rates combine to make up the *Rate per (operating) hour* of equipment. They are:

▼ ownership expense, which includes depreciation, insurance, taxes, storage and interest on investment, and

▼ operating expense, which consists of repairs, fuel, oil and lube, tires and operating labor.

How to Use This Form

The foreman or office engineer should transfer hours from each operator's time card to this form every day. Once the foreman is back in the office, your bookkeeper can charge the proper accounts and update the equipment records (see the Equipment Ledger Sheet).

The form has spaces for *Machine number, Machine, Rate per hour, Cost code, Total hours* and *Total cost*. You can also record time for each part of the job by using the cost code columns. Summarize the total hours for each cost code at the bottom of the form.

Distinguish working time from idle time in the *W/I* column. Monitoring idle time can pinpoint management problems like too much equipment on one job, ineffective machinery balance, poor field supervision, or just plain worn-out equipment.

Daily Equipment Report

Construction Company
Address
City, State, ZIP
Phone Number

Date: _____

Prepared by: _____

Contractor: _____

Project name: _____

Weather: _____

I = Idle
W = Working

Machine number	Machine	Rate per hr.	W/I	Cost code					Total hours	Total cost
			W							
			I							
			W							
			I							
			W							
			I							
			W							
			I							
			W							
			I							
			W							
			I							
			W							
			I							
			W							
			I							
			W							
			I							
			W							
			I							
			W							
			I							
			W							
			I							
			W							
			I							
			W							
			I							
			W							
			I							
			W							
			I							
			W							
			I							
	Total cost									

Weekly Equipment Summary

Form Name on Disk: WEEK-EQU

Use this summary sheet to record the total weekly use of equipment, whether it's company-owned or rented. Transfer information from the Daily Equipment Report to this form.

How to Use This Form

In the *Rate* column, use either the hourly rental rate charged by the equipment rental yard or the cost per hour you compute from the Equipment Ledger Sheet.

Multiply total weekly hours (from the *Hrs.* column) by the rate to calculate the *Amount* column (total weekly cost). If the machine is rented, this is the amount you owe. If you own the equipment, it's your cost per week to own and run the equipment. If you're charging it out, be sure to add profit to this figure.

Weekly Equipment Summary

Construction Company
Address
City, State, ZIP
Phone Number

Week ending: _____

Owner: _____

Sheet number: _____ of _____

Project name: _____

Project number: _____

Description of equipment	Equip. no.	M	T	W	T	F	S	S	Hrs	Rate	Amount

Tool List

Form Name on Disk: TOOLLIST

Tools are expensive and have a way of wandering from job to job until they just wander away. Use this simple list to improve accountability for the tools you own. Have the site superintendent update this list each payroll period and turn it in to the office. In the office, check the inventory against a master tool list. As tools are moved from project to project, make sure the responsible party fills out the Tool Receipt. That should put an end to most of the problems you've had with disappearing tools.

Tool List

Construction Company
Address
City, State, ZIP
Phone Number

Date: _____
Owner: _____
Contractor: _____
Project number: _____
Project name: _____

| Number | Tool | Serial Number | Condition | | | Value |
			G	F	P	

Tool Receipt

Form Name on Disk: TOOLRECP

Complete this form when responsibility for tools is transferred from one person to another. Keep blank copies of this form on the job site and at the shop. Any time a tool is picked up, the person responsible signs for the tool, noting where it was *Taken from* and where it's *Delivered to*. The site superintendent, when receiving a tool and receipt, enters the tool on the project Tool List.

Ask all employees to include comments about tool limitations, such as "hammer drill has broken ½" bit." That's important information for the person responsible for keeping the tools in good working order.

Tool Receipt

Construction Company
Address
City, State, ZIP
Phone Number

Date: _____

Tool ID number: _____

Description: _____

_____

_____

_____

Taken from

Project/shop: _____

Project no: _____

Delivered by: _____

Delivered to

Project/shop: _____

Project number: _____

Delivered by: _____

Comments: _____

_____

_____

_____

_____

_____

_____

_____

_____

_____

_____

_____

_____

_____

_____

Truck Inspection Sheet

Form Name on Disk: TRUCKINS

This form records the results of an inspection of company-owned vehicles. Filled out monthly, it also acts as a mileage verification.

If a truck is used by one employee and taken home at night, that person should be responsible for filling out this sheet. Otherwise, whoever is responsible for truck maintenance should see to it that a monthly report is filed.

Truck Inspection Sheet

Construction Company
Address
City, State, ZIP
Phone Number

Date: _____

Vehicle type: _____

Vehicle make: _____

License number: _____

Mileage: _____

Condition

Body	OK	Marginal	Repair	Remarks
Windshield				
Paint				
Lights				
Turn signals				

Condition

Motor	OK	Marginal	Repair	Remarks
Air cleaner				
Battery				
Engine operation				
Hoses				
Oil filter				
Horn				
Ammeter				
Fuel gauge				
Oil pressure				
Temperature gauge				

Truck Inspection Sheet (Continued)

	Condition			
Chassis	**OK**	**Marginal**	**Repair**	**Remarks**
Hand brake				
Foot brake				
Clutch				
Shocks				
Tires				
Spare tire				
Fire extinguisher				
Seat belts				
Flashlight/flares				

Other

Spare keys in place	☐ Yes	☐ No
Accident instructions in glove box	☐ Yes	☐ No
Log up to date	☐ Yes	☐ No
Registration	☐ Yes	☐ No
Evidence of insurance	☐ Yes	☐ No

Submitted by: _____

Field Problem Report

Form Name on Disk: FIELDPRO

All businesses have to deal with daily problems. Your construction company is no exception. Use this Field Problem Report to create a written record when you come up against a serious unexpected problem on any job. Remember, there's an opportunity lurking in every problem. You can learn to avoid similar problems in the future. And the best way to do that is to create a written record that can be circulated to everyone concerned.

How to Use This Form

Of course, you don't need a problem to use this form. Have your superintendent or foreman fill this form out at the end of each day, right after filling out payroll, while the events are still fresh in his or her mind. In the top section of the form record site conditions, such as weather and temperature. There are also lines for noting which subs were on site that day.

The body of the form should be filled out with notes about the day's activities, especially any problems that arose, corrections that were made, schedules missed or made up.

Completing a form like this seems like a waste of time — until you have reason to look back at a particular day. Then the value of the form is obvious. This log can stop arguments in their tracks.

Field Problem Report

Construction Company
Address
City, State, ZIP
Phone Number

Date: _____

Owner: _____

Weather/temperature: _____

Project number: _____

Project name: _____

To:

_____

_____

_____

_____

Subs present at site:

_____

_____

_____

_____

The following was noted:

_____

_____

_____

_____

_____

_____

_____

_____

_____

_____

_____

_____

_____

_____

_____

Copies to: _____

_____

Field Report

Signed: _____

Field Change Report

Form Name on Disk: FIELDCHA

Plan changes are inevitable in every construction project, regardless of the scale of the work. If the project is a large one, with exacting specifications and contractual obligations, you'll want to log every change made or requested in the field. The Field Change Report makes the effort simple and quick.

Some changes are trivial and don't require any paperwork. For example, your plumbing subcontractor will probably require minor changes in the framing to run drain and vent lines. Other changes are more serious. You'll have to decide when it's appropriate to use the Field Change Report. It's usually better to fill out the form and not need it than have the reverse happen. In many cases, completing the Field Change Report will result in the issuing of a change order.

How to Use This Form

This form is best filled out by the site superintendent or site engineer. They're in the best position to see just what the change will involve and its impact on the rest of the job.

The *Reference data* section zeros in on the location of the change, plan detail, or sketch number, including its revision date. Some plan details won't be accurate representations of the real situation. In that case, attach an "as built" sketch to clarify the deficiency and explain the field change.

Cost and schedule impact might be better handled in the office, by the estimator, scheduler, or project manager. But advice from the superintendent or foreman will almost always be welcome.

Field Change Report

Construction Company
Address
City, State, ZIP
Phone Number

Date: _____

Project: _____

Project number: _____

Location: _____

_____

Revision number: _____

Reference data

Specification section no.: _____ Page no.: _____ Paragraph no.: _____

Drawing no.: _____ Details: _____

Sketch no.: _____ Dated: _____ Other: _____

Description

1) Detailed identification of the problem: _____

_____

_____

_____

_____

2) Detailed solution proposed: _____

_____

_____

_____

_____

3) Is this a general problem or an isolated case? _____

4) See sketches on reverse side.   ☐ Yes   ☐ No

5) Affected contractor(s): _____

_____

6) Cost and schedule impact: _____

_____

_____

By: _____   Title: _____

Subcontractor Work Order

Form Name on Disk: SUBWORK

This document puts the subcontractor on notice that additional work will be required. It's an excellent record-keeping tool, especially for warranty work. Notice that the form has space for the date the work order was given and the date the work should be completed. There's also space on the bottom of the sheet for the customer's (or superintendent's) signature and comments.

Use this form when the supervisor finds defective work when completing the Final Project Punch List or when you receive a customer complaint. Either way, the location and description of work requested must be clear and specific. Every item should be noted so both the client and the subcontractor can "check off" and mutually agree that the items are satisfactorily repaired. The method of payment is specified, so everyone involved understands who will pay for the work.

The customer's signature indicates that they are satisfied with the corrections. The comments section should show how your sub handled the problem.

Subcontractor Work Order

Construction Company
Address
City, State, ZIP
Phone Number

Date: _____

Owner: _____

To: _____

Contractor: _____

_____

Project number: _____

_____

Work order number: _____

_____

Completion required by: _____

You are requested to perform the work listed below.

Payment shall be made by: Warranty ☐   Contractor ☐   Owner ☐

Location: _____

_____

_____

Lot: _____

Phone: _____

Office phone: _____

Location	Description	Complete

Comments _____

_____

Date completed: _____ By: _____

Customer's signature: _____

■ Delay Notice

Form Name on Disk: DELAYNOT

This form puts a subcontractor or supplier on notice that project completion is being delayed due to something they have done or failed to do. The purpose of the form is twofold. It gives the offending contractor time to correct the situation. Second, it's the last resort before taking harsher action, such as hiring a substitute contractor, taking legal action, or both.

How to Use This Form

Since this notice might be the basis of legal action, it's important that you document damages that result from the delay. Restate the subcontractor's or supplier's responsibilities. Then show how the job and other subcontractors are being affected.

Send this letter by registered mail with return receipt requested to create a record of delivery.

Delay Notice

Construction Company
Address
City, State, ZIP
Phone Number

Date: _____

Owner: _____

Contractor: _____

Project number: _____

Project name: _____

To: _____

Attention: _____

_____

_____

Notice number: _____

Contract date: _____

It is apparent that you are causing delay to the project. We request that you do whatever is necessary to get back on schedule, including but not limited to:

_____ Overtime work

_____ Adding additional crew

_____ Better organization of efforts

_____ Using more experienced personnel

_____ Supplying needed tools and materials

Note:

_____

_____

_____

_____

_____

_____

_____

_____

_____

_____

By: _____   Copy to: _____

Memorandum of Delay

Form Name on Disk: MEMDELAY

It's a shame, but many contractors find themselves acting the role of babysitter for subs that can't get their work done on time. Some subs even have a hard time remembering when they promised to be on the job. Others forget what they're supposed to do when they finally arrive.

Most contracts don't allow for time extensions unless notice is given within a specific time period. Use this Memorandum of Delay to give notice to owners, architects, and banks that the project is being delayed.

How to Use This Form

When your phone calls are ignored, consider sending the subcontractor a Delay Notice. Use registered mail with return receipt requested. At the same time, send the Memorandum of Delay to the client, the architect, and anyone else who will be affected by the delay.

Generally, time to complete the contract can be extended without a change order. But if the job requires strict compliance with a schedule, you may also have to prepare a change order.

Memorandum of Delay

Date: _____

Construction Company   To: _____

Address   Address: _____

City, State, ZIP   City, State, ZIP: _____

Phone Number   Project number: _____

Project name: _____

A delay has occurred due to circumstances beyond our control on the following dates:

_____

_____

_____

_____

For a total of _____ working days.

This delay has been caused by:

☐ Weather   ☐ Lack of requested information

☐ Extra work   ☐ Incomplete drawings & specifications

☐ Governmental actions   ☐ Other:

Note:

_____

_____

_____

_____

_____

_____

Potential Backcharge Notice

Form Name on Disk: POTBAKNO

This notice is one of those forms you hope to avoid using. Still, you'll be glad to have this form on hand, at least occasionally. It's used to inform a subcontractor that some part of their work is deficient and must be corrected.

The good news is that this form usually does the job. For some reason, a notice like this, delivered by mail, has the clout of several phone calls.

How to Use This Form

A few checks in the appropriate boxes are all that's needed to get your point across. The job information section contains, in addition to the date, the job name, number, and space for the notice number. That lets you record how many of these notices you have sent. There's also space to record the contract number so there should be no confusion on which job is in question.

After the job information, there's a list of items that describe the reason for the potential backcharge. Just check the appropriate box or boxes. Next there's an "actions" section where you note what you expect to be done or what you expect the backcharge to be.

Finally, there's a space for you to add notes. Make your notes clear and concise and attach copies of documentation or photos that explain the charge.

Potential Backcharge Notice

Construction Company
Address
City, State, ZIP
Phone Number

Date: _____
To: _____
Notice number: _____
Contract number: _____
Project number: _____
Project name: _____

It is apparent that we will incur additional expense due to the following:

☐ Correcting defective work   ☐ Debris removal

☐ Finishing uncompleted work   ☐ Other: _____

☐ Damage to finished surfaces   ☐ Other: _____

☐ Please complete the work noted in accordance with the Contract so backcharges can be avoided.

☐ Estimated backcharge cost $_____

☐ Please refer to Article _____ of the Contract

Note: _____
_____
_____
_____
_____
_____
_____
_____
_____
_____
_____
_____
_____
_____
_____
_____

Accident Report by Supervisor

Form Name on Disk: ACCREPO

This form will help management meet accident reporting requirements established by law and by your insurance carrier. Make sure the supervisor understands that it's to be filled out immediately after the accident.

The supervisor should fill in the form as soon as possible after treating the victim and correcting any unsafe conditions. The more completely it's filled out, the better. Send the original to the main office the same day and keep a copy on site.

Accident Report by Supervisor

Construction Company
Address
City, State, ZIP
Phone Number

Date: _____
Owner: _____
Contractor: _____
Project name: _____

Name of injured _____ Social Security number: _____

Home address of injured _____

Company _____ Age _____ ☐ M   ☐ F

Date of injury _____ Time _____ ☐ AM ☐ PM

Occupation _____ How long _____

Type of injury _____

Part injured _____

What was employee doing at time of injury? _____

Where and how did the accident occur? _____

_____

_____

Specify machine, tool, substance or object that directly injured employee: _____

_____

Was medical treatment sought?   Yes ☐   No ☐

Where and by whom? _____

Was employee unable to work after injury? _____

If yes, for how long was he absent from job? _____

List names and addresses of witnesses: _____

_____

_____

This report filed
by: _____

Date: _____

Corrective action taken:

Describe any unsafe acts or conditions contributing to accident _____

_____

Explain specifically the corrective action taken _____

_____

Safety Meeting Report

Form Name on Disk: SAFETY

This is your report of safety meetings. It's proof that you have made a diligent effort to keep your employees informed on safety issues. If a worker is injured in a fall after you had safety meetings, it's an accident. If the same worker is injured in a fall and you *didn't* have safety meetings, you were negligent.

Use the form to record notes about "tailgate meetings" held to discuss safety and health topics. Have each employee sign the form on the lines marked *Attendance*, offering further proof that you made an effort to train employees and provide a safe working environment. Then have the supervisor sign and date the form at the bottom.

No contractor expects employees to be injured. Maybe that's why many contractors feel that time and effort spent on safety education is time and effort wasted. But think for a minute about your cost of workers' compensation coverage. In many cases, the cost of workers' comp can be reduced significantly by implementing a good safety program.

How to Use This Form

This form needs to be filled out completely or its value diminishes. Some contractors fill out the items to be discussed and then give it to the superintendent, along with backup material to be used as the topic for discussion. This guarantees that all issues will be covered. Backup material will probably be pages copied out of a safety manual. Your workers' comp carrier will be happy to supply safety materials for your use.

Safety Meeting Report

Construction Company
Address
City, State, ZIP
Phone Number

Date: _____

Conducted by: _____

Conducted at: _____

Meeting time: _____

Project number: _____

Project name: _____

Items discussed: _____

_____

_____

_____

_____

_____

_____

_____

_____

_____

_____

_____

_____

_____

_____

_____

_____

_____

_____

Attendance:

_____   _____

_____   _____

_____   _____

_____   _____

_____   _____

Signed by: _____

Job Site Safety Checklist

Form Name on Disk: JOBSITE

This is a guide for periodic review of job site safety conditions. It should be completed by the site superintendent. Ask your superintendent to review this checklist at the beginning of each job and weekly thereafter.

This form lists 36 key safety requirements. After each item, there's space available to check whether each requirement is being observed. If there's a violation, note the location. There's space for other items and comments at the bottom of the form.

Job Site Safety Checklist

Construction Company
Address
City, State, ZIP
Phone Number

Date: _____
Owner: _____
Contractor: _____
Project name: _____
Inspected by: _____

Personal protection

	Yes	No	Location
1. Hard hats worn by all employees and visitors	____	____	_____
2. Hearing protective devices worn by workers where noise levels are high	____	____	_____
3. Eye and face protection worn by workers exposed to potential eye or face injury	____	____	_____

Housekeeping

4. Passageways and stairs clear of debris	____	____	_____
5. Sidewalks free of construction materials and debris	____	____	_____
6. Toilet facilities maintained	____	____	_____
7. Adequate illumination in work areas and stairways	____	____	_____

General

8. Job site accident prevention program posted	____	____	_____
9. OSHA official notice poster posted	____	____	_____
10. Employee injury logs kept current	____	____	_____
11. Fire extinguishers provided	____	____	_____
12. First-aid kit provided	____	____	_____
13. Emergency telephone numbers posted	____	____	_____
14. Warning signs posted near hazardous work areas	____	____	_____

Floors and wall openings

15. Barrier guards provided where there is a drop more than 4 ft. at a wall opening	____	____	_____
16. Floor and roof edges 4 ft. or more above floor or ground level provided with railings	____	____	_____

Job Site Safety Checklist (Continued)

	Yes	No	Location

Scaffolding

17. Railings provided when a platform is 7½ ft. or more from floor or ground level

18. Scaffolding set plumb with adequate foundation bearing plates

19. Scaffold guyed or tied to structure

20. Platform planks laid tightly together to prevent material and tools from falling through

21. Platform planks extend over end supports not less than 6 inches

Ladders

22. Ladders in good condition

23. Proper-height ladders in use

24. Access ladders extend 3 ft. beyond floor or roof and are secured against slipping

Machinery and tool guarding

25. Saw blade guards in place and operating properly

26. Pulley belts and wheels enclosed with guards

27. Cut-off saws provided with automatic blade returns

Welding

28. Valve protection caps in place except when cylinders are in use

29. Cylinders in upright position while in use

30. Cylinder valves closed when work is finished

31. Cylinders secured to prevent being knocked over

32. Proper eye protection worn by welders

Job Site Safety Checklist (Continued)

	Yes	No	Location

Electrical

33. Differing receptacles and attachment plugs not interchanged _____ _____ _____

34. Cords free of cuts exposing wiring _____ _____ _____

35. Cords out of vehicular paths _____ _____ _____

36. Male plug ends unmodified _____ _____ _____

Other:

_____

_____

_____

_____

_____

_____

_____

_____

_____

_____

The above checklist is not all-inclusive. Reference shall be made to the OSHA Construction Safety Orders for complete requirements.

Comments: _____

_____

_____

_____

Copy to: _____

By: _____

Safety Agreement

Form Name on Disk: SAFEAGRE

Several government agencies have authority to make routine inspections. It's to your benefit to make sure all employees are briefed on basic safety issues. You can prove that they have had safety training by getting this form read, filled out, and signed by every employee in the field.

At your next tailgate meeting, have employees review the list on the Safety Agreement and sign it. Keep a copy in the job office and send the original to the main office. If an inspector asks if an employee has been informed of a safety issue, you have proof that you tried to get the information across during a regular safety meetings.

Safety Agreement

Construction Company
Address
City, State, ZIP
Phone Number

Date: _____

Employee: _____

Social security number: _____

Project number: _____

Project name: _____

I have been shown the location of the first-aid kit, emergency telephone numbers and fire extinguisher.

I have received instruction in the use of the fire extinguisher, safety goggles, hard hat, and other equipment particular to my trade.

I have been issued a hard hat and will wear it at all times when working on the job site.

I have received a copy of the Job Site Accident Prevention Program; I have read it, I understand it, and will comply with each and every provision.

In case of injury, I will report it either to the superintendent or foreman.

I will report any unsafe conditions to the superintendent or foreman.

Signed: _____

Project Closeout Checklist

Form Name on Disk: PROJCLOS

Remember, the end of a project for the contractor is the beginning of the project for the owner. That's why it's so important that project closeout be handled with care. Try to make the owner's transition into the new building as smooth as possible. The impression you leave during this part of the project is what the client will remember most, and relate most often to their friends and associates!

The Project Closeout Checklist will help you remember all the little details needed to finalize a project. It also serves as a resource guide, clearly defining the person in the chain of command responsible for each checklist item.

How to Use This Form

Obviously, no list is going to hit on every closeout item for every type of construction job. That's why we've left spaces at the bottom of the list to add your own closeout items. If you're using a computer, simply type in additional items as you need them.

Assign either the construction manager, the site superintendent, or the foreman to each task. By putting an X in the cell under the job title at each task, the assignment is clear and the responsibility is delegated.

Items like the owner's manual, letter of recommendation, and customer follow-up letter are small matters. But they add up to a large image enhancement for your company.

Project Closeout Checklist

Construction Company
Address
City, State, ZIP
Phone Number

Date: _____

Owner: _____

Contractor: _____

Project number: _____

Project name: _____

The following is a checklist of items that should occur when finalizing a project:

		Construction manager	Site superintendent	Foreman
1.	Coordinate final utility and service connections.			
2.	Complete acceptance checklists.			
3.	Arrange for final agency inspection.			
4.	File Notice of Completion.			
5.	Thoroughly clean the project.			
6.	Conduct an acceptance walk-through with the contractors and with the client.			
7.	Process final payment from client or lender.			
8.	Assist in systems start-up.			
9.	Obtain warranties and lien releases from subs.			
10.	Create owner's manual with warranties and project literature.			
11.	Procure as-built drawings.			
12.	Obtain maintenance and operating instructions.			
13.	Initiate preventive maintenance program as appropriate.			
14.	Assist in teaching operating and maintenance staff when needed.			
15.	Obtain and store spare parts and materials as required.			
16.	Dispose of excess materials.			
17.	Remove temporary facilities, tools and equipment.			
18.	Recap the actual schedule and job costs for the data bank.			
19.	Remove data from computer memory after all cost entries have ceased.			
20.	Transfer and obtain sign-off for keys.			
21.	Obtain letter of recommendation from client.			
22.	Follow up with client survey 30 days after close of job.			

Project Closeout Checklist (Continued)

	Construction manager	Site superintendent	Foreman
23.			
24.			
25.			
26.			
27.			
28.			
29.			
30.			
31.			

Project Closeout Letter

Form Name on Disk: PROCLOSE

This letter spurs a subcontractor to complete the last work needed under the contract so payment can be made. It requests warranties, shop drawings, maintenance manuals and "as builts," those easy-to-forget items that never seem to get finished.

Main this letter (or better yet, fax it) to each subcontractor as they wrap up their work on the project. Include a blank Warranty Form. The mention of that last payment usually gets a speedy response.

Project Closeout Letter

Construction Company
Address
City, State, ZIP
Phone Number

Date: _____

Owner: _____

Contractor: _____

Project number: _____

Project name: _____

_____

_____

_____

_____

Dear _____ :

In order to enable closeout of the contract and facilitate final payment, we request that the following be completed and submitted:

1. All pertinent warranty, shop drawings, and maintenance manuals.
2. Review and sign standard warranty form enclosed.

Please send us these items as quickly as possible so final payment is not delayed.

Sincerely,

_____

Final Project Punch List

Form Name on Disk: FINALPRO

Wrapping up all the loose ends at completion of a construction job is never easy. But this form helps the process by getting the owner and the contractor to put the details in writing. A written Final Project Punch List reminds the owner to be diligent in spotting problems. This is the last chance to get work corrected.

For the project manager, this form becomes the list of tasks on the final "pickup" prior to completion.

How to Use This Form

The contractor or superintendent completes the *Description* column during the project's final contractor/client walk-through. Note deficiencies, omissions, repairs, fixes, or touchups as they're discovered.

Office personnel should review the document to see if any backcharge or withholding is in order. Then they should assign work to the person responsible for managing the list (superintendent, project manager, foreman, or pickup man). As the work is completed, the worker fills in the *Date complete* column. After all the items are done, the owner initials the *Owner's approval* column to indicate satisfaction with the work done.

There's space at the bottom of the form for signatures of both contractor and owner.

Final Project Punch List

Construction Company
Address
City, State, ZIP
Phone Number

Date: _____

Owner: _____

Project name: _____

Item no.	Description	Date complete	Owner's approval (initial)
1.			
2.			
3.			
4.			
5.			
6.			
7.			
8.			
9.			
10.			
11.			
12.			
13.			
14.			
15.			
16.			
17.			
18.			
19.			
20.			
21.			
22.			
23.			

Contractor: _____   Owner: _____

General Office Forms

Interoffice Memo

Form Name on Disk: INTEROFF

You won't need this form until your office staff grows large enough to require written memos. When that happens, use this form. It commands notice and demands a reply.

A memo's greatest virtue (and perhaps its largest drawback) is its permanence. People tend to save written memos. That's particularly useful when it comes time to reward performance or search for failures. Keep a copy of the memo in your files.

This form has check boxes to make it easy to use. That makes it more likely that you'll use it more often.

Of course, an interoffice memo doesn't have to stay in your office. You can also send memos to the field. They're a good way to communicate with your site superintendent.

Interoffice Memo

Construction Company
Address
City, State, ZIP
Phone Number

Date: _____

To: _____

From: _____

Subject: _____

Project number: _____

Project name: _____

Please:

☐ Review and recommend   ☐ Shop drawings attached   ☐ Approve

☐ Follow up and report   ☐ Return   ☐ For your information

Note:

_____

_____

_____

_____

_____

_____

_____

_____

_____

_____

Reply:

_____

_____

_____

_____

_____

_____

Memo

Form Name on Disk: MEMO

Fax machines and telephone answering machines have reduced the popularity of written memos. Electronic mail (E-mail), which sends memos from computer to computer across a network, may replace the fax and answering machine eventually. But we've included this form because it still has its uses. Sent as registered mail, it's proof that you made an effort to contact someone. Also, if you want to leave a paper trail, a written memo is ideal.

How to Use This Form

Fill it out, send it, and then hope it gets to the right person. Then hope that person reads it and then answers it. Then hope the response gets to you.

Memo

Construction Company
Address
City, State, ZIP
Phone Number

Date: _____

To: _____

From: _____

Subject: _____

Project name: _____

Project number: _____

_____
_____
_____
_____
_____
_____
_____
_____
_____
_____
_____
_____
_____
_____
_____
_____
_____
_____
_____
_____
_____
_____
_____
_____

☐ Please reply   ☐ No reply necessary   Signed: _____

Fax Cover Sheet

Form Name on Disk: FAXCOVER

Fax machines make the U.S. mail look like the Pony Express. A fax is an indispensable tool in most construction offices. And like any good tool, it does the job better, faster and cheaper than what it's replacing. A fax is transmitted almost instantly. You get confirmation of receipt (on some machines) and can expect an immediate reply.

There are plenty of emergencies in the construction business. Getting written information in minutes rather than days can save both time and expense. Use your fax to transmit bids, requests for proposal, details, shop drawings, and sketches, to name just a few.

How to Use This Form

This is a generic fax cover sheet and its purpose is threefold. It's a transmittal letter, a "table of contents" for the faxed information, and it provides space for a short handwritten note to be included in the fax.

This form is the ultimate in speed and simplicity. Just fill in the blanks to get your information across simply and clearly. To save even more time, fill in your company name and fax number ahead of time and make a few dozen copies. That way you'll have a stock of these forms ready for immediate use.

Every time you fax a document, fill out and send a copy of this form with it. This cover sheet tells the recipient who the fax is from, why it's being sent, and what action is needed. Be sure it also includes your company's name, mailing address and both your fax and voice phone numbers.

Remember to fill in the blank that follows *Number of pages including the cover sheet.* This is the best way to ensure that everything you send is received.

Incidentally, since we're discussing faxed communications and documents, here's a tip to keep in mind when you're on the receiving end of a fax. Remember that unless you have a plain paper fax machine, fax images tend to fade. If you're going to need a file copy, make a photocopy and file that. It's an extra step, but it only takes a moment and ensures that any fax you have on file will always be legible.

Fax Cover Sheet

Construction Company
Address
City, State, ZIP
Phone Number

Date: _____

To: _____

Attention: _____

Fax number used: _____

From: _____

Return fax number: _____

Project name: _____

Number of pages including the cover sheet: _____

If any of these fax copies are illegible, or you do not receive the same number of pages stated above, please contact us immediately at telephone number: _____

Remarks: _____

_____

_____

_____

_____

_____

_____

_____

_____

_____

_____

_____

_____

_____

_____

_____

Transmittal Form

Form Name on Disk: TRANSFRM

Transmittal Form is just a fancy way to say "short letter." The Transmittal Form passes information quickly and precisely, especially when you use it to send documents out of the office. Use a transmittal form like this when sending information about materials, contracts, requests for bids, awards of contract, prints, plans, shop drawings, samples and change orders.

How to Use This Form

Clearly identify in the form:

1) What is being sent

2) What you want the recipient to do with it

Where appropriate, include job information such as name, number, codes, and descriptions.

To save time, make up a dozen or so copies of this Transmittal Form for each new job. Fill in all the job information on an original and make a few dozen copies. If you use a computer, save a version of this file with all the job information filled in. Use that as the original for all transmittal letters on the job.

Transmittal Form

Construction Company
Address
City, State, ZIP
Phone Number

Date: _____
Company: _____
Attention: _____
From: _____
Project name: _____

Regarding: _____

We are sending you: Copies   Date   Description

   ☐ As requested   _____   _____   _____

   ☐ Attached   _____   _____   _____

   ☐ Under separate cover   _____   _____   _____

For your:

   ☐ Records   Memo: _____

   ☐ Use and information   _____

   ☐ Approval   _____

   ☐ Review and comment   _____

   ☐ Use and distribution   _____

Via:

   ☐ Overnight mail   Remarks: _____

   ☐ Mail   _____

   ☐ Hand delivered   _____

   ☐ Fax   _____

Telefax number: _____   Copies to: _____

Number of pages (including this page): _____   _____

Signed: _____

Emergency Telephone Directory

Form Name on Disk: EMERGTEL

Fill out this form and post a copy in plain view by every phone on the job site. There's space for a map and directions to the nearest hospital or emergency care center. Give copies to your foremen and superintendents.

Emergency Telephone Directory

Construction Company
Address
City, State, ZIP
Phone Number

Date: _____

Project name: _____

Name	Day phone	Night phone
Owner: _____	_____	_____
Contractor: _____	_____	_____
Construction manager: _____	_____	_____
Construction superintendent: _____	_____	_____
Fire	_____	_____
Ambulance	_____	_____
Hospital	_____	_____
Police	_____	_____

Utilities

Gas company	_____	_____
Electric company	_____	_____
Water company	_____	_____
Telephone company	_____	_____
Underground service	_____	_____
_____	_____	_____
_____	_____	_____

Hospital address: _____

(Place map here)

All key personnel should have a copy of this information. A copy should be posted in the field office adjacent to the telephone.

Field Directory

Form Name on Disk: FIELDDIR

Create this directory when the job starts. It should show phone numbers for each contractor, subcontractor and supplier that's involved in the job. Emergency numbers are located at the top of the list. Your job superintendent will use this form the most. But distribute a copy to each of the crews expected to work on the job, to your subcontractors, and maybe even to key suppliers.

Field Directory

Construction Company
Address
City, State, ZIP
Phone Number

Date revised: _____

Project name: _____

Emergency numbers   Phone number

    Fire   _____

    Ambulance _____

    Doctor _____

    Hospital _____

    Police _____

    Gas company _____

    Electric company _____

    Water company _____

    Telephone company _____

Public agencies

City or agency	Contact	Phone number	Fax number
_____	_____	_____	_____
_____	_____	_____	_____
_____	_____	_____	_____
_____	_____	_____	_____

Architect/engineer

_____	_____	_____	_____
_____	_____	_____	_____

Contractors/suppliers

Company name	Contact	Phone number	Fax number
_____	_____	_____	_____
_____	_____	_____	_____
_____	_____	_____	_____
_____	_____	_____	_____
_____	_____	_____	_____
_____	_____	_____	_____
_____	_____	_____	_____

■ Office Directory

....

Form Name on Disk: OFFDIR

This form should list all the phone numbers your staff is likely to need, from emergency numbers, public agencies, office extensions, consultants, architects, engineers, contractors, suppliers and even the home numbers of key employees.

Everyone in your office should have a current copy. Because a directory tends to grow and change, assign someone the task of updating it on a regular basis. When the update is ready, it's easy to combine distributing it with collecting old versions for disposal.

This form is organized by category. If used on a computer, you can use the search function in a word processing program to locate the category you need.

Office Directory

Construction Company
Address
City, State, ZIP
Phone Number

Date revised: _____

Emergency numbers   Phone number

    Fire   _____

    Ambulance   _____

    Police   _____

    Gas company   _____

    Electric company   _____

    Water company   _____

    Telephone company   _____

_____   _____

Public agencies

City or agency	Contact	Phone number	Fax number
_____	_____	_____	_____
_____	_____	_____	_____
_____	_____	_____	_____

Office extensions

Name	Extension	Name	Extension
_____	_____	_____	_____
_____	_____	_____	_____
_____	_____	_____	_____

Consultants

Company name	Contact	Phone number	Fax number
_____	_____	_____	_____
_____	_____	_____	_____
_____	_____	_____	_____

Architects/engineers

Company name	Contact	Phone number	Fax number
_____	_____	_____	_____
_____	_____	_____	_____

Office Directory (Continued)

Contractors/suppliers

Company name	Contact	Phone number	Fax number
_____	_____	_____	_____
_____	_____	_____	_____
_____	_____	_____	_____
_____	_____	_____	_____
_____	_____	_____	_____
_____	_____	_____	_____
_____	_____	_____	_____
_____	_____	_____	_____
_____	_____	_____	_____
_____	_____	_____	_____
_____	_____	_____	_____
_____	_____	_____	_____
_____	_____	_____	_____

Employees

Name	Classification	Home phone	Emergency number
_____	_____	_____	_____
_____	_____	_____	_____
_____	_____	_____	_____
_____	_____	_____	_____
_____	_____	_____	_____
_____	_____	_____	_____
_____	_____	_____	_____
_____	_____	_____	_____
_____	_____	_____	_____
_____	_____	_____	_____
_____	_____	_____	_____

First Contact Sheet

Form Name on Disk: FIRSTCON

The first time a potential customer contacts your business, they should get a courteous, businesslike response. That's why it's important to train everyone who answers your phone. Make sure receptionists have a stack of these First Contact Sheets available. It prompts them to ask the necessary questions in a logical and orderly manner. The form also provides a place to collect important sales lead information. These questions will also separate serious prospect from the merely curious.

How to Use This Form

Keep a supply of these forms near the telephone. When a potential customer calls, start by asking for their name and address. Fill in the spaces as appropriate.

On average, you're going to get only about one-quarter of the jobs you go after. You can improve the odds a little with some gentle probing right at the beginning. A question like "What's your budget for this project?" will help prospects do a reality check. Another important question is "Do you plan to get bids from other contractors? If so, how many?" You may decide not to waste time on someone who's obviously bid shopping.

First Contact Sheet

Construction Company
Address
City, State, ZIP
Phone Number

Appointment date: _____

Customer name: _____

Customer address: _____

City, State, ZIP: _____

Salesman: _____

Address of project: Customer information:

_____   Home phone: _____

_____   Office phone: _____

_____   Fax number: _____

Does customer own house?   ☐ Yes   ☐ No

How project will be financed?   _____

Customer budget: _____ to _____

When is work planned to start and finish?   Start _____ Finish _____

Does customer have an architect?   ☐ Yes   ☐ No

Is customer taking other bids?   ☐ Yes   ☐ No

      If yes, how many?   _____

How did customer get our name?   _____

Type of project

☐ Addition	☐ Garage	☐ Roofing
☐ Alterations	☐ Kitchen	☐ Siding
☐ Bath	☐ Patio	☐ Windows
☐ Carport	☐ Porch	☐ Other:
☐ Deck	☐ Renovation	

_____

Directions to job site: Bid outcome

_____   Date of bid _____

_____   Bid price $ _____

_____   ☐ Acceptance date _____

_____   ☐ Rejected, awarded to _____

_____   Work scheduled to start _____

Contractor/Supplier Questionnaire

Form Name on Disk: CONSUPQ

To paraphrase the old cliché, a contractor is only as strong as his weakest subcontractor. The Contractor/Supplier Questionnaire helps screen out undesirable companies before you put your reputation in their hands.

Mail or fax this questionnaire, with its cover letter, to subcontractors and potential suppliers. When filled out completely, it has all the information a prime contractor needs to make a decision. Larger companies bidding on government jobs will find the small business and minority-owned section valuable in selecting services.

The questionnaire asks for all the pertinent phone numbers (including office, fax and mobile) and insurance policy numbers (including workers' compensation and liability).

If you decide to use the subcontractor or supplier, transfer the information to the appropriate logs, including the Subcontractor Insurance Verification Log, and Field and Office Directories.

Contractor/Supplier Questionnaire

Construction Company
Address
City, State, ZIP
Phone Number

Date: _____

Owner: _____

Contractor: _____

Project name: _____

Telephone number: _____

Company name: _____

Fax number: _____

Address: _____

Contact person: _____

Mobile number: _____

Type of business

Contractor (specify) _____

License number: _____

Supplier (specify) _____

Worker's comp. number: _____

Other (specify) _____

Liability insurance number: _____

Type of organization (check one)

Individual ☐   Limited partnership ☐   General partnership ☐

Names of partners: _____

Joint venture ☐   Names of participants: _____

Corporation ☐   Officer's names: _____

General

1. Do you qualify as a "small business"?   Yes ☐   No ☐
   As qualified by:_____

2. Is your company or joint venture "woman-owned"?   Yes ☐   No ☐

3. Is your company or joint venture "minority-owned"?   Yes ☐   No ☐

   If "minority-" or "woman-owned" complete the following ownership interest box.

Ownership or joint venture interest (please circle one):

Alaskan Native	Hispanic	Asian	White
Black	American Indian	Pacific Islanders	Woman

Number of owners: _____

% asset owned: _____

■ Questionnaire Cover Letter

Form Name on Disk: QUESTCOV

This is a cover letter for the Contractor/Supplier Questionnaire. Fill out the cover letter and send it with the questionnaire. The cover letter is a courteous request for the recipient's cooperation. The cover letter also explains where to return the Contractor/Supplier Questionnaire.

Construction Company
Address
City, State, ZIP
Phone Number

Date: _____

Owner: _____

Contractor: _____

Project number: _____

Project name: _____

_____

_____

_____

Dear _____ :

Thank you for your interest in _____ .

To help us learn more about your capabilities and qualifications, please complete the enclosed questionnaire and return it to:

_____

_____

_____

Attention: _____

If you have any questions, please do not hesitate to call.

Sincerely,

_____

Enclosures

Subcontractor Insurance Verification Log

Form Name on Disk: SUBINS

The purpose of this log is to organize, in one place, all the information about insurance coverage for each of your subcontractors. You'll need this information several times (during your annual workers' comp audit, for example) while construction proceeds. This form will keep all the information on hand and available. Set this information up on your computer and you can sort the file by expiration date in a second or two. That makes it easy to identify subcontractors with expired insurance coverage.

How to Use This Form

Whenever you contract with a sub, get that sub to fill out the Contractor/Supplier Questionnaire. Mark off the check boxes (to the left of the *Expires* line) in the *Workers' compensation* and *General liability* columns when you receive the information. The boxes show at a glance which of your subs have responded and which subs haven't. After you mark the check box, transfer the *Expires, Certificate #* and *Ins. carrier* information to this log.

Subcontractor Insurance Verification Log

Construction Company
Address
City, State, ZIP
Phone Number

Date: _____

Owner: _____

Contractor: _____

Project number: _____

Project name: _____

Verification of receipt of subcontractor's insurance certificates:
(Check off when received and fill in expiration date, certificate number, and insurance carrier)

Subcontractor	Workers' compensation	General liability	Federal ID number
	☐ Expires:_____ Certificate #:_____ Insurance carrier:	☐ Expires:_____ Certificate #:_____ Insurance carrier:	
	☐ Expires:_____ Certificate #:_____ Insurance carrier:	☐ Expires:_____ Certificate #:_____ Insurance carrier:	
	☐ Expires:_____ Certificate #:_____ Insurance carrier:	☐ Expires:_____ Certificate #:_____ Insurance carrier:	
	☐ Expires:_____ Certificate #:_____ Insurance carrier:	☐ Expires:_____ Certificate #:_____ Insurance carrier:	
	☐ Expires:_____ Certificate #:_____ Insurance carrier:	☐ Expires:_____ Certificate #:_____ Insurance carrier:	
	☐ Expires:_____ Certificate #:_____ Insurance carrier:	☐ Expires:_____ Certificate #:_____ Insurance carrier:	
	☐ Expires:_____ Certificate #:_____ Insurance carrier:	☐ Expires:_____ Certificate #:_____ Insurance carrier:	

■ Rejection Letter

Form Name on Disk: REJECT

Use this form to notify a bidding subcontractor that the proposal of another subcontractor was selected. That's both common courtesy and routine practice by the best and most professional prime contractors. Less professional outfits don't bother. They notify only the winner. The rest are left to wonder.

It takes only a minute or two to print this letter and an envelope if you use a computer and word processor. Informing your subcontractors that you'll consider them for the next bid is just plain good business. If printing an envelope and mailing a letter is too much trouble, just print the letter and send it by fax. That's even less work.

Construction Company   Date: _____

Address   Owner: _____

City, State, ZIP   Contractor: _____

Phone Order   Project number: _____

                 Project name: _____

_____

_____

_____

_____

Dear _____ :

After thorough consideration and evaluation of the bids for the above referenced project, we have issued the contract to another bidder. We appreciate the interest you have shown and will look forward to the possibility of working with you in the future.

Thank you for your participation in the bidding process.

Sincerely,

_____

Enclosures

Deficiency Notice

Form Name on Disk: DEFNOTIC

Use this form to remind a subcontractor or supplier about a defect. It informs them that they are deficient in some area and explains how they can correct the deficiency. The form can also be used as a follow-up to requests for product information, samples, shop drawings or other information.

Boxes to check make this form fast and easy to use. Combined with a fax machine, there's no better way to get your message out. If you need proof of receipt, sending it by registered mail might be more appropriate than transmittal by fax.

This form is proof that you gave notice of a defect and that you are prepared to take the next step, even legal action, if necessary. So be sure to keep a copy of the form on the job or in your correspondence folder.

How to Use This Form

Check off the items you need and fill in the date you need them. Use the space provided in the *Note* portion of the form to cite the section of the contract, drawings, or specifications that define what was supposed to be done. Then identify what additional work has to be done to comply with the contract documents. That should go a long way toward getting the attention of the sub or supplier.

Deficiency Notice

Construction Company
Address
City, State, ZIP
Phone Number

Date: _____
To: _____
From: _____
Owner: _____
Project number: _____
Project name: _____

The following items have not been submitted to us.

Return by: _____

- ☐ Contract
- ☐ Purchase order
- ☐ Certificate of insurance
- ☐ Sub-schedule
- ☐ Submittals
- ☐ Cost breakdown

- ☐ Warranty
- ☐ Shop drawings
- ☐ As-built drawings
- ☐ Samples
- ☐ Colors/texture
- ☐ Materials list

- ☐ Minority compliance form
- ☐ Product literature
- ☐ Other: _____

_____
_____
_____

Please forward this material immediately for our review.

Note:
_____
_____
_____
_____
_____
_____
_____
_____
_____
_____
_____
_____
_____
_____

Time Management Worksheet

Form Name on Disk: TIMEWORK

This flexible daily form includes scheduled appointments, a to-do list, and weekly goals. Kept in a three-ring binder, this sheet becomes the daily log of your business activity, available for historical reference.

How to Use This Form

The left side of this form lets you record appointments scheduled throughout the day, from 6:00 AM until 7:00 PM, divided into half-hour segments.

The right side of the form includes your *Action record* and a column for estimating the *Time* you'll need to spend to complete each action. Estimate the time needed for each phase of each job to avoid overloading the schedule.

The *Goals for this week* section helps you look past the daily items and reminds you of larger goals a little further out on the horizon.

Time Management Worksheet

Date: Mon.   Tues.   Wed.   Thurs.   Fri.   Sat.   Sun.

Time		Appointments	Action record	Time
6:00				
7:00				
8:00				
9:00				
10:00				
11:00				
Noon				
1:00				
2:00				
3:00				
4:00				
5:00				
6:00				
7:00				

Goals	1.
for	2.
the	3.
week:	4.

Project Startup Checklist

Form Name on Disk: PROSTART

Once a contract is signed, this Project Startup Checklist acts as a reminder for all the details needed to get the job moving. It also assigns responsibility to appropriate personnel at the beginning of the job.

How to Use This Form

Modify this checklist to fit the way you start each project. It should identify who is responsible for each activity. If your organization doesn't have an estimator or project manager (or if you're both the estimator and project manager), change the headings to match your own situation. In any case, take the time to review each item on this list. That should save you many frustrating hours of backpedaling or waiting during the shakeout period at the start of every project.

Project Startup Checklist

Construction Company
Address
City, State, ZIP
Phone Number

Date: _____

Owner: _____

Contractor: _____

Project number: _____

Project name: _____

Following is a checklist of items that should occur prior to beginning work on a project:

	Estimator	Project manager	Supervisor	Foreman
1. Submit the new job info sheet.				
2. Determine the basic organization of the project.				
3. Assign key staff members.				
4. Review the prime contract.				
5. Define the scope of work.				
6. Introduce staff to the project.				
7. Prepare the contract control sheet.				
8. Define procurement authority.				
9. Establish the project work and cost code system.				
10. Receive approval for and enter the budget into the computer.				
11. Make sure all participating departments are aware of the new project and are staffed to handle the work load.				
12. Safety insurance requirements.				
13. Prepare the project and procurement schedules.				
14. Determine anticipated cash flow pattern.				
15. Set up office and job site project files.				
16. Publish the project meeting schedule.				

Project Startup Checklist (Continued)

	Estimator	Project manager	Supervisor	Foreman
17. Hold a pre-construction conference with appropriate parties involved in construction of the project.				
18. Establish lines of communication among project participants.				
19. Resolve drawing and specification questions.				
20. Designate the field crew.				
21. Reserve appropriate materials, tools, and equipment from the company inventory.				
22. Make a visual and photographic survey of existing conditions before starting work. Verify condition of adjacent off-site items.				
23. Verify physical boundaries of work.				
24. Determine site logistics.				
25. Prepare a job site accident prevention program.				
26. Post the job site accident prevention program required safety posters and emergency phone numbers.				
27. Arrange for temporary facilities.				
28. Review quality control procedures, including required tests and inspections.				
29. Review the job site security.				
30. Install project sign.				
31. Obtain a building permit.				

Material Schedule

Form Name on Disk: MATLSCHD

Good contractors are natural-born list makers – and this is one list that should save you both time and trouble. Use this form to show where components such as doors, windows and fixtures will be installed. There's a column for *Item/description* (such as code number or name), *Location*, and nine columns where you fill in details such as style, color, texture or handing.

For example, suppose you're using the form as a window schedule. The first column would describe the window, perhaps with an item code. The next column would identify the room where the window will be hung. Then, fill in the column heads that cover window specifics such as handing, glazing, color, jamb size, cladding, or R-value.

When used in a word processing or spreadsheet program, you can sort the data by window size, location, manufacturer or any other characteristic you want. You could even sort the list by code number (for the window salesman), by room (for the installer), by color (for the painter), and by cost (for the owner).

Material Schedule

Construction Company
Address
City, State, ZIP
Phone Number

☐ Window schedule

☐ Door schedule

☐ Appliance schedule

☐ Other: _____

Date: _____ Revised: _____

Project name: _____

Item/description	Location									

■ Job Cost Report

Form Name on Disk: JOBCOSTR

This form is a good way to collect cost data on the types of work you handle. Keeping up with cost changes is one of the most labor-intensive chores for the accounting people in your company, whether they use a computer or not. Without the aid of a computer, the only way to get an accurate accounting of job costs is to use a form like this.

Use this Job Cost Report to record costs for either a single phase of a project or the whole project. How you use the form depends on the size of the job and the level of detail you want to track.

How to Use This Form

This is a bookkeeping form, not an estimating form. It records the *Date, Description,* then the costs for *Labor, Material, Equipment rental, Subcontracts,* and *Other.* Fill it out with information gleaned from payroll, accounts payable, equipment rental sheets, and the original job estimate.

If you're using the form to record costs for a larger job, you'll probably need one sheet for each phase – one for foundation, one for framing, one for finish if your company does these things, and one for each of the subcontracted phases. On a small job, one sheet will be all the space you need to record all project costs.

Whichever way you use it, fill in the boxes near the top of the form for *Total estimate, Actual* and *Variance.* Then you can tell at a glance how actual job costs compared with estimated costs.

Construction Company
Address
City, State, ZIP
Phone Number

Date: _____
Owner: _____
Project number: _____
Project name: _____

Date	Description	Labor	Materials	Equipment rental	Sub-contracts	Other	Total to date

Procurement Schedule

Form Name on Disk: PROCURE

This form works well whether the project is simple or complex. On a simple job, fill out only the columns you need. As the complexity and size of a project grows, so do the problems associated with scheduling and procurement. With hundreds and even thousands of items being purchased and delivered at different times, you need some system to keep order. The Procurement Schedule has columns that can help you track materials by number or item description.

How to Use This Form

To begin with, fill out the *Number* and *Item description*. Next, if there are *Submittals* involved, fill in the dates they were *Received* and *Approved*.

Order date should match the date of the purchase order (if you use them). *Shipping time, Delivery on* and *Call confirm* are useful for scheduling and for follow-up telephone calls when material deliveries are delayed. In this *Received* column, enter the date you received the material. The *Scheduled installation* column is the earliest date that installation is possible.

The final column is labeled *Critical installation*. This is the absolute latest date that the item can be installed without delaying completion of the project.

Specification Change

Construction Company
Address
City, State, ZIP
Phone Number

Date: _____

Owner: _____

Contractor: _____

Project name: _____

Project number: _____

Specification number: _____

Detail sheet/number: _____

Received specification change from:

Name: _____

Company: _____

Phone: _____

Project address:

_____

_____

_____

Specification change information:

_____

_____

_____

_____

_____

_____

_____

_____

_____

_____

_____

_____

_____

_____

_____

_____

_____

_____

_____

Employee Data Sheet

Form Name on Disk: EMPDATA

When a new employee is hired, he or she should begin work by filling out an Employee Data Sheet. File the original in the employee's personnel folder.

Be careful to record the employee's correct social security number. Ask about any special medical conditions that would limit the employee's ability to perform on a job site. If there are physical limitations, the superintendent or foremen should be informed of them before the employee is allowed on a job site.

Keep Employee Data Sheets available for use in an emergency. On remote sites, provide the superintendent or foreman with a copy of this sheet for each employee.

Employee Data Sheet

Date: _____

Construction Company
Address
City, State, ZIP
Phone Number

Position: _____

Start date: _____

Interviewed by: _____

Employee name: _____

              Last   First

Address: _____

_____

Telephone: _____

Social security number: _____

Birthdate: _____

In case of emergency contact:

Primary contact: _____   Secondary contact: _____

Phone: _____   Phone: _____

Address: _____   Address: _____

_____   _____

Emergency medical information:

_____

_____

_____

_____

_____

_____

_____

_____

■ Driving Record Verification

Form Name on Disk: DRIVEREC

This form is used to verify employee driving records. Your insurance carrier will probably insist on a list of drivers of company vehicles. Drivers with poor records will probably be excluded from driving. By filling out and signing this form, employees give permission for you to request a report on their driving record from the state.

Have each new employee who will be driving a company vehicle fill out and sign this form. Fax a copy to your automobile insurance carrier and put another copy in the employee's personnel file.

Driving Record Verification

Construction Company
Address
City, State, ZIP
Phone Number

Date: _____

Employee: _____

Address: _____

_____

Phone number: _____

Driver's license number: _____

State: _____

Please answer the following questions:

1. Has your license ever been suspended or revoked? ☐ Yes ☐ No

    If yes, please explain: _____

    _____

2. Have you ever been cited for driving under the influence? ☐ Yes ☐ No

    If yes, please explain: _____

    _____

3. Have you received any moving violations within the past 3 years? ☐ Yes ☐ No

    If yes, please explain: _____

    _____

4. Have you been involved in any accidents within the past 3 years? ☐ Yes ☐ No

    If yes, please explain: _____

    _____

I give permission to allow a verification of my driving record to be performed.

I certify that the above information is true and correct.

Signed: _____ Date: _____

Employee Evaluation

Form Name on Disk: EMPEVAL

If your company has employees who can be expected to stay on the payroll for many months or years, you should evaluate their performance regularly. Promotion, raises, layoffs and profit sharing contributions may be affected by this evaluation.

This form is designed to make the evaluation procedure as objective and fair as possible. Enter scores from 1 to 5 for each of the four categories. *Quality of work, Quantity of work, Attitude,* and *Initiative* are all very general qualities. We've left a blank space at the bottom of this form for you to add a category of your own choice. For example, job knowledge, leadership, attendance, or trustworthiness.

Schedule employee evaluations at regular intervals, not just before you have to trim the payroll. And let each employee know that he or she is being evaluated. Show them the form so they get a clear picture of company expectations. This encourages each employee to set personal goals.

How to Use This Form

The site superintendent, crew chief or immediate supervisor should fill out this form. Tally results back at the office just by adding the scores together and dividing the result by the number of rated categories.

There's also a space for *Narrative* comments. Use this section to evaluate subjective categories of job performance. Examples include leadership, teaching ability or affability. A fair rating of any of these qualities isn't possible using a strictly numeric system. When the evaluation is complete, it should become the subject of a conference between the employee and the employee's supervisor. Finally, file a copy of the evaluation in the employee's personnel folder.

Employee Evaluation

Construction Company
Address
City, State, ZIP
Phone Number

Date: _____

Employee: _____

Job title: _____

Start date: _____

Last review: _____

Evaluated by: _____

Rating:

1. Unsatisfactory performance
2. Minimum requirements met
3. Average, expected level
4. Consistently exceeds requirements
5. Exceptional performance

Instructions:

Fill in the rating that best fits the employee's overall performance in relation to the category listed. The rating must be accompanied by a narrative. The overall rating is the average score of all the categories.

Quality of work: _____ Narrative: _____
_____
_____

Quantity of work: _____ _____
_____

Attitude/relationships with others: _____
_____
_____

Initiative & self reliance: _____
_____
_____
_____
_____

Employee Time Card

Form Name on Disk: EMPLOYTC

Accurate estimates are the key to making money in the construction industry. The key to accurate estimates is knowing your costs. The only way to do that is to track actual costs on every job you have. That's never easy. Recording actual job costs will probably be one of your greatest challenges.

Tracking material costs is fairly easy. Collect all the material invoices for any job. Do a little analysis of what materials went where. Then figure the material costs per unit right down to the last nickel. It's harder to figure actual labor costs per unit installed.

No matter how you track labor costs, the time card has to be your starting point. This book has four time cards. One of the four should be ideal for the job cost recording system you use. Of the four time cards, this form is the simplest. As the forms increase in complexity, they also collect more information. More of the work details get reported to your office — and your tradesmen spend more time writing essays on time cards. You decide how much time can be spent on this chore and how much information is required.

For instance, if your accounting system simply lumps labor into one category on each job, it's overkill to have employees list the work they do by time and category. But if you're billing for time worked, use a form that tracks employee time by work classification. Keep in mind that too much detailed information can cost as much as not enough.

How to Use This Form

This time card has spaces for *Date,* the *Client/job* (name), *Task,* and the *Hours* worked. Employees fill in the form daily, entering each task description. It's up to the bookkeeper to interpret these descriptions.

This form works fine where the contractor is also the superintendent or at least visits the job frequently. In that case, it should be easy to match the work being done with the worker's written description of it. Deciphering task descriptions correctly requires some knowledge of the job and the units used in estimating the work.

This card is fine if job costing doesn't have to be too detailed. Use this card on a time and materials job where the client can be expected to scrutinize time cards and the office needs time cards only for payroll purposes.

In most cases, the written explanations on this card won't provide enough information for true job costing. You'll need a time card with a little more sophistication.

Employee Time Card

Construction Company
Address
City, State, ZIP
Phone Number

Period ending: _____

Employee name: _____

Date	Client/job	Task	Hours

Unit Cost Time Card

Form Name on Disk: UNITCARD

Larger construction companies usually have the foreman fill out employee time cards. Some companies even have both the employee and the foreman fill out separate cards. That provides a convenient way to verify labor hours. Regardless of the complexity of the time card you use, try to simplify the labor cost recording process. Aim to eliminate time in the office spent looking up codes or writing them down more than once. Of course, doing the payroll on a computer can speed and simplify the work.

This card is the most complex of the four time cards in this book. It can be used in any construction business. But the detailed work coding and unit costing makes it ideal for subcontractors who are trying to nail down their unit labor costs. You'll need a sophisticated job costing system in the office to use all the information collected on this card. If you can't use all this information, there's no sense collecting it.

How to Use This Form

This time card has space to list work codes down the left side of the form. Use your computer to produce a code list that's right for your company. Each day, the user simply puts the hours worked next to the work code most closely matching the work done.

The *Units* column next to the *Hours* column is for units installed during the hours recorded. So if an electrician installs 80 single gang boxes in an 8-hour day, the card should show 80 in the *Units* column. Your office clerk will do the math: 10 boxes an hour is one tenth of an hour per box.

Unit Cost Time Card

Construction Company
Address
City, State, ZIP
Phone Number

Date: _____

Employee: _____

Week ending: _____

Work code	Thursday		Friday		Sat/Sun		Monday		Tuesday		Wednesday	
	Hours	Units	Hours	Units	Hours	Units	Hours	Units	Hours	Units	Hours	Units

Total reg. hours												
Total O/T hours												

O/T approved by: _____   Total reg. hrs: _____   Total O/T hrs: _____

Gross	FIT	FICA	SIT	Other	Other

Total deductions: _____   Net pay: _____

Employee Time Sheet

Form Name on Disk: EMPLTIME

This time sheet is simple yet lets you do some job cost recording. It's a weekly time card, but it also includes space to record custom work codes and work descriptions. We've also included space at the bottom where your payroll clerk can enter totals for the various job categories. That saves entering this information on another form.

How to Use This Form

Start with work categories and code numbers that match the workers' compensation categories and codes used in your state. Insurance carriers in some states let you divide a worker's time into several categories and pay for workers' comp coverage under each category. In other states that practice is prohibited and you must pay the highest rate that applies to the worker. If payroll for a worker can be segregated by category, track each classification separately. This usually helps you to lower your workers' comp burden. Of course, you'll need good records to back up your claims.

We've left the *Work codes* blank for you to fill in with a typewriter or computer. In some cases, you'll have more job cost classifications than workers' comp classifications. If you need to track them, simply add a letter to the original classification number. For example, suppose you need to track finish carpentry and rough carpentry as different job cost items. Suppose also that the code number for all residential carpentry is 5645 under the worker's comp rating system in your state. For rough carpentry, use a code of R5645. For finish carpentry, use F5645.

The table to the right of the job codes is for recording total hours by job type. Each day that a worker does a specific type of work, enter the time in the box opposite the code. Fill in the next box in the same row if the worker does more of the same work during the pay period. For example if a worker does rough carpentry Monday for 4 hours, put a 4 in the first box to the right of R5645 Rough Carpentry. If the same worker does rough carpentry again on Wednesday for 6 hours, put a 6 in the next box. Add across the rows to total the hours spent on rough carpentry for the week.

Employee Time Sheet

Construction Company
Address
City, State, ZIP
Phone Number

Week ending: _____

Employee name: _____

Employee number: _____

Monday:

Job name	Job #	Work code	Hours

Subtotal hours: _____

Thursday:

Job name	Job #	Work code	Hours

Subtotal hours: _____

Tuesday:

Job name	Job #	Work code	Hours

Subtotal hours: _____

Friday:

Job name	Job #	Work code	Hours

Subtotal hours: _____

Wednesday:

Job name	Job #	Work code	Hours

Subtotal hours: _____

Saturday:

Job name	Job #	Work code	Hours

Subtotal hours: _____

Total hours: _____

Work codes   **Job names**

_____ _____

_____ _____

_____ _____

_____ _____

_____ _____

_____ _____

Total

Time Card — Categorized & Time Card Categories

Form Name on Disk: TIMECARD & TIMECAT

This time card is a modified version of a system designed by Alexander Brennen. He devised a coding system that linked his estimating system to his job costing system. The estimating system divided residential construction tasks into 32 categories, beginning with Permits and ending with Extra Work. These are listed on the form Time Card Categories. Each major category can be divided into as many subdivisions as necessary. For example, layout, clear and grub, and survey all fall under the category of Site Prep.

How to Use This Form

Since this coding system is too extensive to commit to memory, give a copy of the job categories and time sheets to each employee. If you're using the form on a computer, customize it to fit the categories needed in your business. Most residential builders tend to do the same type of construction over and over. Changing the categories to fit your business should be worth the time and trouble.

It's important to demonstrate to employees how to use the card. Make sure they understand what each category includes. Be sure they know that a code numbers is required for each task they perform each day.

When the time cards come back to the office each week, it's a simple process to compare actual and estimated labor costs.

Time Card - Categorized

Construction Company
Address
City, State, ZIP
Phone Number

Date: _____

Employee: _____

Pay period ending: _____

Job number / task	Monday	Tuesday	Wednesday	Thursday	Friday	Sat/Sun	Total

Daily totals: _____ _____ _____ _____ _____ _____ _____

Job number / task	Monday	Tuesday	Wednesday	Thursday	Friday	Sat/Sun	Total

Daily totals: _____ _____ _____ _____ _____ _____ _____

Total hours worked: [ ]

Time Card Categories

Date: _____

PE Permits
Misc.
SP Site Prep
Layout
Clear & grub
Survey
Floor protection
EX Excavation
Rough grade
Piers or postholes
Drainage/footings
Backfill
Haulage
DE Demolition
Temp. bracing
Demo roofing
Demo framing
Demo concrete
Demo stucco
Demo misc.
DR Drainage
Membrane
Filter cloth
Gravel
Drainpipe
CO Concrete
Forming walls
Forming slab
Form misc.
Tieing rebar
Pouring
Stripping forms
Rebolt exist. fdtn.
FR Framing
Mudsills
Holdowns
Walls
Straps
Roof rafters
Trusses
Soffit framing
Misc. beams
Subfloor
Shearwall ply
Roof ply
Stair framing
Misc. framing
Scaffolding
Skylight framing

DE Decks
Foundation
Framing
Decking
Railing
Benches
Trellis
Gate
Flashing
Stairs
FE Fences
Set posts
Frame
Finish
Gate
RF Roofing
Tarpaper
Asphalt shingles
Flashing
1x4 skip sheath
Wood shingles
Gutters
Downspouts
EPDM membrane
WI Windows
Set
Flashing
Skylights
ET Exterior Trim
Windows
Doors
Fascia
Soffit
Misc.
SI Siding
Tarpaper
Flashing
Wood (specify)
Shingles
Plywood
Wall lattice
ST Stucco
Paper
Wire
Metal
Stucco
FP Fireplace
Fireplace
Chimney

IN Insulation
Rigid
Walls R11
Roof R30
Floor R19
Title 24
SR Sheetrock
RC1 Channel
Hanging
Taping
DO Doors
Prehang
Set
Weatherstrip
Locks
Make door
IT Interior Trim
Window
Door
Base
Stair base
Shelves
Paneling
Ceiling moldings
Handrails
Interior stairs
Misc.
PA Painting
Caulking & prep.
Painting
CA Cabinets
Milling
Sanding
Hardware
Kicks
Installation
Finishing
CT Countertops
Underlayment
Fabricate
Install
TI Tile
Furring
Wonderboard
FI Finish Work
Set appliances
Hardware
Misc.

EL Electrical
Prep.
Rough
Finish
PL Plumbing
Prep.
Rough
Finish
ME Mechanical
Ducts
Flues
Furnace
Hood
Misc.
FL Floors
Underlayment
Patching
Vinyl
CL Cleanup
Dump runs
Site cleanup
MI Misc.
(Describe)

MA Management
Supervisor
Bidding
Drafting
Misc.
EW Extra Work
Attach separate sheet

Weekly Time Card

Form Name on Disk: WEEKTIME

This type of time card is especially useful when you have a large crew doing the same type of work. An example would be a painting crew of five or six on the same job for several days.

The foreman is in the best position to fill out this type of card. It's designed to accommodate seven employees, but you can double that number by using the PM rows for other employees.

How to Use This Form

Fill in the name of each worker in the *Employee name* column. There are seven sets of *In* and *Out* columns and seven *Ttl hrs* (total hours) columns. Use these columns to record the times when each employee started and finished work for the day. The foreman should send the card to the payroll clerk who then runs totals across each row for each employee.

Weekly Time Card

Construction Company
Address
City, State, ZIP
Phone Number

Date: _____
Week ending: _____
Pay period starts: _____
Sheet number: _____
Project name: _____

#	Employee name		In	Out	Ttl hrs	In	Out	Ttl hrs	In	Out	Ttl hrs	In	Out	Ttl hrs	In	Out	Ttl hrs	In	Out	Ttl hrs	In	Out	Ttl hrs	Ttl hrs for wk
1		AM																							
		PM																							
2		AM																							
		PM																							
3		AM																							
		PM																							
4		AM																							
		PM																							
5		AM																							
		PM																							
6		AM																							
		PM																							
7		AM																							
		PM																							
	Totals																								

Preliminary Notice

Form Name on Disk: PRELIM

Every state has a mechanic's lien law. These laws are written to protect those who do work or furnish materials that improve land and buildings. If you aren't paid for what you supply or the work you do, the law gives you a lien against the property until your bill is paid. A lien is like a mortgage. It follows the property when the property is sold and isn't discharged by bankruptcy of the owner.

A lien isn't automatic, of course. You have to comply with state law to gain lien rights. And the law varies from state to state. Most states require that you give the property owner a copy of this notice to preserve your rights under the law. This form meets the requirements of California and many other states. The form required by your state will probably be similar (but may not be identical).

This preliminary notice can be used by subcontractors, material suppliers, equipment renters, architects, engineers and other non-contractor claimants on both public and private construction projects.

In most states the law requires a preliminary notice to be sent to the owner of property within 20 days of the date that materials are furnished or labor performed. It notifies the property owner (and the lender) that the property may be subject to a mechanic's lien and stop notices. This notice give owners the opportunity to protect themselves by demanding a signed release before paying for work that's been done.

How to Use This Form

Contractors know when their subcontractors and material suppliers have been paid. You write the checks. Your client, on the other hand, has no proof that you've made those payments. It's common to hear stories about disreputable contractors taking final payment and then failing to pay their subs and suppliers. Then the subs and suppliers file a lien on the owner's property to secure payment. The result may be that the owner has to pay twice to clear the lien – once to the general contractor and again to the subcontractor.

By filing this preliminary notice, architects, engineers, subs and suppliers put the owner and lender on notice that they should demand releases before paying the general contractor. If you're a subcontractor, send this notice (by registered mail) to both the owner and lender. That gives you all the rights available under your state's mechanic's lien law.

Preliminary Notice

Construction Company
Address
City, State, ZIP
Phone Number

Date: _____

Owner: _____

Contractor: _____

Project name: _____

To: _____

_____

_____

Notice is hereby given, pursuant to Sections _____ and _____ of the Civil Code as follows:

That the undersigned_____, whose address is _____

_____ has, at the request of _____

furnished or will furnish materials, supplies, equipment and/or perform labor, for use upon property

located at _____, County of _____.

That said materials, supplies, and equipment were furnished and/or labor was performed beginning on

_____.

That this preliminary notice is sent in compliance with the Laws of the State of _____, and is

sent within twenty (20) days after the initial furnishing of materials and/or performance of labor.

Dated this _____ day of _____, 19_____.

Name: _____

Address: _____

_____

Signature: _____

Title: _____

Notice to property owner:

If bills are not paid in full for the labor, services, equipment, or materials furnished or to be furnished, a
mechanic's lien may be filed against the property, leading to the loss, through court foreclosure
proceedings, of all or part of your property even though you have paid your contractor in full.
You may wish to protect yourself against this consequence by (1) requiring your contractor to furnish
a signed release by the person or firm giving you this notice before making payment to your contractor or
(2) any other method or device which is appropriate under the circumstances.

Waiver of Lien (Partial)

Form Name on Disk: WAIVLIEN

This partial lien release waives your right to file a lien for work done up to the date on the form. Use it when you receive a progress payment during construction.

The portion of the lien waived is the dollar amount of the progress payment. Fill in the amount that matches the *total due* on a Percentage Complete Invoice, and send this waiver with your invoice. The property description can be an address or the legal description. Both of those can be found on the Job Information sheet.

Waiver of Lien (Partial)

Construction Company
Address
City, State, ZIP
Phone Number

Date: _____

Owner: _____

Contractor: _____

Project number: _____

Project name: _____

State of: _____

County of: _____

To whom it may concern:

_____ has been employed by _____

to furnish _____

_____

for the building with the address of: _____ City of: _____

County of: _____ State of: _____

Lot number _____ Section _____ Township _____ Range _____

Now that _____

the undersigned, has received the sum of _____

dollars and other good and valuable considerations, receipt acknowledged, we waive and release any and all

lien, or right to lien on above described building and premises under the statutes of the state of _____

relating to mechanic's liens, on account of labor or materials, or both, furnished or to be furnished, by the

undersigned to or on account of _____

for said building or premises.

Witnessed this _____ day of _____, 19 _____

Signature _____ Witness _____

Material or Labor Waiver of Lien

Form Name on Disk: MATLWAIV

No matter what state you work in, the purpose of the mechanic's lien laws is to ensure that subs, workers and material suppliers get paid for the goods and services they provide. The Waiver of Lien is a signed legal document declaring that materials and labor supplied for a specific project have been paid for and that you are waiving your lien rights in return for payment. Although lien laws differ around the country, this "generic" version is intended to work in any state. But before you use any of these forms, *verify that they meet the requirements in your state.*

This form is designed for the final payment, since there's no provision for future work.

How to Use This Form

The Waiver of Lien is usually presented with the invoice. *Job description* comes from the Job Information sheet; the sum should match the invoice amount.

Material or Labor Waiver of Lien

Construction Company
Address
City, State, ZIP
Phone Number

Date: _____

Owner: _____

Contractor: _____

Project number: _____

Project name: _____

State of: _____

County of: _____

To whom it may concern:

_____ has been employed by _____

to furnish _____

_____

for the building with the address of _____ City of: _____

County of: _____ State of: _____

Lot number _____ Section _____ Township _____ Range _____

Now that _____

the undersigned, has received the sum of _____

dollars and other good and valuable considerations, receipt acknowledged, we waive and release any and all

lien, or right to lien on above described building and premises under the statutes of the state of _____

relating to mechanic's liens, on account of labor or materials, or both, furnished or to be furnished, by the

undersigned to or on account of _____

for said building or premises.

Witnessed this _____ day of _____, 19 _____

_____   _____
Signature   Witness

Nonresponsibility Notice

Form Name on Disk: NONRESP

The Nonresponsibility Notice gives owners who have not contracted for work on property they own a way to avoid liens. For example, assume a contractor is doing tenant improvement work in leased space. The contractor has a contract with a tenant. The owner of the building wants to protect his building from mechanic's liens if the lessee doesn't pay for work done. The property owner would file a Nonresponsibility Notice.

This too is a California form, but many states use a similar form. Check with your state contractor's board to see if you can use it. If you've loaded this form into your computer, it's easy to make minor modifications.

How to Use This Form

The notice is filled out by the owner of the building and, in California, recorded with the county recorder. Notice that the signature on the form has to be notarized. A copy of the form should be posted in a conspicuous place on the job site.

Nonresponsibility Notice

Construction Company
Address
City, State, ZIP
Phone Number

Date: _____

Owner: _____

Contractor: _____

Project number: _____

To whom it may concern:

Notice is hereby given that the undersigned _____ is the Owner of the

premises situated at _____ County of _____

_____, State of _____ more particularly described as follows:

_____

legal description of property

That the name of the Lessee of the premises is _____

residing at _____

That the first date on which the undersigned obtained knowledge that construction or repairs were being made on

the above described property was on the _____ day of _____, 19_____

and notice is posted in compliance with the Laws of the State of _____ within ten (10)

days of acquiring such knowledge, and copy of the same has been filed in the Office of the County Recorder
where the above-described property is situated.

And that the undersigned disclaims any liability or responsibility, either express or implied, for any work,
including the furnishing of materials or the performance of labor, that has been done, or is being done, or will
be done, on the above-described premises.

Dated this _____ day of _____, 19_____

Name: _____

Address: _____

_____

Signature: _____

State of _____

County of _____ **ss,**

On this _____ day of _____, in the year 19 _____ before me, _____

_____ **Notary Public**, personally appeared _____

personally known to me (or proved to me on the basis of satisfactory evidence) to be the person that executed
this instrument on behalf of the _____ and acknowledged to me that the _____ executed it.

Notary Public in and for said State of _____

Thank You Letter

Form Name on Disk: THANKYOU

It took many years, but the Detroit auto makers finally learned their lesson. No matter what their actors said in the commercials, when you're selling lemons, the public will discover that you're selling lemons. Spend millions praising your product, if you want. But the public won't be fooled for long.

Construction contracting is no different. In fact, studies have shown that construction contractors rate right down there with lawyers, politicians and car salesmen as people least likely to be trusted. Accept that as a given. Then find ways to separate yourself from the type of contractors who give this industry a bad name. Thank you notes are a good place to start.

How to Use This Form

Send this note with the final invoice, after filling in your company name. But don't send this note until the work is really finished. Use the Final Project Punch List to be sure your client is truly satisfied. Some contractors include with the note an inexpensive but thoughtful gift. A T-shirt, flowers or a bottle of champagne are popular choices. That creates a feeling of good will at the end of the job. It's also a good idea to follow up a month or two later with a questionnaire.

Thank You Letter

Construction Company   Date: _____

Address   Client: _____

City, State, ZIP   Address: _____

Phone Number   City, State, ZIP: _____

With the receipt of this invoice we complete our cycle of service to you, our client. It has been a pleasure working with you. We hope our service was prompt and efficient. If by chance you have any questions, please call us immediately.

Once again, thank you for calling _____ for your remodeling project. If we can help in the future, please contact us.

Sincerely,

_____

Customer Satisfaction Survey

Form Name on Disk: CUSTSURV

As a construction contractor, your most valuable asset is your reputation in the community. That's the reason for this form. If your customers aren't satisfied with the work you're doing, you want to be the first to know. Satisfied customers build a successful contracting business. This form will both identify problems (which is the first step in building satisfaction) and demonstrate that you're concerned about quality and reliability.

The form thanks your customer for the business and at the same time invites them to comment on the service provided. Why not just ask the customer face to face? We've found that a letter elicits more frank, truthful responses than you would get in a face-to-face conversation.

One of the hardest tasks in the construction business is dealing with unhappy customers. And as hard as it is to hear criticism of your work, that's the only way to improve customer satisfaction. Send this sheet shortly after completing every job. Every few months, tally the responses and see where your business needs improvement. Then follow up to make those improvements.

Customer Satisfaction Survey

Construction Company
Address
City, State, ZIP
Phone Number

Date: _____

Client: _____

Address: _____

_____

City, State, ZIP _____

Project name: _____

Dear _____ :

Thank you for the opportunity to work on your project. We are glad you called upon us and hope that if future needs arise you will call us again.

We hope the quality of our work pleased you. Any input you have regarding our performance would be greatly appreciated. Your comments are an important part of our quality assurance program. Would you please take the time to fill out this form so that future clients will gain from your and our experience?

Were your needs met promptly?

Before the job	☐ Yes	☐ No
During the job	☐ Yes	☐ No
After the job	☐ Yes	☐ No

Did the project . . .

start on time?	☐ Yes	☐ No
complete on time?	☐ Yes	☐ No
finish cleanly?	☐ Yes	☐ No

Were our workers/subs courteous?

☐ Yes ☐ No

Did we fulfill our agreements?

☐ Yes ☐ No

Did you receive the value you expected?

☐ Yes ☐ No

Was the quality of the work as expected?

☐ Yes ☐ No

Will you consider us for future projects?

☐ Yes ☐ No

Please write in any additional comments . . .

_____

_____

_____

_____

May we use your name as a reference on future jobs? ☐ Yes ☐ No

Signature _____   Date _____

Form Name on Disk: COMPEVAL

This letter will help you determine what your customers think of your work. It's a long form and takes several minutes to fill out. But it gives you a good picture of how your clients view your company's performance.

Send this form to each client on completion of a job. Enclose a self-addressed stamped envelope and you're almost sure to get a response. Consider offering a free T-shirt or cap with the company logo on it when the form is returned.

The returned forms are like a report card on your company. If you're producing satisfied customers, use surveys results in your advertising – "90% of our clients rated our overall construction performance as good or excellent . . ."

Company Evaluation

Construction Company   Date: _____
Address   Client: _____
City, State, ZIP   Address: _____
Phone Number   City, State, ZIP: _____
                                      Project name: _____

1. How did you find out about our company? _____

2. Do you feel our crew and subcontractors respected your property? ☐ Yes ☐ No
    If no, please explain any difficulties you might have had: _____
    _____
    _____
    _____

3. How would you rate our company's overall construction performance?
    ☐ bad   ☐ good   ☐ excellent

4. How would you rate our administrative performance?
    ☐ bad   ☐ good   ☐ excellent

5. How would you rate our professionalism?
    ☐ bad   ☐ good   ☐ excellent

6. How did you feel we handled the day-to-day phases of your job?
    ☐ bad   ☐ good   ☐ excellent

7. What could we have done to make your project run more smoothly? _____
    _____
    _____

8. Are you happy with your completed project?   ☐ Yes ☐ No
    What, if anything, would you have done differently? _____
    _____
    _____

9. How effectively and timely were problems dealt with? _____

10. May we use you as a telephone reference?   ☐ Yes ☐ No

Please feel free to include any additional comments.

Thank you very much for your valuable input.

Installation Instructions

Files on the Construction Forms & Contracts disk are highly compressed in ZIP format. You won't be able to use them until they've been decompressed. The INSTALL program decompresses the files of your choice and writes them to your hard disk.

Begin by turning your computer on. Close Windows and exit from your menu program so you have the DOS prompt (such as C:\>) on the screen.

1. Put the Construction Forms & Contracts disk in your 3.5" floppy drive (such as A:).

2. Change control to that drive (such as by typing A:). Press Enter.

3. At the command prompt (such as A:), type INSTALL. Press Enter.

4. Notice the recommended destination is C:\FORMBOOK. Press Enter to confirm this choice or Esc to exit without installing anything.

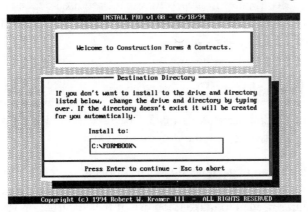

5. Install Pro checks the files available on the Construction Forms & Contracts disk.

```
Reading H:\EXCEL.ZIP configuration.
              Please wait...
```

6. Install Pro lists the five file formats available for installation. See the column headed File Name.

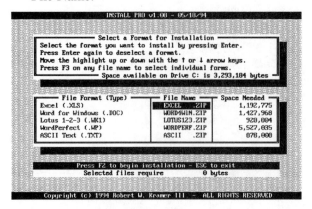

The next step will be selecting files to be written to your hard disk.

Enough Space Available?

All 125 construction forms are on disk in each of five file formats (Excel, Lotus, Word, WordPerfect and ASCII). You probably want to install only one of the five file formats. But you can install any of the five (or even all five formats) if there's enough space available on your hard disk. Check the number on the line that starts *Space available . . .* in the top window at the right side of your screen. In the example above:

    · Space available on Drive C: is 3,293,184 bytes ·

Space needed for installing all forms in each of the five formats is listed in the column headed *Space Needed.* In the example above, see the lines:

    · Space Needed
          1,192,775

Space required for the files you've selected will appear near the bottom of the screen when you begin selecting files. See the line that begins *Selected files require . . .* Note that the required disk space is an estimate. Actual space required depends on the way your hard disk is formatted. In the example above, selecting WORD4WIN.ZIP will show:

    Selected files require   1,427,968 bytes

Decisions, Decisions, Decisions

Which version of Construction Forms & Contracts should you install? The best choice will be the format that works with the program you know best and like most.

Choice #1 – If you're an experienced user of Lotus or Excel or WordPerfect or Word, select the file appropriate for that program. Each of these programs has all the features needed to make good use of the construction forms and contracts on disk.

Choice #2 – If you aren't familiar with any of the word processing or spreadsheet programs listed, install ASCII.ZIP. This set of forms works fine with many simple editing programs. The Applications Directory that follows explains how to get one of these editing programs at little or no cost.

Choice #3 – If you can't be bothered with getting a new editing program, install ASCII.ZIP and use the editing program you already have. It's called EDIT.COM and it was written to the DOS directory of your hard disk when DOS 5 or 6 was installed.

Choice #4 – If all else fails, install ASCII.ZIP and use the editing program called NCU Edit. That program will be written to your hard disk automatically when you install ASCII.ZIP. NCU Edit may be all you'll ever need to make good use of these forms.

Make a Selection and Press F2

To select a file for installation, move the highlight up or down with the ↑ or ↓ key. Then press Enter. (Be sure Num Lock is off.) Then press F2 to install.

▼ Leave the highlight on EXCEL.ZIP if you use Excel 4 or Excel 5 or Quattro Pro for Windows or Claris Works for Windows.

▼ Move the highlight down to LOTUS123.ZIP if you use Lotus 1-2-3 for DOS or Lotus 1-2-3 for Windows.

▼ Move the highlight down to WORD4WIN.ZIP if you use Word for Windows 2 or Word 6.

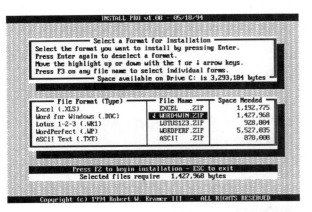

▼ Move the highlight down to WORDPERF.ZIP if you use WordPerfect 5.1 for DOS, WordPerfect for Windows or AmiPro for Windows.

▼ Move the highlight down to ASCII.ZIP if you use WordStar 2000, Q&A for DOS or if you don't have any of the programs listed above.

Press Enter to select the file name to be installed. A ✓ (check mark) will appear beside the file name you've selected. In the illustration at the left, WORD4WIN.ZIP (the construction forms in Word for Windows format) has been selected.

To Cancel a Selection

To cancel your selection, use the ↑ or ↓ key to move the highlight to the name selected. Press Enter again and the check mark will disappear.

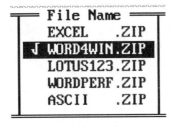

Selected

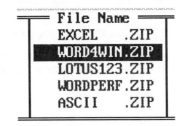

Selection Cancelled

All or Just a Few?

When a .ZIP file name is selected, all 125 construction forms in that format will be installed. The next section explains how to select specific construction forms for installation. To install just a few of the construction forms, skip the next step and jump down to the following section, "Selecting Individual Forms for Installation."

Press F2 to Install

When you've made your selection, press the F2 key and all forms selected will be written to your hard disk. If you decide to abort installation without writing any files to disk, press the Esc key.

Selecting Individual Forms for Installation

If free space is limited on your hard drive, consider installing only the forms you need immediately. Later you can install any other forms you need. Here's how to select only a few of the 125 forms for installation.

1. Begin by following steps 1 through 6 at the beginning of this section, "Installation Instructions."

2. Use the ↑ or ↓ key to put the highlight on one of the five .ZIP file names listed under File Name.

3. With none of the .ZIP file names checked, press the F3 key. You'll see the first five of the 125 construction forms in that file format.

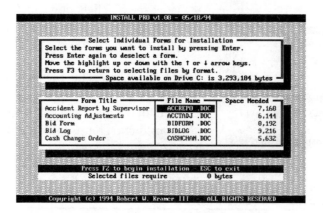

4. Move the highlight up or down the list of construction forms with the ↑ or ↓ key.

5. Titles of the construction forms are listed under the heading *Form Title*. File names on the installation disk are listed under the heading *File Name*. Space needed on your hard drive is listed under *Space Needed*.

6. Press Enter to put a ✓ (check mark) next to the names of individual files to be installed. The illustration below shows BIDFORM.DOC and BIDLOG.DOC with a check mark, indicating that these two forms are selected for installation.

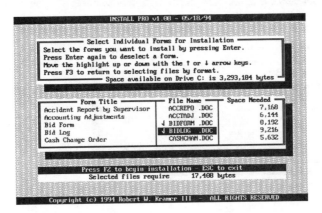

7. To cancel a selection, use the ↑ or ↓ key to move the highlight back to the file name checked. Press Enter again and the check mark will disappear.

8. Continue scrolling down the list of 125 forms by pressing the ↓ key.

9. When finished selecting individual forms, press F3.

10. Press F2 to complete installation. Install Pro will run the PKUNZIP utility to extract selected forms to your hard drive.

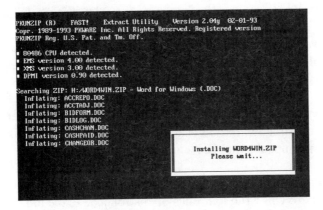

11. When installation is complete, you'll be returned to the DOS prompt (unless you selected forms from the file ASCII.ZIP).

12. If you decided to install ASCII.ZIP, you'll have to answer a question about the printer you plan to use. The paragraphs below explain how to answer this question.

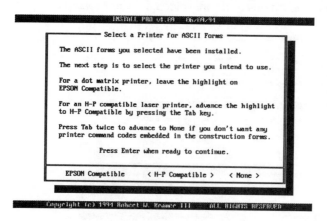

A Question About Your Printer

There's an advantage to using the construction forms with a word processing or spreadsheet program. All decisions about your printer have already been made. If you install the file ASCII.ZIP, you have to configure the forms to be compatible with your printer. Even worse, some printers may not be able to use these ASCII forms. The only way to find out for sure is to try it. Here's how:

▼ If you have a dot matrix printer, it's probably Epson compatible. Leave the highlight on *EPSON Compatible* and press Enter. Install Pro will write Epson printer control codes to the four top lines of each form you selected for installation.

▼ If you have a laser printer, it's probably H-P compatible. Move the highlight to *H-P Compatible* by pressing the Tab key. Install Pro will write PCL printer control codes to the top four lines of each form you selected for installation.

▼ Select *None* by pressing Tab twice if you don't want any printer control codes written to the construction forms. That's the only practical choice if your printer is neither Epson compatible nor H-P compatible.

Press Enter to complete writing of printer control codes. If you selected either Epson or H-P codes, Install Pro will write four lines of control code to the top of each form you selected for installation.

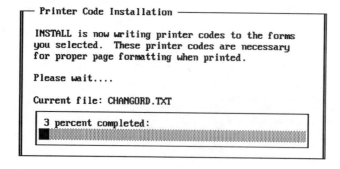

Printing from the DOS Prompt

Even if you didn't have printer control codes embedded in the construction forms, you'll still be able to print the forms. At the DOS prompt, just type the command:

TYPE FORMNAME.TXT >LPTx

In this command, replace *formname* with the name of the form you want to print. Replace *x* with the number of the port your printer uses. That's usually number 1. For example, to print COSTBOOK.TXT to a printer attached to LPT1 you would type:

TYPE COSTBOOK.TXT >LPT1

Need Help? Call 619-438-7828

Installation of these forms should be pretty simple on most computers. If you're having trouble, don't waste a lot of time struggling with what may be an easy problem. Call Craftsman Book Company's software support department at 619-438-7828.

Editing ASCII Forms

Construction forms and contracts are written using a character set know as *PC-8 code page 437*. To create these forms, we've used ASCII characters with values greater than 127. The editing programs listed in the section that follows (the Applications Directory) work fine with the forms on disk. Other editors may strip off the seventh bit of each of these characters. If so, what should be lines and boxes will appear as capital letters. There may be a simple remedy for this. Look through the documentation for your text editor. See if there's a way to turn off stripping of the seventh (or high) bit. Then make sure your editor ignores page formatting when printing the form. Margins, headers, footers, form feeds, pitch and line spacing should not be set by your editor unless you installed ASCII.ZIP with no printer codes.

Installing Most (But Not All) Forms

Here's how to save time if you want to install most (but not all) files in one of the five formats. Move the highlight to the file name of your choice, such as WORD4WIN.ZIP. Press Enter to select that name. Then press F3. You'll notice that all form names have been selected (have a ✓). Press Enter on any name selected to skip installation of that form. The check mark will disappear and that form will not be installed. Press F2 to complete installation.

Be Careful When Reinstalling

You can install Construction Forms & Contracts as many times as you want. But be aware that second and later installations may overwrite any changes you've made to forms installed previously. Install Pro will provide a warning and offer to skip overwriting when you reinstall Construction Forms & Contracts.

When you customize a form by making changes, it's a good idea to save the revised form to a new name or to a different directory. That prevents accidental overwriting of a customized form.

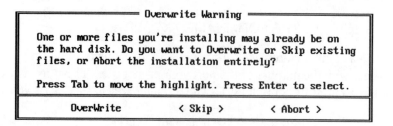

```
╒══════════════════ Overwrite Warning ══════════════════╕
│                                                        │
│  One or more files you're installing may already be on │
│  the hard disk. Do you want to Overwrite or Skip existing │
│  files, or Abort the installation entirely?            │
│                                                        │
│  Press Tab to move the highlight. Press Enter to select. │
╞════════════════════════════════════════════════════════╡
│     OverWrite          < Skip >          < Abort >     │
╘════════════════════════════════════════════════════════╛
```

The following pages explain how to use Construction Forms & Contracts with the word processing program, spreadsheet program or editing program of your choice.

Applications Directory

The following pages explain how to use Construction Forms & Contracts on Disk with the word processing, spreadsheet or editing program of your choice. The program you select should be the program you know best and like most.

1. Ami Pro, Claris Works, Excel, Lotus 1-2-3, Quattro Pro, Word for Windows and WordPerfect are all good choices. Each of these programs has all the features needed to make good use of the construction forms and contracts on disk.

2. Boxer and Visual Display Edit (VDE Edit) can use the forms and contracts on disk and are available at no cost if you know how to use a computer bulletin board. See the explanation that begins on page 421.

3. MS-DOS Editor is installed on every new computer that uses DOS. If you don't have any of the programs listed above, try the MS-DOS Editor. It should be in the DOS directory on your hard disk.

4. If you don't have any of the programs listed above and can't find the MS-DOS Editor, use NCU Edit. It's included on the Construction Forms & Contracts disk and is installed automatically to your hard disk when you elect to install forms in ASCII format. You can learn NCU Edit in a few minutes and will be surprised at how much you can get done with this small, simple program.

■ Index of Programs

■ Ami Pro 3.0 for Windows

Install forms from the file WORDPERF.ZIP on the Construction Forms & Contracts disk. The installation procedure is explained in the section "Installation Instructions" beginning on page 333.

Begin Ami Pro and click on File

Click on Open.

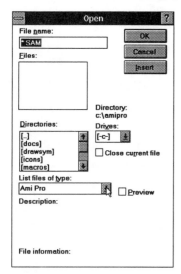

◄ The *Open* dialog box appears. Click the down arrow on the right of the box *List files of type:*

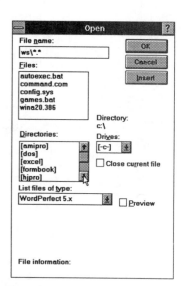

Ami Pro displays a list of file types. Click and hold the down arrow on the lower right of the list box until you see the WordPerfect 5.x file type. ►

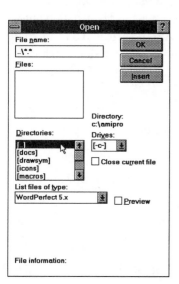

◄ Click on WordPerfect 5.x

Double click on the double dots [..] in the Directories box until they disappear.

Click and hold the down arrow until you ► see [formbook] listed under Directories.

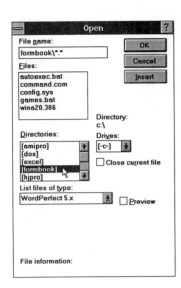

◀ Double click on [formbook].

Under *File name*, change the *.* to
*.WP. Press Enter. Notice that all the
forms you installed with a .WP file type
appear in the *Files* box at the upper left.
To scroll down the list of file names,
click and hold the mouse cursor on the
down arrow at the lower right of the
Files box. See the mouse cursor in the
illustration at the right. Form names are
listed in alphabetical order.

▶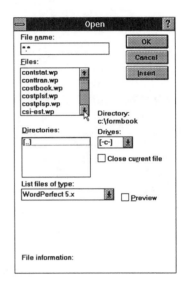

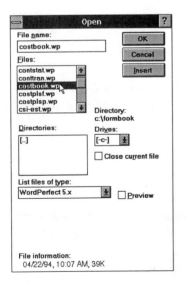

◀ Double click on the name of the form
you want to use.

Ami Pro then asks you to select *Import
Options*. Click on Apply styles. Then
click on OK.

▶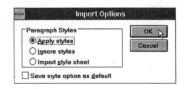

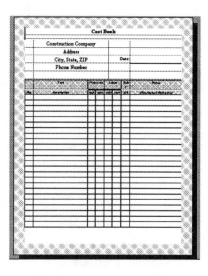

◀ Ami Pro will then load the form and display it on your screen.

Changing the Type Style

Construction Forms & Contracts for Ami Pro are in WordPerfect 5.1 for DOS format. WordPerfect 5.1 for DOS does not use True Type fonts. Computers that use Windows usually use True Type fonts. When opening a form, your computer will try to substitute a type font that's appropriate. But the font selected depends on the printer you use and type fonts you've installed with Windows. If some headings are too wide for a column or if type spills off the page, change to another type style or size. Here's how: With the construction form displayed on the screen, select the type you want to change. Hold the Ctrl key down and type the letter A to open the *Modify Style* dialog box. Then either:

☑ Click on the type font you prefer, or

☑ Click on the size font you prefer.

☑ Then click on OK.

Changing the Margins

Some construction forms may not fit on one page when printed with some printers. If part of a form spills over onto a second page, try resetting the margins:

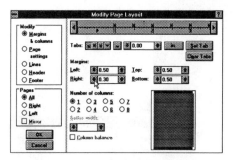

☑ Click on Page

☑ Click on Modify Page Layout

☑ Reduce the top, bottom, left and right margins to the minimum your printer can handle. That's about 0.30" (three tenths of an inch) on most laser printers.

☑ Click on OK

If that doesn't solve the problem, try reducing the form length by deleting a line or reducing the form width by making one column a little narrower.

Save a Revised Form to a New File Name

When you customize a form by making changes, it's a good idea to save the revised form to a new file name or to a different directory. That prevents accidental overwriting of a customized form if you decide to reinstall forms from the Construction Forms & Contracts disk.

Saving in Ami Pro

Construction Forms & Contracts are in WordPerfect format. To save your customized documents in Ami Pro format:

☑ Click on File

☑ Click on Save As

☑ Type, for example, C:\FORMBOOK\COSTBOK1.SAM for the name you want to give this document

☑ Click on OK

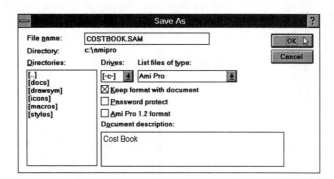

Reinstalling Construction Forms & Contracts

Occasionally you may customize a contract or form and then decide you like the original document better. It's easy to reinstall any single contract or form on the Construction Forms & Contracts disk. See "Selecting Individual Forms for Installation" on page 336.

Boxer for DOS

Boxer is an excellent shareware editing program. It's available at no cost from CompuServe, many computer bulletin boards and the Contractor's Bulletin Board (319-242-0060). See the instructions on page 421. If you use Boxer, install forms from the file ASCII.ZIP on the Construction Forms & Contracts disk. The installation procedure is explained in the section "Installation Instructions" beginning on page 333.

◀ To begin Boxer, type B and press Enter. Press the F10 key once. The top menu bar becomes active and one of the menu bar options is highlighted. Type F to open the File menu.

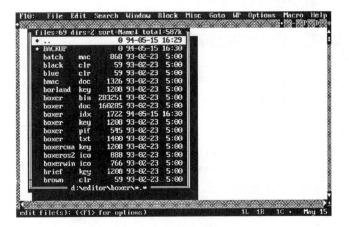

◀ Type O to show the file and directory list.

◀ Press the Tab key. The cursor moves to the bottom of the screen where you're prompted to select a filter (a directory name where the construction forms are stored). Type the drive letter, a colon, a backslash, and the directory name where you installed the forms, such as C:\FORMBOOK

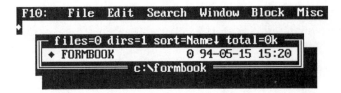

◀ Press the Enter key once and a small directory box appears near the top of the screen.

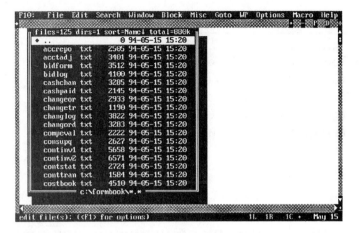

◀ Press Enter. Notice that all the forms you installed appear in the *Files* box. Press the ↑ or ↓ key until the highlight is on the name of the form you want to open. See the *Files* box in the illustration at the left. Form names are listed in alphabetical order.

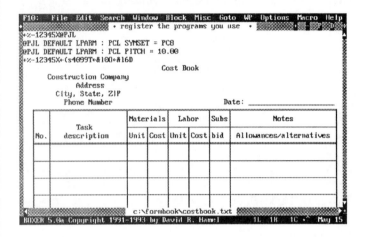

◀ With the highlight on the form of your choice, press Enter. Press Enter again to confirm that selection. Boxer loads the form and displays it on your screen.

If you selected either a laser (H-P compatible) printer or a dot matrix (Epson compatible) printer when installing the forms, the top four lines of all forms will be printer control codes. These control codes are instructions to your printer and will not appear in the printed forms. Printer codes select:

☑ Printing in either portrait (upright) or landscape (sideways) style, and

☑ Line spacing, symbol set, typeface, and pitch.

The instruction manual for your printer has more information on control codes for your printer. As long as you use the same printer, the control codes on your forms should not be changed. You may not be able to print landscape style forms with some dot matrix printers.

Making Changes with Boxer

You can change letters and numbers (text) anywhere on the construction forms by typing over. First, be sure you're not in insert mode. If the cursor is a blinking underline, you're in insert mode. Press the Ins key to turn the cursor into a blinking solid block (and to leave insert mode). Note that typing over any vertical or horizontal line will remove that line.

Drawing Lines with Boxer

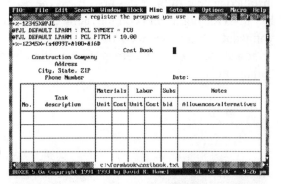

◀ Use the ←, ↑, → or ↓ key to move the cursor to where you would like to draw a line. Press the F10 key. The top menu bar becomes active and one of the menu bar options is highlighted. Use the ← or → key to move the menu bar highlight to Misc.

◀ Press the ↓ key to open the Misc options menu.

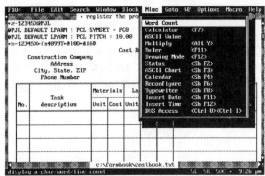

◀ Type the letter D for draw. At the bottom of the screen Boxer will ask which line style you would like to draw. Use the ← or → key to highlight your choice. Then press Enter.

◀ Use the ←, ↑, → or ↓ key to draw a line or box. Press Esc twice when finished.

Save a Revised Form to a New File Name

Construction Forms & Contracts are in ASCII format. When you customize a form by making changes, it's a good idea to save the revised form to a new file name or to a different directory. That prevents accidental overwriting of a customized form if you decide to reinstall forms from the Construction Forms & Contracts disk.

ClarisWorks 1.0 for Windows

Install forms from the file EXCEL.ZIP on the Construction Forms & Contracts disk. The installation procedure is explained in the section "Installation Instructions" beginning on page 333.

Begin ClarisWorks. The new document dialog box appears. Click on Spreadsheet and click on OK. Then click on File.

Click on Open.

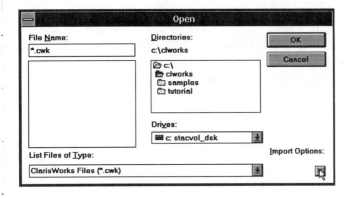

◀ The *Open* dialog box appears. Click on the Import Options button until a series of buttons appear at the bottom of the dialog box.

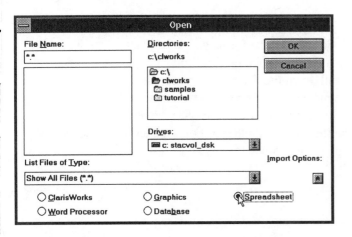

◀ Click on Spreadsheet.

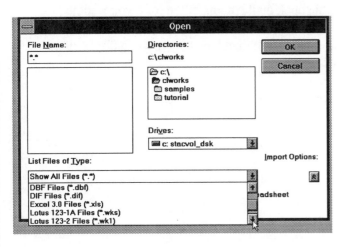

◀ Click the down arrow on the right of the *List Files of Type* box to see the list of file types. Click and hold the down arrow on the lower right side of the list box until you see the Excel 3.0 (*.xls) Files type. Click on Excel 3.0 Files (*.xls) type.

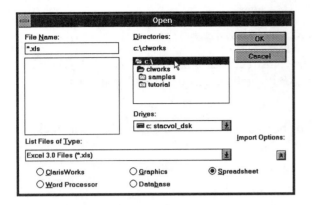

Double click on C:\ in the *Directories* box.

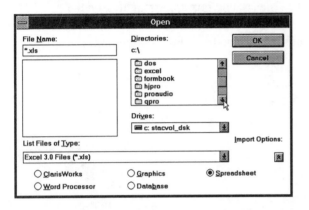

Click and hold the down arrow on the lower right of the *Directories* box until you see the formbook directory. Double click on formbook.

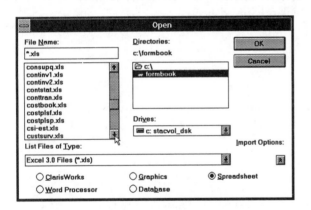

Notice that all the forms you installed with an .XLS file type appear in the *File Name* box to the left. To scroll down the list of file names, click and hold the mouse cursor on the down arrow at the lower right of the *File Name* box. See the mouse cursor in the illustration at the left. Form names are listed in alphabetical order.

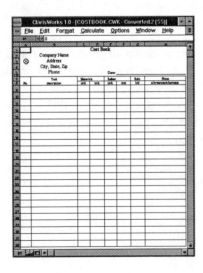

Double click on the name of the form you want to use. ClarisWorks converts the .XLS format to .CWK. ClarisWorks will then load the form and display it on your screen.

Changing the Type Style

When opening a form, your computer will try to select a type font that's appropriate for your printer. But the font selected depends on the printer you use and type fonts installed with Windows. If some headings are too wide for a column or if type spills off the page, change to another type style or size. Here's how: With the construction form displayed on the screen, select the type you want to change.

To change the font, begin by clicking on Format:

☑ Click on Font

☑ Click on the type font you prefer, or

☑ Click on OK

To change the size, begin by clicking on Format:

☑ Click on Size

☑ Click on the point size you prefer

☑ Click on OK

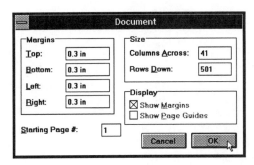

Changing the Margins

Some construction forms may not fit on one page when printed with some printers. If part of a form spills over onto a second page, try resetting the margins:

☑ Click on Format

☑ Click on Document

☑ Reduce the top, bottom, left and right margins to the minimum your printer can handle. That's about 0.3" (three tenths of an inch) on most laser printers. Then click on OK.

If that doesn't solve the problem, try reducing the form length by deleting a line or reducing the form width by making one column a little narrower.

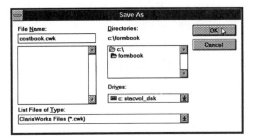

Saving in ClarisWorks

Construction Forms & Contracts are in Microsoft Excel format. You'll probably want to save your customized documents in ClarisWorks format.

☑ Click on File

☑ Click on Save As

☑ In the *File Name* box, type, for example, costbook.cwk

☑ Click on OK

Save a Revised Form to a New File Name

When you customize a form by making changes, it's a good idea to save the revised form to a new file name or to a different directory. That prevents accidental overwriting of a customized form if you decide to reinstall forms from the Construction Forms & Contracts disk.

Reinstalling Construction Forms & Contracts

Occasionally you may customize a contract or form and then decide you like the original document better. It's easy to reinstall any single contract or form on the Construction Forms & Contracts disk. See "Selecting Individual Forms for Installation" on page 336.

■ Excel 5 and Excel 4

Install forms from the file EXCEL.ZIP on the Construction Forms & Contracts disk. The installation procedure is explained in the section "Installation Instructions" beginning on page 333.

Begin Excel and click on File.

Click on Open.

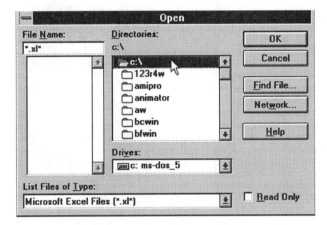

◀ Notice the mouse cursor in the illustration at the left. Double click on C:\.

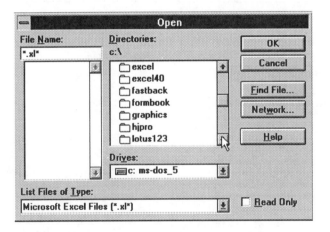

◀ Click and hold the down arrow until you see the directory formbook.

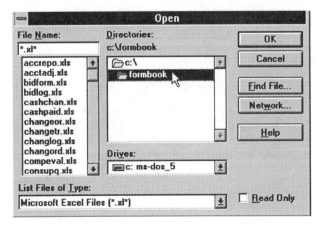

◀ Double click on formbook. Notice that all the forms you installed with an .XLS file type appear in the box at the left.

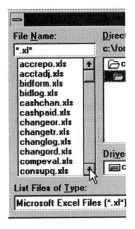

•••

◄ To scroll down the list of file names, click and hold the mouse cursor on the down arrow at the lower right of the *File Name* box. See the mouse cursor in the illustration at the left. Files are listed in alphabetical order.

•••

Then double click on the name of the form you want to use. ►

Excel will open the file selected and display it on your screen.

Changing the Type Style

When opening a form, your computer will try to select a type font that's appropriate for your printer. But the font selected depends on the printer you use and type fonts installed with Windows. If some headings are too wide for a column or if type spills off the page, change to another type style or size. Here's how:

☑ With the construction form displayed on screen, hold the Ctrl key down and type A. That selects the entire document.

☑ Click on Format

☑ Click on Cells

☑ Click on Font

☑ Click on the type font you prefer. See the figure at the left.

☑ Click on OK

Changing the Margins

Some construction forms may not fit on one page when printed with some printers. If part of a form spills over onto a second page, try resetting the margins:

☑ Click on File

☑ Click on Page Setup

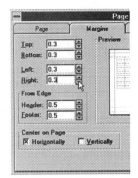

☑ Click on Margins

☑ Reduce the top, bottom, left and right margins to the minimum your printer can handle. That's about 0.3" (three tenths of an inch) on most laser printers.

If that doesn't solve the problem, try reducing the form length by deleting a line or reducing the form width by making one column a little narrower.

Saving in Excel 5

Construction Forms & Contracts are Excel 4.0 documents. When saving a document back to disk in Excel 5, you'll want to update to Excel 5.0 format. Click on File. Click on Save. Then click on Yes.

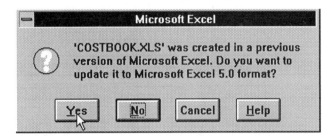

Save a Revised Form to a New File Name

When you customize a form by making changes, it's a good idea to save the revised form to a new file name or to a different directory. That prevents accidental overwriting of a customized form if you decide to reinstall forms from the Construction Forms & Contracts disk.

Reinstalling Construction Forms & Contracts

Occasionally you may customize a contract or form and then decide you like the original document better. It's easy to reinstall any single contract or form on the Construction Forms & Contracts disk. See the section "Selecting Individual Forms for Installation" on page 336.

Lotus 1-2-3 Release 2.01 for DOS

Install forms from the file LOTUS123.ZIP on the Construction Forms & Contracts disk. The installation procedure is explained in the section "Installation Instructions" beginning on page 333.

Lotus 1-2-3 Release 2.01 for DOS will display Construction Forms & Contracts correctly if the file ALLWAYS.ADN is in the same directory where Lotus 1-2-3 is installed. When you begin using Lotus 1-2-3, the file ALLWAYS.ADN will be loaded automatically.

Begin Lotus 1-2-3 for DOS.

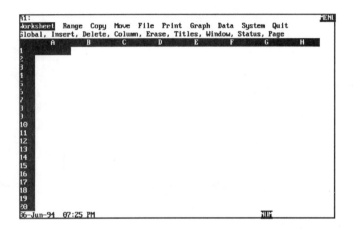

◀ Press the forward slash key (/) and the menu bar will appear at the top of the screen.

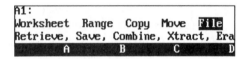

◀ Use the ← or → key to move the highlight to File.

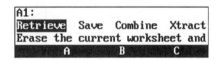

◀ Press Enter. The menu bar changes to display the File options.

◀ Press Enter to Retrieve a file. Names of files available on the Lotus 1-2-3 directory are listed horizontally across the screen.

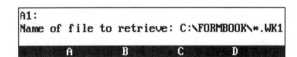

◀ Press Esc twice to erase the list of files available on the Lotus 1-2-3 directory. Then type C:\FORMBOOK*.WK1.

◀ Press Enter, and the names of the first five construction forms will appear across the screen. Forms are listed in alphabetical order.

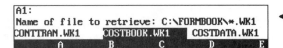

Press the ← or → key to move the highlight to the name of the form you want to open.

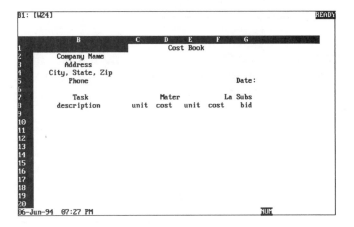

Press Enter, and Lotus 1-2-3 will display a fragment of the form on your screen.

To display a more accurate image of what your printer will reproduce, invoke the ALLWAYS driver. Here's how:

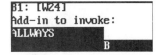

Hold the Shift key down while pressing the F10 key. Release both keys and Lotus will suggest options for an add-in. Press the ← or → key to move the highlight to Invoke.

Press Enter, and Lotus will ask which add-in to invoke. Press the ← or → key to move the highlight to ALLWAYS.

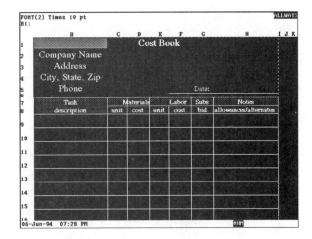

Press Enter, and Lotus will display the form in graphics mode, about the same as it will look when printed on paper.

Some minor changes may be needed before the form prints as intended. These changes are explained on the following pages.

Page Preview

Press the forward slash key (/) once to display the Lotus menu. Then press the ← or → key to move the highlight to Display.

```
FONT(2) Times 10 pt
Worksheet  Format  Graph  Layout  Print  Display
Select display options
```

```
FONT(2) Times 10 pt
Mode Zoom Graphs Colors Qui
Select graphics or text mode

          Mode: Graphics
          Zoom: Normal
    Show graphs: Yes

    Color
      Background: Black
      Foreground: White
       Highlight: Blue
```

◄ Press Enter to see the Display options menu. Press the ← or → key to move the highlight to Zoom.

```
FONT(2) Times 10 pt
Tiny Small Normal Large Hug
Show cells at 60% of their size

          Mode: Graphics
          Zoom: Normal
    Show graphs: Yes

    Color
      Background: Black
      Foreground: White
       Highlight: Blue
```

◄ Press Enter to see Display options. Press the ← or → key to move the highlight to Tiny. Press Enter. Press the ← or → key to Quit. Press Enter. The form is displayed in tiny mode.

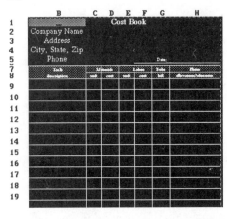

FONT(2) Times 10 pt
B1:

◄ To display the form the same way it will be printed, select Normal mode in Display options.

Changing the Type Style

When opening a form, your computer will try to select a type style and size that's appropriate for your printer. If some headings are too wide for a column or if type spills off the page, change to another type style or size. Here's how:

```
FONT(2) Times 10 pt
Worksheet  Format  Graph  Lay
Font, Bold, Underline, Color,
```

◄ Press the ←,↑,→ or ↓ key to move the cursor to the first cell you want to change. Then press the forward slash key to display the Lotus menu. Advance the highlight to Format with the ← or → key.

```
FONT(2) Times 10 pt
Font  Bold  Underline  Color  Lines
Change the font for a cell or range
                    B         C        D
```

◀ Press Enter to display Format options. Press the
← or→ key to highlight Font. Press Enter.

```
FONT(2) Times 10 pt
Use  Replace  Default  Library  Quit
Use the highlighted font
┌──────────────────────────────────────────┐
│   TYPEFACE                    SIZE         │
│ 1 Triumvirate                 10 point     │
│ 2 Times                       10 point     │
│ 3 Times                       12 point     │
│ 4 Times                       12 point     │
│ 5 Times                       17 point     │
│ 6 Triumvirate Italic          10 point     │
│ 7 Triumvirate                 14 point     │
│ 8 Triumvirate                 20 point     │
└──────────────────────────────────────────┘
```

◀ Press the ← or→ key to highlight Use. Then
press the ↑ or ↓ key to move the highlight to the
font you prefer.

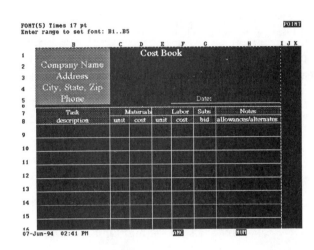

◀ Press Enter, and Lotus displays the form that's
open. Press the ←,↑,→ or ↓ keys to select the
cells you want to change.

Once you've highlighted all the cells you want to
change, press Enter. Lotus will change those cells
to the new font.

Changing the Margins

Some construction forms may not fit on one page when printed with some printers. If part
of a form spills over onto a second page, try resetting the margins.

```
FONT(2) Times 10 pt
Worksheet  Format  Graph  Layout  Print
Set page size, margins, header, footer,
```

◀ Start by pressing the forward slash key (/) to
display the Lotus menu. Then press the ← or →
key to highlight Layout.

```
FONT(2) Times 10 pt
PageSize  Margins  Titles  Borders  Options
Set page width and length

   Page Size: Standard (8.5 by 11 inches)

   Margins (in inches)        Borders
        Left:  0.50              Top:
       Right:  0.50             Left:
         Top:  0.50           Bottom:
      Bottom:  0.50

   Titles
      Header:
      Footer:
```

◀ Press Enter to display the Layout menu. Then
press the ← or → key to move the highlight to
Margins.

```
┌─────────────────────────────────────────────┐
│ Page Size: Standard (8.5 by 11 inches)        │
│                                               │
│ Margins (in inches)          Borders          │
│    Left:   0.50                  Top:          │
│   Right:   0.50                 Left:          │
│     Top:   0.50               Bottom:          │
│  Bottom:   0.50                               │
│                                               │
└─────────────────────────────────────────────┘
```

◀ Use the ← or → key to select the margin you want to change (Left, Right, Top or Bottom). Press Enter to change the highlighted margin.

Lotus 1-2-3 for DOS asks for the new margin setting. Change the margin to the minimum your printer can handle. That's about 0.30" (three tenths of an inch) on most laser printers. Repeat this step for each margin you wish to change. If that doesn't solve the problem, try reducing the form length by deleting a line or reducing the form width by making one column a little narrower.

Saving in Lotus 1-2-3 Release 2.01 for DOS

To save a customized form, press Esc to exit Allways mode. The appearance of the form on your screen changes, but the form itself hasn't changed. Press the forward slash key (/) to display the Lotus menu.

```
┌─────────────────────────────────────────────┐
│ B1: [W24]                                     │
│ Worksheet   Range   Copy   Move   █File█  Pri │
│ Retrieve, Save, Combine, Xtract, Erase,       │
└─────────────────────────────────────────────┘
```

◀ Press the ← or → key to move the highlight to File.

```
┌─────────────────────────────────────────────┐
│ B1: [W24]                                     │
│ Retrieve  █Save█  Combine  Xtract  Erase  List│
│ Store the entire worksheet in a worksheet file│
└─────────────────────────────────────────────┘
```

◀ Press Enter to display File options. Press the ← or → key to move the highlight to Save.

```
┌─────────────────────────────────────────────┐
│ B1: [W24]                                     │
│ Enter save file name: C:\FORMBOOK\COSTBOOK.WK1│
└─────────────────────────────────────────────┘
```

◀ Press Enter, and Lotus 1-2-3 for DOS asks you to enter the file name. Notice that the directory and file name suggested are the same as the original directory and file name.

```
┌─────────────────────────────────────────────┐
│ B1: [W24]                                     │
│ Enter save file name: c:\formbook\costbok1.wk1│
└─────────────────────────────────────────────┘
```

◀ Press Esc three times. The suggested directory and filename disappear and you can type in the new directory and file name. For example, type C:\FORMBOOK\COSTBOK1.WK1.

Press Enter, and Lotus 1-2-3 for DOS saves the form under the new file name.

Save a Revised Form to a New File Name

When you customize a form by making changes, it's a good idea to save the revised form to a new file name or to a different directory. That prevents accidental overwriting of a customized form if you decide to reinstall forms from the Construction Forms & Contracts disk.

Lotus 1-2-3 Release 1 for Windows

Install forms from the file LOTUS123.ZIP on the Construction Forms & Contracts disk. The installation procedure is explained in the section "Installation Instructions" beginning on page 333.

Begin Lotus 1-2-3 Release 1 for Windows and click on File.

Click on Open.

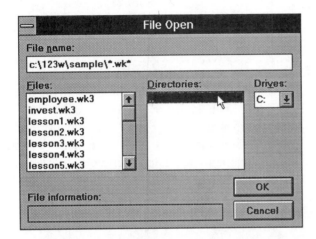

◀ The *File Open* dialog box appears. Double click on the double period [..] in the *Directories* box.

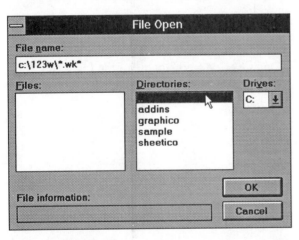

◀ Double click a second time if you still see the double period [..] in the *Directories* box.

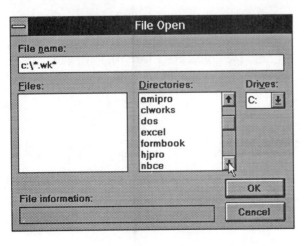

◀ Click and hold the down arrow on the lower right side of the *Directories* box until you see the directory formbook.

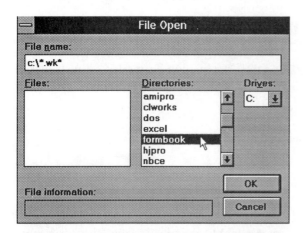

◀ Double click on formbook.

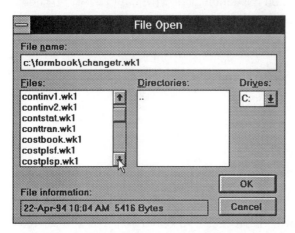

◀ Notice that all the forms you installed with a .WK1 file type appear in the *Files* box to the left. To scroll down the list of file names, click and hold the mouse cursor on the down arrow at the lower right of the *Files* box. See the mouse cursor in the illustration at the left. Form names are listed in alphabetical order.

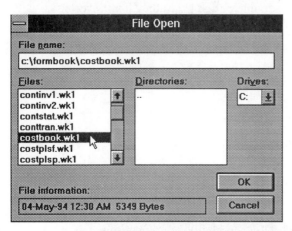

◀ Double click on the name of the form you want to use, such as costbook.wk1.

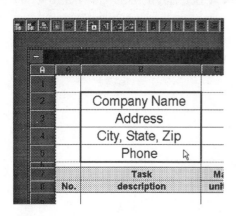

◀ Lotus 1-2-3 Release 1 for Windows will then load the form and display it on your screen.

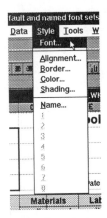

Changing the Type Style

Construction Forms & Contracts for Lotus 1-2-3 are in WK1 for DOS format. WK1 for DOS does not use True Type fonts. Computers that use Windows usually use True Type fonts. When opening a form, your computer will try to substitute a type font that's appropriate. But the font selected depends on the printer you use and type fonts you've installed with Windows. If some headings are too wide for a column or if type spills off the page, change to another type style or size. Here's how:

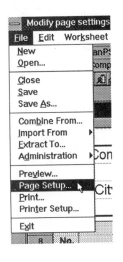

- ☑ Position the mouse cursor over the starting cell you wish to change

- ☑ Click and hold down the left mouse button

- ☑ Drag the mouse cursor until the selection includes all cells you wish to change. A shaded border will surround all selected cells.

- ☑ Click on Style

- ☑ Click on Font

- ☑ The *Style Font* dialog box appears

- ☑ Click on the desired type font

- ☑ Click on OK

Changing the Margins

Some construction forms may not fit on one page when printed with some printers. If part of a form spills over onto a second page, try resetting the margins:

- ☑ Click on File

- ☑ Click on Page Setup

- ☑ The *File Page Setup* dialog box appears. Click in the top, bottom, left or right margins box. Change the margin to the minimum your printer can handle. That's about 0.3" (three tenths of an inch) on most laser printers. Set each margin that needs to be changed.

- ☑ Click on OK

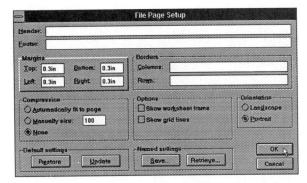

If that doesn't solve the problem, try reducing the form length by deleting a line or reducing the form width by making one column a little narrower.

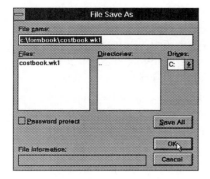

Saving in Lotus 1-2-3 Release 1 for Windows

Construction Forms & Contracts are in Lotus 1-2-3 WK1 format. You can save your customized documents:

☑ Click on File. Click on Save As.

☑ The *File Save As* dialog box appears.

☑ Type the directory and file name, such as c:\formbook\ costbook.wk1

☑ Click on OK

Save a Revised Form to a New File Name

When you customize a form by making changes, it's a good idea to save the revised form to a new file name or to a different directory. That prevents accidental overwriting of a customized form if you decide to reinstall forms from the Construction Form and Contracts disk.

Reinstalling Construction Forms & Contracts

Occasionally you may customize a contract or form and then decide you like the original document better. It's easy to reinstall any single contract or form on the Construction Forms & Contracts disk. See the section "Selecting Individual Forms for Installation" on page 336.

Lotus 1-2-3 Release 4 for Windows

Install forms from the file LOTUS123.ZIP on the Construction Forms & Contracts disk. The installation procedure is explained in the section "Installation Instructions" beginning on page 333.

Begin Lotus 1-2-3 Release 4 for Windows and click on File.

Click on Open.

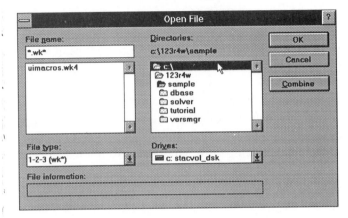

◄ The *Open File* dialog box appears. Double click on C:\ in the *Directories* box.

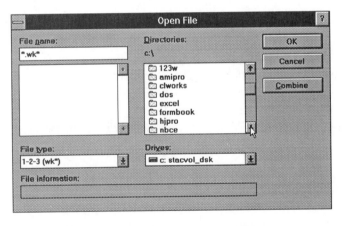

◄ Click and hold the down arrow on the lower right side of the *Directories* box until you see the directory formbook.

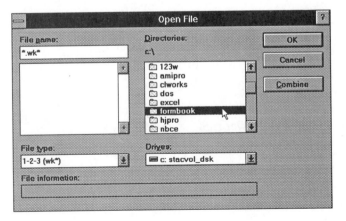

◄ Double click on formbook.

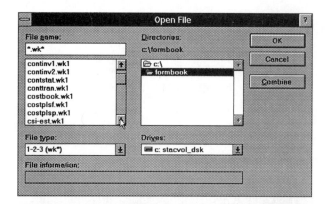

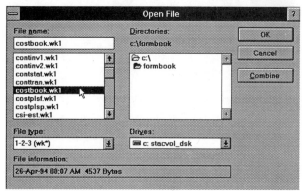

◀ Notice that all the forms you installed with a .wk1 file type appear in the *File name* box at the upper left. To scroll down the list of file names, click and hold the mouse cursor on the down arrow at the lower right of the *File name* box. See the mouse cursor in the illustration at the left. Form names are listed in alphabetical order.

◀ Double click on the name of the form you want to use, such as costbook.wk1.

Lotus 1-2-3 Release 4 for Windows will then load the form and display it on your screen.

Before using this form, you'll want to fit the form to the page and change the type style. See the next two sections.

Changing the Type Style

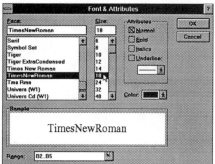

Construction Forms & Contracts for Lotus 1-2-3 are in WK1 for DOS format. WK1 for DOS does not use True Type fonts. Computers that use Windows usually use True Type fonts. When opening a form, your computer will try to substitute a type font that's appropriate. But the font selected depends on the printer you use and type fonts you've installed with Windows. If some headings are too wide for a column or if type spills off the page, change to another type style or size. Here's how:

☑ Position the mouse cursor over the starting cell you wish to change. Click and hold down the left mouse button. Drag the mouse cursor vertically or horizontally to select all cells you wish to change. Release your left mouse button.

☑ Click your right mouse button while the mouse cursor is somewhere within the area you just selected. A pull down menu appears at the cursor location.

☑ Click on Font & Attributes.

☑ The *Font & Attributes* dialog box appears. Click and hold the down arrow button on the lower right side of the *Face* box until the desired font name appears.

☑ Click on the font face you prefer.

☑ Click on the size font you prefer.

☑ Click on OK.

Make the Form Fit the Page

Construction Forms & Contracts for Lotus are in WK1 format and won't fit the page when first loaded by Lotus 1-2-3 Release 4 for Windows. To make any form fit the page:

☑ Click on File.

☑ Click on Page Setup.

☑ In the Size box, click on the down arrow

☑ Click on *Fit all to page* (as shown below).

☑ Click on OK.

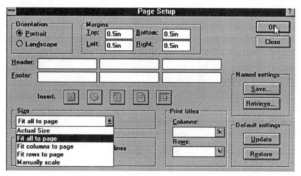

On multi-page forms, click on *Fit columns to page* instead of *Fit all to page*. For landscape forms (wider than they are tall), be sure to click on the Landscape button under Orientation in the Page Setup dialog box.

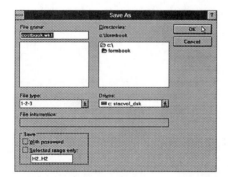

Saving in Lotus 1-2-3 Release 4 for Windows

Construction Forms & Contracts are in Lotus 1-2-3 WK1 format. To save your customized documents in WK4 format, click on File, click on Save As. The *Save As* dialog box appears.

Type in the name of the file.

Click on OK.

Save a Revised Form to a New File Name

When you customize a form by making changes, it's a good idea to save the revised form to a new file name or to a different directory. That prevents accidental overwriting of a customized form if you decide to reinstall forms from the Construction Forms & Contracts disk.

Reinstalling Construction Forms & Contracts

Occasionally you may customize a contract or form and then decide you like the original document better. It's easy to reinstall any single contract or form on the Construction Forms & Contracts disk. See "Selecting Individual Forms for Installation" on page 336.

■ MS-DOS Editor

MS-DOS Editor is part of Microsoft DOS. It was written to the DOS directory of your computer when MS-DOS 5 or 6 was installed. The file name is EDIT.COM. If you plan to use the MS-DOS Editor, install forms from the file ASCII.ZIP on the Construction Forms & Contracts disk. The installation procedure is explained in the section "Installation Instructions" beginning on page 333.

To begin MS-DOS Editor, change to the DOS directory, such as by typing CD \DOS. Press Enter. Then type EDIT and press Enter. The welcome screen will appear.

◀ Press Esc to clear the welcome screen. Press the Alt key to highlight File on the menu bar at the top of the screen.

◀ Type the letter F to open the File menu. Press the ↓ key once to highlight Open.

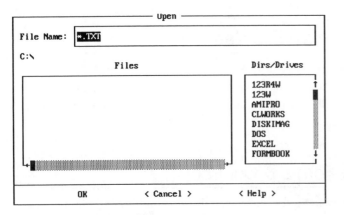

◀ Press Enter. The *Open* file dialog box appears with the cursor flashing at the end of *.TXT in the *File Name* box.

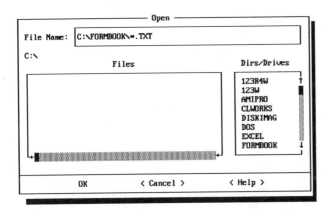

```
┌──────────────── Open ────────────────┐
│ File Name: C:\FORMBOOK\*.TXT          │
│ C:\                                    │
│          Files          Dirs/Drives    │
│  ┌──────────────────┐  ┌──────────┐   │
│  │                  │  │ 123R4W  ↑│   │
│  │                  │  │ 123W     │   │
│  │                  │  │ AMIPRO   │   │
│  │                  │  │ CLWORKS  │   │
│  │                  │  │ DISKIMAG │   │
│  │                  │  │ DOS      │   │
│  │                  │  │ EXCEL    │   │
│  │                  │  │ FORMBOOK↓│   │
│  └──────────────────┘  └──────────┘   │
│     OK      < Cancel >     < Help >    │
└────────────────────────────────────────┘
```

◄ Press the Home key. Then type the drive letter, a colon, a backslash, and the directory name where you installed the forms. For example, type C:\FORMBOOK. Then type another backslash (\). See the illustration at the left.

```
┌──────────────── Open ────────────────┐
│ File Name: [*.TXT]                     │
│ C:\FORMBOOK                            │
│          Files          Dirs/Drives    │
│ ┌────────────────────────┐ ┌────────┐ │
│ │ ACCREPO.TXT CHANGLOG.TXT COSTBOOK.TXT  ..  ↑│
│ │ ACCTADJ.TXT CHANGORD.TXT COSTDATA.TXT [-A-] │
│ │ BIDFORM.TXT COMPEVAL.TXT COSTPLSF.TXT [-B-] │
│ │ BIDLOG.TXT  CONSUPQ.TXT  COSTPLSP.TXT [-C-] │
│ │ CASHCHAN.TXT CONTINU1.TXT CSI-EST.TXT [-D-] │
│ │ CASHPAID.TXT CONTINU2.TXT CUSTSURV.TXT [-E-] │
│ │ CHANGEOR.TXT CONTSTAT.TXT DAILYCON.TXT [-F-] │
│ │ CHANGETR.TXT CONTTRAN.TXT DAILYEQ1.TXT [-G-]↓│
│ └──────────────────────────┘ └────────┘ │
│     OK      < Cancel >     < Help >    │
└────────────────────────────────────────┘
```

◄ Press Enter. Notice that all the forms you installed appear in the *Files* box. To move the highlight into the *Files* box, press the Tab key. Then use the ←, ↑, →, or ↓ key to move the highlight to the name of the form you want to print. Forms are listed in alphabetical order.

```
┌ File Edit Search Options              Help ┐
│ ┌──────── COSTBOOK.TXT ────────┐          │
│ ←%-12345X@PJL                              │
│ @PJL DEFAULT LPARM : PCL SYMSET = PC8      │
│ @PJL DEFAULT LPARM : PCL PITCH = 10.00     │
│ ←%-12345X←(s4099T+&l60+&l6D                │
│                         Cost Book          │
│   Construction Company                     │
│         Address                            │
│      City, State, ZIP                      │
│      Phone Number          Date: _____    │
│ ┌──┬──────────┬─────┬─────┬────┬─────────┐ │
│ │  │   Task   │Materials│Labor│Subs│  Notes │ │
│ │No│description│Unit│Cost│Unit│Cost│bid│Allowances/alternatives│
│ ├──┼──────────┼────┼────┼────┼────┼───┼─────┤
│ │  │          │    │    │    │    │   │     │
│ └──┴──────────┴────┴────┴────┴────┴───┴─────┘
│ MS-DOS Editor  <F1=Help> Press ALT to activate menus │
└────────────────────────────────────────────┘
```

◄ When the highlight is on the form name you want, press Enter. MS-DOS Editor loads the form and displays it on your screen.

If you selected either a laser (H-P compatible) printer or a dot matrix (Epson compatible) printer when installing the forms, the top four lines of all forms will be printer control codes. These codes are instructions to your printer and will not appear in the printed forms. Printer codes select:

☑ Printing in either portrait (upright) or landscape (sideways) style, and

☑ Line spacing, symbol set, typeface, and pitch.

The instruction manual for your printer has more information on control codes for your printer. As long as you use the same printer, the control codes on your forms should not be changed. Many dot matrix printers will not be able to print in landscape style.

Making Changes with MS-DOS Editor

You can change letters and numbers (text) anywhere on the construction forms by typing over. First, be sure you're in overtype mode (not insert mode). If the cursor is a blinking underline, you're in insert mode. Press the Ins key to turn the cursor into a blinking solid block. That indicates overtype mode. Note that typing over any vertical or horizontal line will remove that line.

Save a Revised Form to a New File Name

Construction Forms & Contracts are in ASCII format. When you customize a form by making changes, it's a good idea to save the revised form to a new file name or to a different directory. That prevents accidental overwriting of a customized form if you decide to reinstall forms from the Construction Forms & Contracts disk.

◀ To save a file to a new name, press Alt to highlight the File menu option on the top menu bar. Then type the letter F to open the file menu. Press the ↓ key until the highlight is on Save As.

◀ Press Enter to open the *Save As* dialog box. The cursor will be flashing at the end of the file name, such as COSTBOOK.TXT

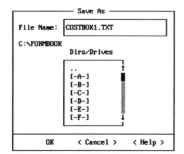

◀ Type the name you want to give to the new file, such as COSTBOK1.TXT.

Press Enter and MS-DOS Editor saves your form to the new file name.

Reinstalling Construction Forms & Contracts

Occasionally you may customize a contract or form and then decide you like the original document better. It's easy to reinstall any single contract or form on the Construction Forms & Contracts disk. See the previous section "Selecting Individual Forms for Installation" on page 336.

◼ NCU Edit for DOS

NCU Edit is a small, compact editing program. If you installed the file ASCII.ZIP on the directory C:\FORMBOOK, the NCU Edit program was also installed to C:\FORMBOOK. The installation procedure is explained in the section "Installation Instructions" beginning on page 333.

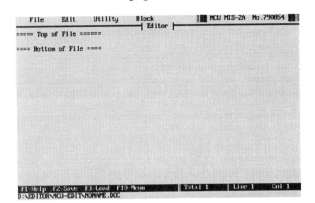

◀ To begin NCU Edit, change control to the directory where the construction forms were installed. For example, at the C:\> prompt, type CD \FORMBOOK and press Enter. Then type SUPERED and press Enter.

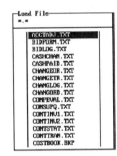

◀ Press the F3 key. The *Load File* dialog box displays a list of files you installed. Notice that forms are listed in alphabetical order.

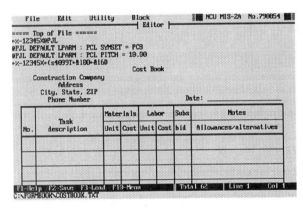

◀ Use the ↓ or ↑ key to move the highlight to the name of the form you want to print. Then press Enter. NCU Edit loads the form and displays it on your screen.

If you selected either a laser (H-P compatible) printer or a dot matrix (Epson compatible) printer when installing the forms, the top four lines of all forms will be printer control codes. These codes are instructions to your printer and will not appear in the printed forms. Printer codes select:

☑ Printing in either portrait (upright) or landscape (sideways) style, and

☑ Line spacing, symbol set, typeface, and pitch.

The instruction manual for your printer has more information on control codes for your printer. As long as you use the same printer, the control codes on your forms should not be changed. You may not be able to print landscape style forms with some dot matrix printers.

Making Changes with NCU Edit

You can change letters and numbers (text) anywhere on the construction forms by typing over. For practice, use the ←,↑,→, or ↓ key to move the highlight to the words Construction Company on any construction form. Type the name of your construction company.

If you typed over the words Construction Company, NCU Edit is in overtype mode. To switch to insert mode, press the Ins key once. Now anything you type is inserted and the balance of the line moves to the right. To return to overtype mode, press the Ins key. Note that typing over any vertical or horizontal line will remove that line.

Drawing Lines with NCU Edit

There may be times when you need to change the location of vertical or horizontal lines on a form or even add new lines. Your keyboard doesn't show any keys that will make lines and boxes. But it's possible to make lines and boxes using the extended ASCII character set. With a construction form open on your screen, try this:

Use the ←,↑,→, or ↓ key to move the cursor to where you want to draw a vertical line. Press the Num Lock key to turn Num Lock on. Then hold the Alt key down while typing the number 0179 on the numeric keypad at the right of your keyboard. Release the Alt key and you will see a vertical line. Use the same procedure to create any symbol shown on the ASCII Conversion Chart on page 374.

Inserting Lines

To insert a line in NCU Edit, change to insert mode by pressing the Ins key. Then press Enter and you've added a line. Press Ins again to leave insert mode.

Moving and Deleting Blocks of Text

Use the ←,↑,→, or ↓ key to move the cursor to the beginning of text you want to move or delete. Press and hold the Shift and Ctrl keys while typing the letter B. Then move the cursor to the end of text you want to move or delete. Press and hold the Shift and Ctrl keys while typing K. Move the cursor to where the block should be inserted and press Shift-Ctrl-M to move the block selected or Shift-Ctrl-O to copy the text selected. Press the F1 key to see a summary of these block management keystrokes.

Printing a Form

Press the F10 key to see the File menu. Press the → key twice to move the highlight to Utility. Press the ↓ key three times to move the highlight to Print File. Press Enter and the form will begin to print.

Save a Revised Form to a New File Name

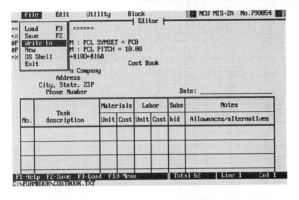

When you customize a form by making changes, it's a good idea to save the revised form to a new file name or to a different directory. That prevents accidental overwriting of a customized form if you decide to reinstall forms from the Construction Forms and Contracts disk. To save a file to a new name, press F10. The File option menu pulls down from the top menu bar. Press the ↓ key twice to move the highlight to Write to.

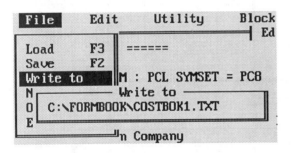

◄ Press Enter. The *Write to* dialog box appears.

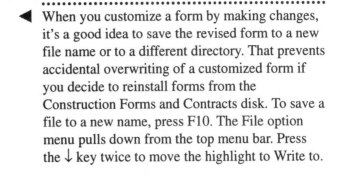

◄ Type the drive letter, a colon, a backslash, and the name you want to give to the new file.

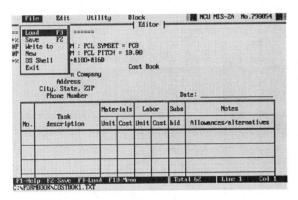

◄ Press Enter to write the form to disk. The Write to dialog box clears and you are back to the File options menu.

Press the Esc key to clear the menu or the ↓ key twice and Enter to exit NCU Edit.

Reinstalling Construction Forms & Contracts

Occasionally you may customize a contract or form and then decide you like the original document better. It's easy to reinstall any single contract or form on the Construction Forms & Contracts disk. See the section "Selecting Individual Forms for Installation" on page 336.

ASCII Conversion Chart

(PC-8 Code Page 437)

0	16	32	48	64	80	96	112	128	144	160	176	192	208	224	240
NUL	PLE	SP	0	@	P	`	p	Ç	É	á	░	└	╨	α	≡
SOH	DC1	!	1	A	Q	a	q	ü	æ	í	▒	┴	╤	ß	±
STX	DC2	"	2	B	R	b	r	é	Æ	ó	▓	┬	╥	Γ	≥
ETX	DC3	#	3	C	S	c	s	â	ô	ú	│	├	╙	π	≤
EOT	DC4	$	4	D	T	d	t	ä	ö	ñ	┤	─	╘	Σ	⌠
ENQ	NAK	%	5	E	U	e	u	à	ò	Ñ	╡	┼	╒	σ	⌡
ACK	SYN	&	6	F	V	f	v	å	û	ª	╢	╞	╓	µ	÷
BEL	ETB	'	7	G	W	g	w	ç	ù	º	╖	╟	╫	τ	≈
BS	CAN	(	8	H	X	h	x	ê	ÿ	¿	╕	╚	╪	Φ	°
HT	EM	)	9	I	Y	i	y	ë	Ö	⌐	╣	╔	┘	Θ	∙
LF	SUB	*	:	J	Z	j	z	è	Ü	¬	║	╩	┌	Ω	·
VT	ESC	+	;	K	[	k	{	ï	¢	½	╗	╦	█	δ	√
FF	FS	,	<	L	\	l	|	î	£	¼	╝	╠	▄	∞	ⁿ
CR	GS	-	=	M	]	m	}	ì	¥	¡	╜	═	▐	ø	²
SO	RS	.	>	N	^	n	~	Ä	₧	«	╛	╬	▌	ε	■
SI	US	/	?	O	_	o	⌂	Å	ƒ	»	┐	╧	▬	∩	

Q&A 4.0 for DOS

Install forms from the file ASCII.ZIP on the Construction Forms & Contracts disk. The installation procedure is explained in the section "Installation Instructions" beginning on page 333.

```
┌──────────────────────────────────────┐
│            Q&A MAIN MENU               │
│ ─────────────────────────────────────│
│                                        │
│  F - File         │  W - WordPerfect   │
│  R - Report       │                    │
│  W - Write        │                    │
│  A - Assistant    │                    │
│  U - Utilities    │                    │
│  X - Exit Q&A     │                    │
│                                        │
└──────────────────────────────────────┘
```

◀ Begin Q&A 4.0 for DOS and the *Q&A Main Menu* appears.

```
┌──────────────────────────────────────┐
│            Q&A MAIN MENU               │
│ ─────────────────────────────────────│
│                                        │
│  F - File         │  W - WordPerfect   │
│  R - Report       │                    │
│  W - Write        │                    │
│  A - Assistant    │                    │
│  U - Utilities    │                    │
│  X - Exit Q&A     │                    │
│                                        │
└──────────────────────────────────────┘
```

◀ Press the ↓ or ↑ key until the Write menu option is highlighted.

```
┌──────────────────────────────────────┐
│             WRITE MENU                 │
│ ─────────────────────────────────────│
│         T - Type/Edit                  │
│         D - Define page                │
│         P - Print                      │
│         C - Clear                      │
│         G - Get                        │
│         S - Save                       │
│        ───────────────                 │
│         U - Utilities                  │
│         M - Mailing labels             │
└──────────────────────────────────────┘
```

◀ Press Enter and the *Write Menu* appears.

```
┌──────────────────────────────────────┐
│             WRITE MENU                 │
│ ─────────────────────────────────────│
│         T - Type/Edit                  │
│         D - Define page                │
│         P - Print                      │
│         C - Clear                      │
│         G - Get                        │
│         S - Save                       │
│        ───────────────                 │
│         U - Utilities                  │
│         M - Mailing labels             │
└──────────────────────────────────────┘
```

◀ Press the ↓ or ↑ key until the Get menu option is highlighted.

```
Document: C:\QA\
```

```
Document: C:\FORMBOOK\*.TXT
```

◄ Press Enter and Q&A will ask for the directory and file name of the form you want to open.

Press the Home key and then type the drive letter, a colon, a backslash, the directory name, a backslash, a star, a period and the letters TXT. For example, type C:\FORM-BOOK*.TXT.

```
                 LIST OF FILES IN C:\FORMBOOK\*.TXT

\..              COMPEVAL.TXT   CUSTSURV.TXT   EMPLOYTC.TXT   FIELDCHA.TXT
ACCREPO.TXT      CONSUPQ.TXT    DAILYCON.TXT   EMPLTIME.TXT   FIELDDIR.TXT
ACCTADJ.TXT      CONTINV1.TXT   DAILYEQ1.TXT   EQUPLEDG.TXT   FIELDPRO.TXT
BIDFORM.TXT      CONTINV2.TXT   DAILYMAT.TXT   ESTCHECK.TXT   FINALPAY.TXT
BIDLOG.TXT       CONTSTAT.TXT   DAILYWOR.TXT   ESTRECAP.TXT   FINALPRO.TXT
CASHCHAN.TXT     CONTTRAN.TXT   DEFNOTIC.TXT   EXPENSE.TXT    FINISCHD.TXT
CASHPAID.TXT     COSTBOOK.TXT   DELAYNOT.TXT   FAXCHANG.TXT   FIRSTCON.TXT
CHANGEOR.TXT     COSTDATA.TXT   DRIVEREC.TXT   FAXCOVER.TXT   FIXFEEPR.TXT
CHANGETR.TXT     COSTPLSF.TXT   EMERGTEL.TXT   FAXEDPO.TXT    HISTPROJ.TXT
CHANGLOG.TXT     COSTPLSP.TXT   EMPDATA.TXT    FAXQUOTE.TXT   HOURRATE.TXT
CHANGORD.TXT     CSI-EST.TXT    EMPEVAL.TXT    FHACOST.TXT    INTEROFF.TXT
```

◄ Press Enter. All the forms you installed with a .TXT file type appear in the *List of Files* box. Notice that form names are listed in alphabetical order.

```
                 LIST OF FILES IN C:\FORMBOOK\*.TXT

\..              COMPEVAL.TXT   CUSTSURV.TXT   EMPLOYTC.TXT   FIELDCHA.TXT
ACCREPO.TXT      CONSUPQ.TXT    DAILYCON.TXT   EMPLTIME.TXT   FIELDDIR.TXT
ACCTADJ.TXT      CONTINV1.TXT   DAILYEQ1.TXT   EQUPLEDG.TXT   FIELDPRO.TXT
BIDFORM.TXT      CONTINV2.TXT   DAILYMAT.TXT   ESTCHECK.TXT   FINALPAY.TXT
BIDLOG.TXT       CONTSTAT.TXT   DAILYWOR.TXT   ESTRECAP.TXT   FINALPRO.TXT
CASHCHAN.TXT     CONTTRAN.TXT   DEFNOTIC.TXT   EXPENSE.TXT    FINISCHD.TXT
CASHPAID.TXT     COSTBOOK.TXT   DELAYNOT.TXT   FAXCHANG.TXT   FIRSTCON.TXT
CHANGEOR.TXT     COSTDATA.TXT   DRIVEREC.TXT   FAXCOVER.TXT   FIXFEEPR.TXT
CHANGETR.TXT     COSTPLSF.TXT   EMERGTEL.TXT   FAXEDPO.TXT    HISTPROJ.TXT
CHANGLOG.TXT     COSTPLSP.TXT   EMPDATA.TXT    FAXQUOTE.TXT   HOURRATE.TXT
CHANGORD.TXT     CSI-EST.TXT    EMPEVAL.TXT    FHACOST.TXT    INTEROFF.TXT
```

◄ Press the ←, ↑, → or ↓ key to move the highlight to the name of the form you want to open. For example, highlight COSTBOOK.TXT.

```
              IMPORT DOCUMENT

      Unknown document file format.
      Is it one of the following?
      Make a selection, or press
      Esc to cancel:

      A - ASCII
      S - Special ASCII
      W - WordStar Editor
      L - Lotus 1-2-3 or Symphony
```

◄ When the form you want to open is highlighted, press Enter. The *Import Document* menu appears.

```
+%-12345X@PJL
@PJL DEFAULT LPARM : PCL SYMSET = PC8
@PJL DEFAULT LPARM : PCL PITCH = 10.00
+%-12345X+(s4099T+&l00+&l6D
                           Cost Book
    Construction Company
         Address
      City, State, ZIP
      Phone Number                    Date: _____

       |              |Materials| Labor |Subs |      Notes
       | Task         |---------|-------|-----|---------------------
  No.  | description  |Unit|Cost|Unit|Cost|bid | Allowances/alternatives
       |              |    |    |    |    |    |
       |              |    |    |    |    |    |
       |              |    |    |    |    |    |

ls ·|T|·1···|·T|·2···|·T|·3···|·T|·4···|···|·5···|···|·6···|·7···|·8
COSTBOOK.TXT                Num          1 % 1   Line 1 of 62

Esc-Exit  F1-Help  F2-Print  Shift+F7-Restore  F7-Search  F8-Options  ↑F8-Save
```

◄ Press Enter to open the file as an ASCII document. Q&A will display the form on your screen.

If you selected either a laser (H-P compatible) or dot matrix (Epson compatible) printer when installing the forms, the top four lines of all forms will be printer control codes. These codes are instructions to your printer and will not appear in the printed forms. Printer codes select:

☑ Printing in either portrait (upright) or landscape (sideways) style, and

☑ Line spacing, symbol set, typeface and pitch.

The instruction manual for your printer has more information on control codes for your printer. As long as you use the same printer, the control codes on your forms should not be changed. Many dot matrix printers will not be able to print in landscape style.

Changing Forms in Q&A

You can change letters and numbers (text) anywhere on the construction forms by typing over. First, be sure you're in overtype mode (not insert mode). If the cursor is a blinking solid block, insert mode is on. Press the Ins key and the cursor will turn into a blinking underline, indicating that insert mode is off.

Drawing Lines with Q&A

There may be times when you need to change the location of vertical or horizontal lines on a form or even add new lines. Your keyboard doesn't show any keys that will make lines and boxes. But it's possible to make lines and boxes with Q&A. With a construction form open on your screen, try this:

```
        OPTIONS MENU

  L - Lay out page
  D - Documents
  A - Align text
  B - Block operations
  P - Print commands
  O - Other options
```

◀ Press the ←,↑,→ or ↓ key to move the cursor to where you want to start drawing a line. Press your F8 key once. The *Options Menu* appears.

```
  H - Edit Header
  F - Edit Footer
  P - Define Page
  S - Set tabs
  N - Newpage
  D - Draw
```

◀ Press the Tab key to move the highlight to the right of the *Options Menu*.

```
H - Edit Header
F - Edit Footer
P - Define Page
S - Set tabs
N - Newpage
D - Draw
```

◀ Press the ↓ or ↑ key to highlight Draw.

```
+%-12345X@PJL
@PJL DEFAULT LPARM : PCL SYMSET = PC8
@PJL DEFAULT LPARM : PCL PITCH = 10.00
+%-12345X+(s4099T+&l00+&16D
                              Cost Book
    Construction Company
           Address
        City, State, ZIP
        Phone Number                    Date: _____
      ┌────────────┬─────────┬─────────┬─────┬──────────────────┐
      │            │Materials│  Labor  │Subs │      Notes       │
      │    Task    ├────┬────┼────┬────┼─────┼──────────────────┤
 No.  │ description│Unit│Cost│Unit│Cost│ bid │Allowances/alternatives│
      ├────────────┼────┼────┼────┼────┼─────┼──────────────────┤
      │            │    │    │    │    │     │                  │
      ├────────────┼────┼────┼────┼────┼─────┼──────────────────┤
      │            │    │    │    │    │     │                  │
      ├────────────┼────┼────┼────┼────┼─────┼──────────────────┤
      │            │    │    │    │    │     │                  │
└s─┴┬┴1┴┴┴┬┴┴┴2┴┬┴┴┴3┴┬┴┴┴4┴┴┴┴┴┴5┴┴┴┴┴6┴┴┴┴┴┴7┴┴┴┴┴┴8
COSTBOOK.TXT                Num         2 % 50  Line 4 of 62

Esc-Exit  → ← ↓ ↑   Shift → ← ↓ ↑   F6-Pen up   F8-Erase  F10-Resume editing
```

◀ Press Enter. Now press the ←,↑,→ or ↓ key to draw lines and boxes.

Press the F10 key to resume normal editing.

Save a Revised Form to a New File Name

When you customize a form by making changes, it's a good idea to save the revised form to a new file name or to a different directory. That prevents accidental overwriting of a customized form if you decide to reinstall forms from the Construction Forms & Contracts disk.

```
┌──────────────────────────┐
│      OPTIONS MENU        │
├──────────────────────────┤
│ L - Lay out page         │
│ D - Documents            │
│ A - Align text           │
│ B - Block operations     │
│ P - Print commands       │
│ O - Other options        │
└──────────────────────────┘
```

◀ To save a file to a new name, press the F8 key. The *Options Menu* appears.

```
┌──────────────────────────┐
│      OPTIONS MENU        │
├──────────────────────────┤
│ L - Lay out page         │
│ D - Documents            │
│ A - Align text           │
│ B - Block operations     │
│ P - Print commands       │
│ O - Other options        │
└──────────────────────────┘
```

◀ Press the ↓ or ↑ key to highlight Other options.

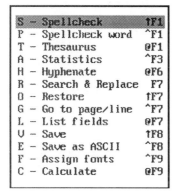

◀ Press the Tab key to move the highlight to the menu box to the right of the *Options Menu*.

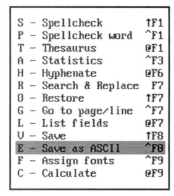

◀ Press the ↓ or ↑ key to highlight Save as ASCII.

```
ASCII file: C:\FORMBOOK\COSTBOOK.TXT
```

```
ASCII file: C:\FORMBOOK\costbok1.txt
```

◀ Press Enter. Q&A asks for the disk drive, directory and filename where the customized form should be saved.

Press the Home key and type the disk drive, directory and file name, such as C:\FORMBOOK\cost-bok1.txt.

Press Enter and Q&A saves the form to the new file name.

Reinstalling Construction Forms & Contracts

Occasionally you may customize a contract or form and then decide you like the original document better. It's easy to reinstall any single contract or form on the Construction Forms & Contracts disk. See "Selecting Individual Forms for Installation" on page 336.

Quattro Pro for Windows

You can install forms from either the file EXCEL.ZIP or the file LOTUS123.ZIP on the Construction Forms & Contracts disk. Quattro Pro for Windows works equally well with either file. The installation procedure is explained in the section "Installation Instructions" beginning on page 333.

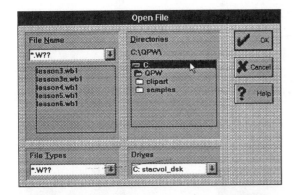

◄ Begin Quattro Pro and click on File. Then click on Open to display the *Open File* dialog box. Double click on C: under *Directories*.

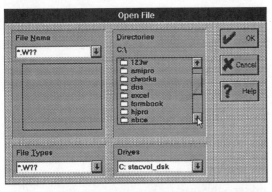

◄ Click on the down arrow at the lower right corner of the *Directories* list box. Hold the mouse button down until you see the directory formbook.

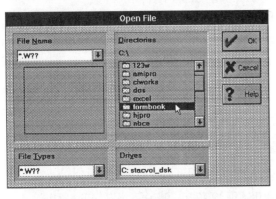

◄ Double click on formbook.

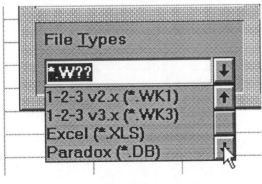

◄ Click the down arrow button on the right side of the *File Types* box. A list of file types appears. Click the down arrow button on the lower right of the list box until the Excel (*.XLS) type is visible. Click on Excel (*.XLS) file type if you installed the file EXCEL.ZIP. Click on 1-2-3 v2.x (*.WK1) if you installed the file LOTUS123.ZIP. These instructions assume that you install the EXCEL.ZIP from Construction Forms & Contracts disk.

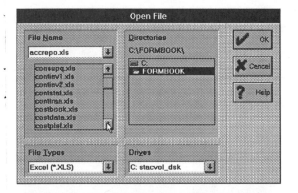

◀ Notice that all the forms you installed with an .xls file type appear in the *File Name* box at the left. To scroll down the list of file names, click and hold the mouse cursor on the down arrow at the lower right of the *File Name* box. See the mouse cursor in the illustration. Form names are listed in alphabetical order.

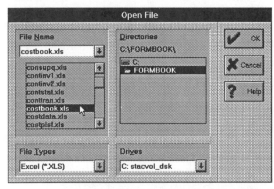

◀ Double click on the name of the form you want to open.

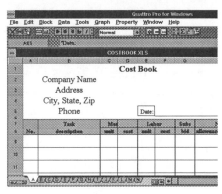

◀ Quattro Pro for Windows will open the form and display it on your screen.

Changing the Type Style

Your computer will try to select a type font that's appropriate for the construction forms and contracts. But the font selected depends on the printer you use and type fonts you've installed with Windows. If some headings are too wide for a column or if type spills off the page, change to another type style or size.

◀ First, select with your mouse the type you want to change. Hold your left mouse button down and drag to select. Then click on Edit. Click on Define Style.

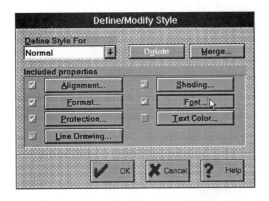

◀ In the *Define/Modify Style* dialog box, click on Font.

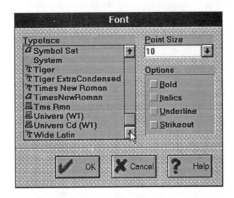

◀ In the *Font* dialog box, click and hold the down arrow at the lower right corner of the *Typeface* box to scroll down the list of fonts available.

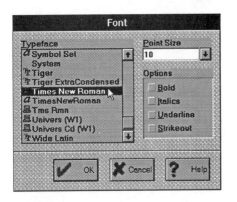

◀ Click on the type font you prefer. Times New Roman is a good choice if that name appears in the *Typeface* box.

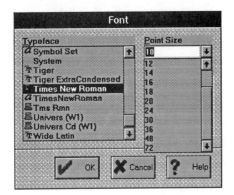

◀ Click on the down arrow button on the right side of the *Point Size* box to see a list of available type sizes.

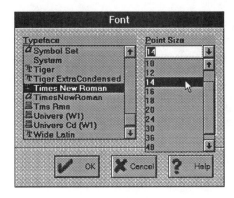

◀ Click on the desired point size. Then click on OK. When the *Define/Modify Style* dialog box appears, click on OK again.

Changing the Margins

Some construction forms may not fit on one page when printed with some printers. If part of a form spills over onto a second page, try resetting the margins:

◀ Click on File and Page Setup.

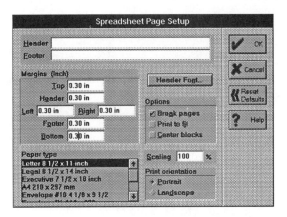

◀ Reduce the top, bottom, left and right margins to the minimum your printer can handle. That's usually about 0.30" (three tenths of an inch) on most laser printers.

Click on OK.

If that doesn't solve the problem, try reducing the form length by deleting a line or reducing the form width by making one column a little narrower.

Saving in Quattro Pro for Windows

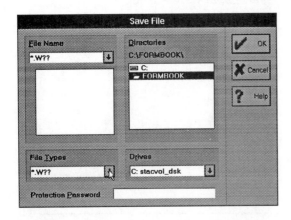

◄ Construction Forms and Contracts are in Microsoft Excel and Lotus 1-2-3 formats. To save a customized form in Quattro Pro format, click on File and click on Save As to open the *Save File* dialog box.

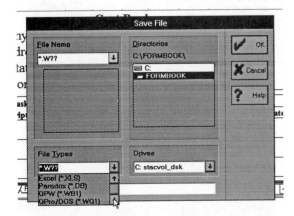

◄ Click on the down arrow on the right side of the *File Types* box. Click and hold the down arrow button at the lower right corner of the list box until you see the QPW (*.WB1) files type.

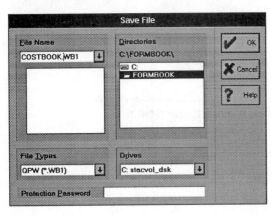

◄ Click on QPW (*.WB1) files type. Click in the *File Name* box. Press your delete key five times to remove the *.WB1. Type the name of the file with a .WB1 extension, such as COSTBOOK.WB1.

Click on OK to complete saving the file.

Save a Revised Form to a New File Name

When you customize a form by making changes, it's a good idea to save the revised form to a new file name or to a different directory. That prevents accidental overwriting of a customized form if you decide to reinstall forms from the Construction Forms & Contracts disk.

■ SEDIT for DOS

SEDIT is a popular shareware editing program. It's available at no cost from CompuServe, many computer bulletin boards and the Contractor's Bulletin Board (319-242-0060). See the instructions on page 421. It's also available from J.E. Smith, 344 Observatory Drive, Birmingham, AL 35206. If you use SEDIT, install forms from the file ASCII.ZIP on the Construction Forms & Contracts disk. The installation procedure is explained in the section "Installation Instructions" beginning on page 333.

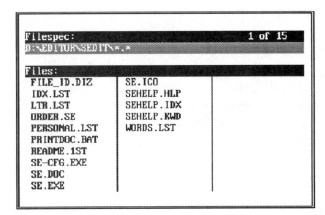

◀ Begin by typing SE. Press Enter. The *Files* dialog box appears.

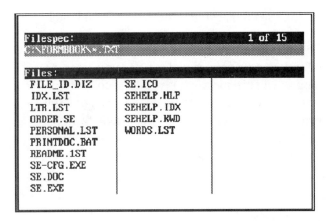

◀ Type the drive letter, a colon, a backslash, the directory name, a backslash and *.TXT. For example, type C:\FORMBOOK*.TXT.

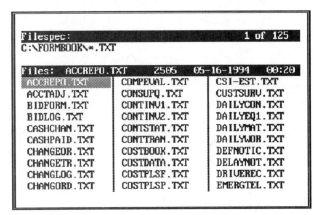

◀ Press Enter. Notice that all the forms you installed appear in the *Files* box. Press the ←, ↑, → or ↓ key to move the highlight to the name of the form you want to load. See the Files box in the illustration at the left. Form names are listed in alphabetical order.

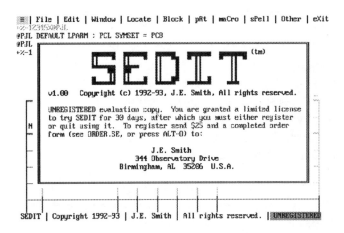

≡ | File | Edit | Window | Locate | Block | pRt | maCro | sPell | Other | eXit
+:-12345X@PJL
@PJL DEFAULT LPARM : PCL SYMSET = PCB
@PJL
+:-1

SEDIT (tm)

v1.00 Copyright (c) 1992-93, J.E. Smith, All rights reserved.

UNREGISTERED evaluation copy. You are granted a limited license
to try SEDIT for 30 days, after which you must either register
or quit using it. To register send $25 and a completed order
form (see ORDER.SE, or press ALT-O) to:

J.E. Smith
344 Observatory Drive
Birmingham, AL 35206 U.S.A.

SEDIT | Copyright 1992-93 | J.E. Smith | All rights reserved. |

◄ When the highlight is on the form of your choice, press Enter. SEDIT loads the form and displays it on your screen. SEDIT also displays a copyright notice and explains how to register your copy of the program. Press the space bar and the copyright notice will disappear.

≡ | File | Edit | Window | Locate | Block | pRt | maCro | sPell | Other | eXit
+:-12345X@PJL
@PJL DEFAULT LPARM : PCL SYMSET = PCB
@PJL DEFAULT LPARM : PCL PITCH = 10.00
+:-12345X+(s4099T+8100+8160

Cost Book

Construction Company
Address
City, State, ZIP
Phone Number   Date: _____

No.	Task description	Materials		Labor		Subs	Notes
		Unit	Cost	Unit	Cost	bid	Allowances/alternatives

SEDIT | Copyright 1992-93 | J.E. Smith | All rights reserved. |

◄ If you selected either a laser (H-P compatible) printer or a dot matrix (Epson compatible) printer when installing the forms, the top four lines of all forms will be printer control codes. These codes are instructions to your printer and will not appear in the printed forms. Printer codes select:

☑ Printing in either portrait (upright) or landscape (sideways) style, and

☑ Line spacing, symbol set, typeface, and pitch.

The instruction manual for your printer has more information on control codes for your printer. As long as you use the same printer, the control codes on your forms should not be changed. You may not be able to print landscape style forms with some dot matrix printers.

Making Changes with SEDIT

You can change letters and numbers (text) anywhere on the construction forms by typing over. First, be sure you're not in insert mode. If the cursor is a blinking solid block, you're in insert mode. Press the Ins key to turn the cursor into a blinking underline (and leave insert mode). Note that typing over any vertical or horizontal line will remove that line.

Drawing Lines with SEDIT

There may be times when you need to change the location of vertical or horizontal lines on a form or even add new lines. Your keyboard doesn't show any keys that will make lines and boxes. But it's possible to make lines and boxes using the extended ASCII character set. With a form open on the SEDIT screen, try this:

```
Restore line      ALT-U
Erase EOL         CTRL-E
Delete line       CTRL-Y
Undelete line     CTRL-U
delete Word       CTRL-T
Insert line       CTRL-N
eXpand TABs       SHIFT-TAB
Control code      CTRL-O
reFormat          CTRL-CR
reformat Quote    CTRL-\
Line draw         ALT--
```

◀ Use the ←, ↑, → or ↓ key to move the cursor to where you want to draw a box. Press the Alt key and hold it down while typing the letter E. The *Edit options* menu drops down.

Press the ↓ key until the highlight is on Line draw.

```
Off
Single
Double
double Horizontal
double Vertical
Erase
```

◀ Press Enter. A small dialog box appears asking which type of line you want to draw. Press the ↓ key until the highlight is on double Horizontal. Select "Off" to turn line draw mode off when done.

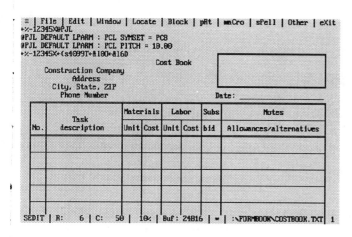

◀ Press Enter and you're back to the form. Press the ←, ↑, → or ↓ key and you're drawing a double horizontal line on the screen.

```
Save file      F2
save All        ALT-F2
Load new        F3
Close file      ALT-F3
Import          CTRL-Z
Export          CTRL-X
Rename          F4
DOS shell       ALT-S
Quit            ALT-X
```

Save a Revised Form to a New File Name

Construction Forms & Contracts are in ASCII format. When you customize a form by making changes, it's a good idea to save the revised form to a new file name or to a different directory. That prevents accidental overwriting of a customized form if you decide to reinstall forms from the Construction Forms & Contracts disk. To save a file to a new name, hold the Alt key down while typing the letter F. Then press the ↓ key until the highlight is on Rename.

Press Enter and type the new file name in the *Enter filename* dialog box.

```
Enter filename: C:\FORMBOOK\COSTBOK1.TXT
```

Press Enter and SEDIT saves your form under the new file name.

VDE (Visual Display Edit) for DOS

VDE is a popular shareware editing program. It's available at no cost from CompuServe and from many computer bulletin boards including the Contractor's Bulletin Board (319-242-0060). See instructions on page 421. It's also available from Eric Meyer, 3541 Smuggler Way, Boulder, CO 80303. If you use VDE, install forms from the file ASCII.ZIP on the Construction Forms & Contracts disk. The installation procedure is explained in the section "Installation Instructions" beginning on page 333.

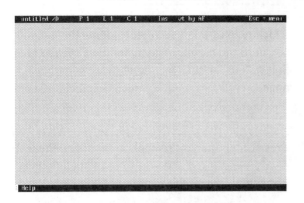

◀ Type VDE to begin using the program. VDE displays the editing screen.

◀ Press and hold the Ctrl key while typing the letter K. Release both keys. Then type the letter L. VDE requests the location and name of the file you want to open.

◀ Type the drive letter, a colon, a backslash and the file name, such as c:\formbook*.txt.

untitled /D	P 1	L 1	C 1	Ins	vt hj AF	^KL
D:\EDITOR\VDE>dir	c:\formbook*.txt					(3504 k free)
ACCREPO .TXT	ACCTADJ .TXT	BIDFORM .TXT	BIDLOG .TXT	CASHCHAN.TXT
CASHPAID.TXT	CHANGEOR.TXT	CHANGETR.TXT	CHANGLOG.TXT	CHANGORD.TXT
COMPEVAL.TXT	COMSUPQ .TXT	CONTINU1.TXT	CONTINU2.TXT	CONTSTAT.TXT
CONTTRAN.TXT	COSTBOOK.TXT	COSTDATA.TXT	COSTPLSF.TXT	COSTPLSP.TXT
CSI-EST .TXT	CUSTSURV.TXT	DAILYCON.TXT	DAILYEQ1.TXT	DAILYMAT.TXT
DAILYWOR.TXT	DEFNOTIC.TXT	DELAYNOT.TXT	DRIVEREC.TXT	EMERGTEL.TXT
EMPDATA .TXT	EMPEVAL .TXT	EMPLOYTC.TXT	EMPLTIME.TXT	EQUPLEDG.TXT
ESTCHECK.TXT	ESTRECAP.TXT	EXPENSE .TXT	FAXCHANG.TXT	FAXCOVER.TXT
FAXEDPO .TXT	FAXQUOTE.TXT	FHACOST .TXT	FIELDCHA.TXT	FIELDDIR.TXT
FIELDPRO.TXT	FINALPAY.TXT	FINALPRO.TXT	FINISCHD.TXT	FIRSTCON.TXT
FIXFEEPR.TXT	HISTPROJ.TXT	HOURRATE.TXT	INTEROFF.TXT	JOBCOSTR.TXT
JOBINFO .TXT	JOBINV .TXT	JOBPROG .TXT	JOBSITE .TXT	JOBSURV .TXT
LETRFOLD.TXT	MATLREQ .TXT	MATLSCHD.TXT	MATLWAIV.TXT	MEMDELAY.TXT
MEMO .TXT	NONRESP .TXT	OFFDIR .TXT	OVERHEAD.TXT	PASTDUE .TXT
PAYSUM .TXT	PERCOMP .TXT	PLANLOG .TXT	POTBAKNO.TXT	PRELIM .TXT
PRIMCONT.TXT	PROBIL1 .TXT	PROBIL2 .TXT	PROCLOSE.TXT	PROCURE .TXT
PROF&LOS.TXT	PROJACCT.TXT	PROJCLOS.TXT	PROJMAN .TXT	PROPOSE .TXT
PROSTART.TXT	PURCHASE.TXT	QUANTITY.TXT	QUESTCOV.TXT	QUOTE .TXT
REJECT .TXT	REMPROP .TXT	SAFEAGRE.TXT	SAFETY .TXT	SCHEDULE.TXT
SPECSEL .TXT	SPEKCHAN.TXT	STATCONT.TXT	STATMENT.TXT	SUBCONTA.TXT
SUBCONTC.TXT	SUBINS .TXT	SUBPOLIC.TXT	SUBWORK .TXT	SUMESTIM.TXT
↕← A-Z\ →	[Enter] new			/ mode	

◀ Press Enter and all the forms you installed with a .TXT file type appear in alphabetical order.

WORK .TXT SUI

/N mode

◀ Press the ←, ↑, → or ↓ key to move the blinking underline until it's under the first letter of the name of the form you want to load. Then press the forward slash (/) key. That positions the cursor at the bottom of the screen near the word mode. Type the letter N so VDE is in non-document mode.

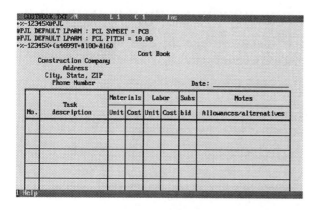

● ●

◀ Press Enter to open the form and VDE displays it on your screen.

If you selected either a laser (H-P compatible) printer or a dot matrix (Epson compatible) printer when installing the forms, the top four lines of all forms will be printer control codes. These codes are instructions to your printer and will not appear in the printed forms. Printer codes select:

☑ Printing in either portrait (upright) or landscape (sideways) style, and

☑ Line spacing, symbol set, typeface, and pitch.

The instruction manual for your printer has more information on control codes for your printer. As long as you use the same printer, the control codes on your forms should not be changed. You may not be able to print landscape style forms with some dot matrix printers.

Making Changes with VDE

You can change letters and numbers (text) anywhere on the construction forms by typing over. Note that typing over any vertical or horizontal line will remove that line. When making changes, be sure insert mode is off. If you see the letters Ins near the top center of the screen, insert mode is on. Press the Ins key to leave insert mode.

Drawing Lines with VDE

There may be times when you need to change the location of vertical or horizontal lines on a form or even add new lines. Your keyboard doesn't show any keys that will make lines and boxes. But it's possible to make lines and boxes using the extended ASCII character set. With a form open on the VDE screen, try this:

● ●

◀ Use the ←, ↑, → or ↓ key to move the cursor to where you want to draw a box. Press and hold the Alt key while typing the letter G. Release both keys. A dialog box appears with a chart of line graphics characters.

◄ Type the letter or number beside the character you want to use. The character you selected is placed in your form.

Save a Revised Form to a New File Name

When you customize a form by making changes, it's a good idea to save the revised form to a new file name or to a different directory. That prevents accidental overwriting of a customized form if you decide to reinstall forms from the Construction Forms & Contracts disk. To save a file to a new name, hold Ctrl key down while you type the letter K. Release both keys. Type the letter E. VDE prompts you for the path and file name for the new file.

```
COSTBOOK.TXT /N          L 6    C 58
Rename work:
```

Type the new file name, such as c:\formbook\costbok1.txt. Then press Enter.

```
COSTBOOK.TXT /N          L 6    C 58
Rename work: c:\formbook\costbok1.txt
```

Reinstalling Construction Forms & Contracts

Occasionally you may customize a contract or form and then decide you like the original document better. It's easy to reinstall any single contract or form on the Construction Forms & Contracts disk. See the section "Selecting Individual Forms for Installation" on page 336.

Word 6 for Windows and Word for Windows 2.0

Install forms from the file WORD4WIN.ZIP on the Construction Forms & Contracts disk. The installation procedure is explained in the section "Installation Instructions" beginning on page 333.

Begin Word 6 or Word for Windows 2.0 and click on File.

Click on Open.

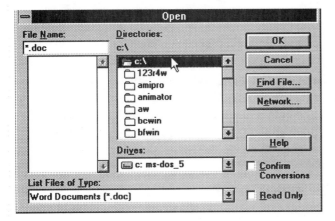

◄ Notice the mouse cursor in the illustration at the left. Double click on C:\.

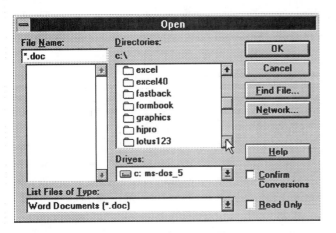

◄ Click and hold the down arrow until you see the directory formbook.

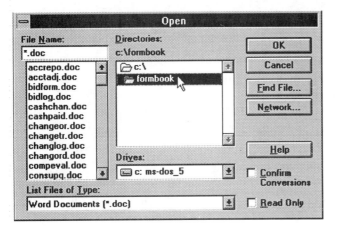

◄ Double click on formbook. Notice that all the forms you installed with a .DOC file type appear in the box at the left.

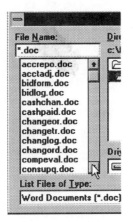

◀ To scroll down the list of file names, click and hold the mouse cursor on the down arrow at the lower right of the *File Name* box. See the mouse cursor in the illustration at the left. Form names are listed in alphabetical order.

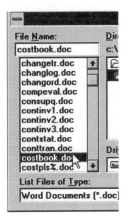

◀ Then double click on the name of the form you want to use.

Word 6 will open the file selected and display it on your screen.

Changing the Type Style

When opening a form, your computer will try to select a type font that's appropriate for your printer. But the font selected depends on the printer you use and type fonts installed with Windows. If some headings are too wide for a column or if type spills off the page, change to another type style or size. Here's how:

☑ With the construction form displayed on screen, hold the Ctrl key down and type A. That selects the entire document.

☑ Click on Format

☑ Click on Font

☑ Click on the type font you prefer

☑ Click on the size font you prefer

☑ Click on OK

Changing the Margins

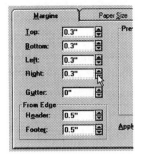

Some construction forms may not fit on one page when printed with some printers. If part of a form spills over onto a second page, try resetting the margins:

- ☑ Click on File

- ☑ Click on Page Setup

- ☑ Click on Margins

- ☑ Reduce the top, bottom, left and right margins to the minimum your printer can handle. That's about 0.3" (three tenths of an inch) on most laser printers.

- ☑ Click on OK when done

If that doesn't solve the problem, try reducing the form length by deleting a line or reducing the form width by making one column a little narrower.

Saving in Word 6

Construction Forms & Contracts are Word for Windows 2.0 documents. When saving the form back to disk in Word 6, you'll want to save as a Word document.

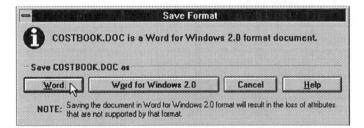

Save a Revised Form to a New File Name

When you customize a form by making changes, it's a good idea to save the revised form to a new file name or to a different directory. That prevents accidental overwriting of a customized form if you decide to reinstall forms from the Construction Forms & Contracts disk.

Reinstalling Construction Forms & Contracts

Occasionally you may customize a form and then decide you like the original form better. It's easy to reinstall any single form on the Construction Forms & Contracts disk. See "Selecting Individual Forms for Installation" on page 336.

■ WordPerfect 5.1 for DOS

Install forms from the file WORDPERF.ZIP on the Construction Forms & Contracts disk. The installation procedure is explained in the section "Installation Instructions" beginning on page 333.

◄ Begin WordPerfect 5.1. Press the F5 key and you'll be prompted for a directory and filename to open.

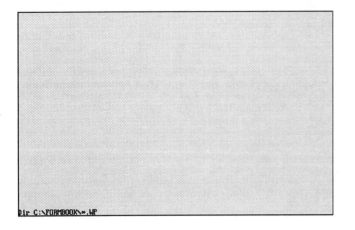

◄ Type, for example, C:\FORMBOOK*.WP to change to the formbook directory. Press Enter to see a list of construction forms in WordPerfect format. Notice that form names are listed in alphabetical order.

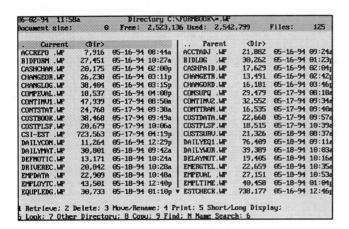

◄ Use the ←,↑,→ or ↓ key to move the highlight to the form you want to open.

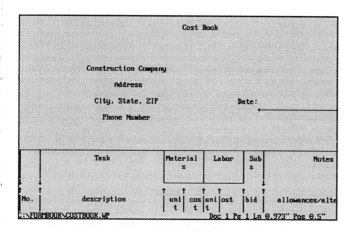

▶ Type number 1 to display the form on your screen.

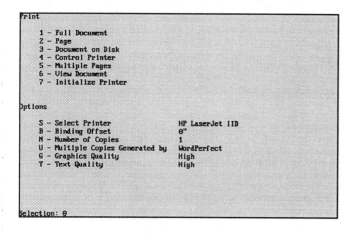

▶ WordPerfect 5.1 for DOS doesn't show documents exactly the way they will be printed. But here's a way to see a more accurate preview. Hold the Shift key down and tap F7 to display the *Print* menu.

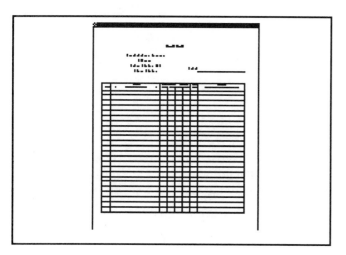

▶ Type number 6 and WordPerfect will display a more accurate representation of the form.

Press F1 to exit preview and return to the Print menu. Type number 1 to print the form or press F7 to resume editing.

Construction Forms & Contracts are WordPerfect tables. Unless you're an expert WordPerfect user, you'll probably have trouble making anything more than simple changes to any form. But you should be able to change a few words, change the type style and reset the margins without too much trouble.

Changing the Type Style

The type style WordPerfect uses depends on the printer you've installed. If type is too wide for some columns, change to a smaller size or a different style. Begin by selecting the words you want to change.

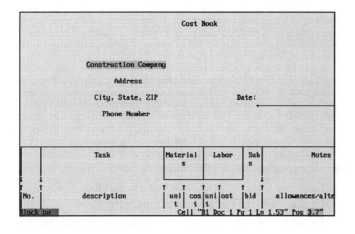

◀ Use the ←,↑,→ or ↓ key to move the cursor under the first letter of the first word you want to change. Press F12 (or hold Alt down while pressing F4). WordPerfect blinks "Block on" at the lower left corner of the screen. Use the ←,↑,→ or ↓ key to move the cursor to just after the last word you want to change. In the illustrations, the words Construction Company are selected.

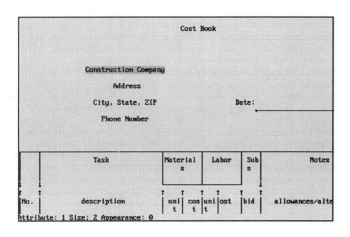

◀ Hold the Ctrl key down and press F8. Notice the words at the bottom left of the screen. To change the size of the words selected, type number 1. To change the appearance of the words selected, type number 2. Be sure to press F12 again to leave block mode.

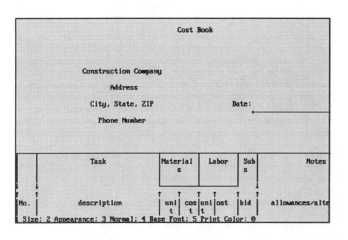

◀ To change to a different font, move the cursor to the beginning of the text you want to change. Hold the Ctrl key down and press F8.

```
Base Font

  Courier 10cpi
  Courier 10cpi (Legal)
  Courier 10cpi Bold
  Courier 10cpi Bold (Legal)
  Courier 10cpi Italic
  Courier 10cpi Italic (Legal)
* Courier 12cpi
  Courier 12cpi (Legal)
  Courier 12cpi Bold
  Courier 12cpi Bold (Legal)
  Courier 12cpi Italic
  Courier 12cpi Italic (Legal)
  Line Printer 16.67cpi
  Line Printer 16.67cpi (Legal)




 Select; N Name search: 1
```

◀ Type number 4 to see a list of fonts available.

```
Base Font

* Courier 10cpi
  Courier 10cpi (Legal)
  Courier 10cpi Bold
  Courier 10cpi Bold (Legal)
  Courier 10cpi Italic
  Courier 10cpi Italic (Legal)
  Courier 12cpi
  Courier 12cpi (Legal)
  Courier 12cpi Bold
  Courier 12cpi Bold (Legal)
  Courier 12cpi Italic
  Courier 12cpi Italic (Legal)
  Line Printer 16.67cpi
  Line Printer 16.67cpi (Legal)




 Select; N Name search: 1
```

◀ Use the ↑ or ↓ key to move the highlight to the font of your choice.

Type number 1 to select that font. The font change remains in effect until WordPerfect encounters another font code. Press the F11 key or hold Alt down and press F3 to reveal the font codes.

Changing the Margins

Some construction forms may not fit on one page when printed with some printers. If part of a form spills over onto a second page, try resetting the margins. Here's how:

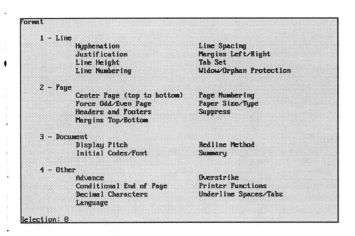

◀ Hold the Shift key down and type F8 to see the *Format* menu.

```
Format: Line

  1 - Hyphenation                No

  2 - Hyphenation Zone - Left    10%
                        Right    4%

  3 - Justification              Full

  4 - Line Height                Auto

  5 - Line Numbering             No

  6 - Line Spacing               1

  7 - Margins - Left             0.5"
                Right            0.5"

  8 - Tab Set                    Rel: 0", every 0.5"

  9 - Widow/Orphan Protection    No


Selection: 0
```

◀ Type number 1 to see the *Format: Line* options menu.

```
Format: Line

  1 - Hyphenation                No

  2 - Hyphenation Zone - Left    10%
                        Right    4%

  3 - Justification              Full

  4 - Line Height                Auto

  5 - Line Numbering             No

  6 - Line Spacing               1

  7 - Margins - Left             0.3"
                Right            0.31"

  8 - Tab Set                    Rel: 0", every 0.5"

  9 - Widow/Orphan Protection    No


Selection: 0
```

◀ Type number 7 and adjust the margins to the minimum your printer can handle. That's about 0.3" (three tenths of an inch) on most laser printers. Press Enter when you're satisfied with the changes.

```
Format: Page

  1 - Center Page (top to bottom)   No

  2 - Force Odd/Even Page

  3 - Headers                       HA Every page

  4 - Footers

  5 - Margins - Top                 0.5"
                Bottom              0.5"

  6 - Page Numbering

  7 - Paper Size                    8.5" x 11"
      Type                          Standard

  8 - Suppress (this page only)


Selection: 0
```

◀ Then press Enter again until the Format menu appears. To change the top and bottom margins, type number 2. The *Format: Page* menu appears.

```
Format: Page

  1 - Center Page (top to bottom)   No

  2 - Force Odd/Even Page

  3 - Headers                       HA Every page

  4 - Footers

  5 - Margins - Top                 0.3"
                Bottom              0.3"

  6 - Page Numbering

  7 - Paper Size                    8.5" x 11"
      Type                          Standard

  8 - Suppress (this page only)


Selection: 0
```

◀ Type number 5 to change the top and bottom margins. Again, the minimum margin for most laser printers is 0.3" (three tenths of an inch). Press Enter twice to resume editing.

Saving in WordPerfect 5.1 for DOS

When you customize a form by making changes, it's a good idea to save the revised form to a new file name or to a different directory. That prevents accidental overwriting of a customized form if you decide to reinstall forms from the Construction Forms & Contracts disk.

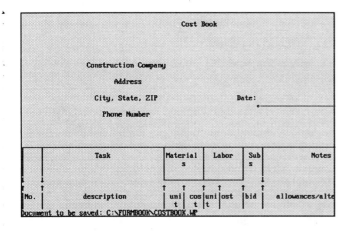

◀ To save a revised form to a new file name, press F10. At the lower left corner of the screen, you're prompted to type the directory and new file name.

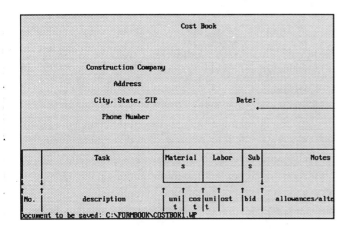

◀ Type, for example, C:\FORMBOOK\COST-BOK1.WP and press Enter. WordPerfect 5.1 saves your customized form to the new file name.

Reinstalling Construction Forms & Contracts

Occasionally you may customize a contract or form and then decide you like the original document better. It's easy to reinstall any single form or contract from the Construction Forms & Contracts disk. See "Selecting Individual Forms for Installation" on page 336.

WordPerfect 5.2 for OS/2

Install forms from the file WORDPERF.ZIP on the Construction Forms & Contracts disk. The installation procedure is explained in the section "Installation Instructions" beginning on page 333.

Begin WordPerfect 5.2 for OS/2.

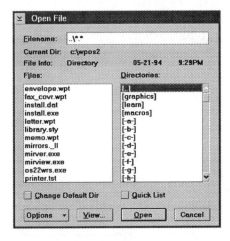

◀ Press the F4 key to see the *Open File* dialog box. Double click on the double dots (..) in the *Directories* box.

◀ Click and hold the down arrow on the lower right corner of the *Directories* box until you see the directory [formbook].

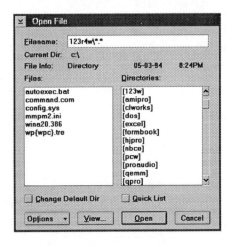

◀ Double click on [formbook].

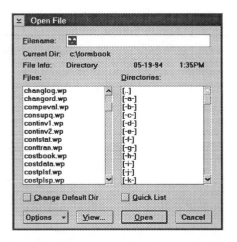

◀ Notice that all the forms you installed in the formbook directory appear in the *Files* box. To scroll down the list of file names, click and hold the mouse cursor on the down arrow at the lower right of the *Files* box. See the illustration at the left. Form names are listed in alphabetical order.

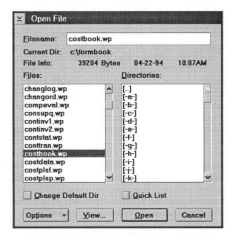

◀ Double click on the name of the form you want to use.

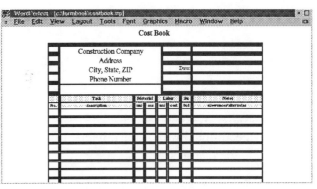

◀ WordPerfect 5.2 for OS/2 opens the form and displays it on your screen.

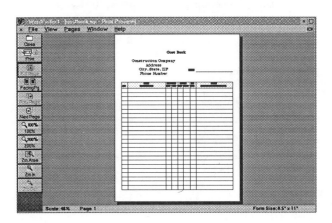

◀ To see a preview of the form, hold the Shift key down while pressing F5. The entire page is displayed on your screen.

To return to editing view, click on the Close button in the upper left corner of the screen.

Changing the Type Style

When opening a form, your computer will try to select a type font that's appropriate for your printer. But the font selected depends on the printer you use and the type fonts installed with OS/2. If some headings are too wide for a column or if type spills off the page, change to another type style or size. Here's how:

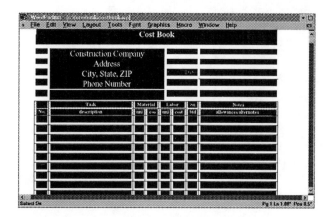

◄ With the construction form displayed on screen, hold both the Ctrl and Shift keys down while pressing the End key. That selects the entire document.

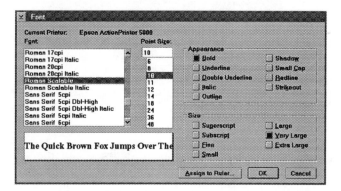

◄ Press F9 to open the *Font* dialog box.

Click on the up or down arrow on the right side of the *Font* box until you see the font you prefer. Then click on that font. Next, click on the font size you prefer in the *Point Size* box. When the font and size are correct, click on OK at the lower right of the screen.

Changing the Margins

Some construction forms may not fit on one page when printed with some printers. If part of a form spills over onto a second page, try resetting the margins.

Hold the Ctrl key down while pressing the F8 key. Release both keys to display the *Margins* dialog box. Click in the Left Margins box and change that margin to the minimum your printer can handle. That's about 0.300" (three tenths of an inch) on most laser printers. Repeat this step for each of the three remaining margins. When finished, click on OK.

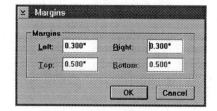

If that doesn't solve the problem, try reducing the form length by deleting a line or reducing the form width by making one column a little narrower.

Saving in WordPerfect 5.2 for OS/2

Construction Forms & Contracts are in WordPerfect 5.1 for DOS format. You'll probably want to save customized forms in WordPerfect 5.1/5.2 for OS/2 format. Begin by pressing the F3 key to open the *Save As* dialog box. Type, for example, COSTBOK1.WP and click on Save. WordPerfect 5.2 for OS/2 will save the form under the new file name and return to the editing screen.

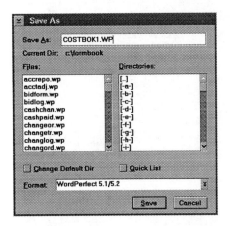

Save a Revised Form to a New File Name

When you customize a form by making changes, it's a good idea to save the revised form to a new file name or to a different directory. That prevents accidental overwriting of a customized form if you decide to reinstall forms from the Construction Forms & Contracts disk.

Reinstalling Construction Forms & Contracts

Occasionally you may customize a contract or form and then decide you like the original document better. It's easy to reinstall any single contract or form on the Construction Forms & Contracts disk. See "Selecting Individual Forms for Installation" on page 336.

◾ WordPerfect 6.0 for DOS

Install forms from the file WORDPERF.ZIP on the Construction Forms & Contracts disk. The installation procedure is explained in the section "Installation Instructions" beginning on page 333.

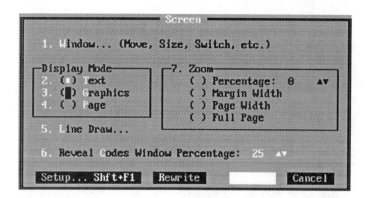

◀ Begin WordPerfect 6.0 for DOS. Be sure the display mode is set to graphics: Hold the Ctrl key down and press F3. At the *Screen* dialog box, type 3 to change the display mode to Graphics.

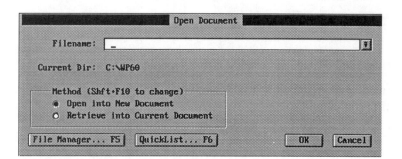

◀ Hold the Shift key down and press F10 to display the *Open Document* dialog box. WordPerfect asks for the file name you want to open.

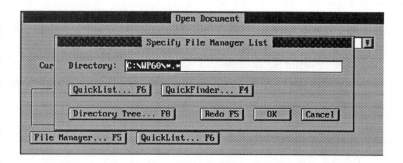

◀ Press F5 and the *Specify File Manager List* dialog box appears.

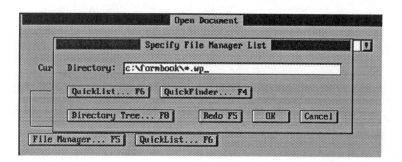

◀ Type the drive letter, directory and file type, such as C:\FORMBOOK*.WP in the *Directory* box.

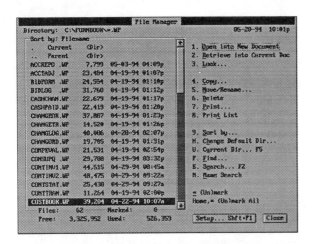

▶ Press Enter. All the forms you installed with a .WP file type appear under the *Sort by: Filename* box at the left. Form names are listed in alphabetical order. Move the highlight down the list of file names with the ↓ key until it's on the name of the form you want to open.

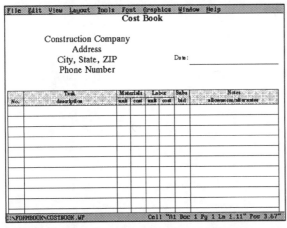

▶ Press Enter and the form you selected is displayed on the screen.

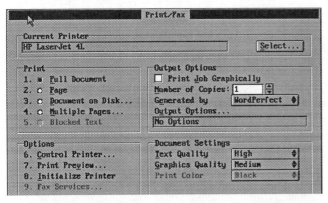

▶ To see a preview of the form, hold the Shift key down while you press F7. The *Print/Fax* dialog box appears.

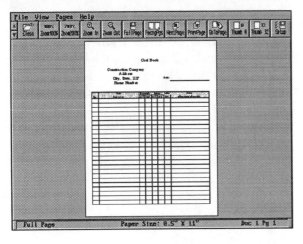

▶ Type the number 7 to see a preview of the entire form.

To exit Preview mode, press Esc twice.

Changing the Type Style

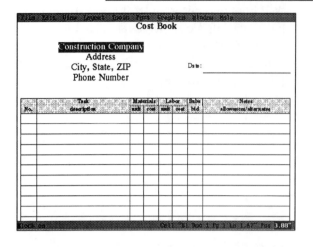

◀ The type size and style used on the Construction Forms and Contracts disk may not be a good choice for your printer. If the type doesn't look right or if type spills off the page, change to a style and size that's better for your printer. With the construction form displayed on screen, position your cursor just before the words you want to change. Press F12. Use the ←,↑,→ or ↓ keys to highlight type you want to change.

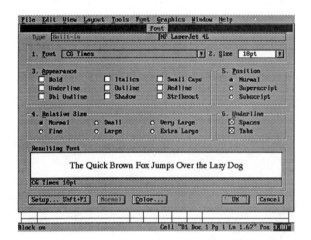

◀ To change the type selected, hold the Ctrl key down while pressing F8. The *Font* dialog box appears.

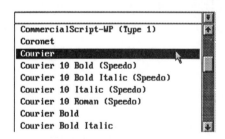

◀ Type the number 1. The Font list box drops down. Use the ↑ or ↓ key to move the highlight to the font you prefer. To select the font that's highlighted, press Enter.

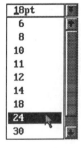

◀ Type the number 2 and press the ↓ key to open the Size list box. Use the ↑ or ↓ key to move the highlight to the font size you prefer.

Press Enter twice when you're satisfied with the type style and size. Only type selected on your form will be changed to the new size and style.

Changing the Margins

Some construction forms may not fit on one page when printed with some printers. If part of a form spills over onto a second page, try resetting the margins:

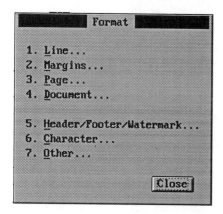

◄ Hold the Shift key down while pressing F8. Release both keys. The *Format* dialog box appears.

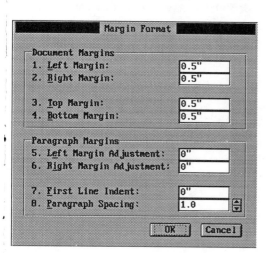

◄ Type the number 2. The *Margin Format* dialog box appears.

Adjust document margins to the minimum your printer can handle. That's about 0.3" (three tenths of an inch) on most laser printers. Press Enter three times to accept the changes and resume editing. If that doesn't solve the problem, try reducing the form length by deleting a line or reducing the form width by making one column a little narrower.

Saving in WordPerfect 6.0 for DOS

Construction Forms & Contracts are in WordPerfect 5.1 for DOS format. The first time you open each form, WordPerfect 6.0 for DOS automatically converts the document to 6.0 format. To save the form to disk, press F10. The *Save Format* dialog box appears.

Press Enter twice to open the *Save Document* dialog box.

Type in c:\formbook\costbok1.wp and press Enter.

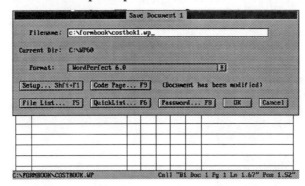

Click on OK to save the form in WordPerfect 6.0 for DOS format.

Save a Revised Form to a New File Name

When you customize a form by making changes, it's a good idea to save the revised form to a new file name or to a different directory. That prevents accidental overwriting of a customized form if you decide to reinstall forms from the Construction Forms & Contracts disk.

Reinstalling Construction Forms & Contracts

Occasionally you may customize a contract or form and then decide you like the original document better. It's easy to reinstall any single contract or form on the Construction Forms & Contracts disk. See "Selecting Individual Forms for Installation" on page 336.

WordPerfect 6.0 for Windows

Install forms from the file WORDPERF.ZIP on the Construction Forms & Contracts disk. The installation procedure is explained in the section "Installation Instructions" beginning on page 333.

Begin WordPerfect 6.0 for Windows

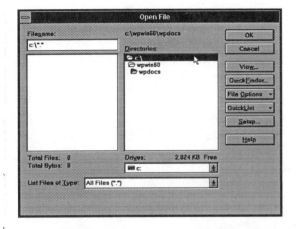

◀ Hold the Ctrl key down while typing the letter O to see the *Open File* dialog box. Double click on C:\ in the *Directories* box.

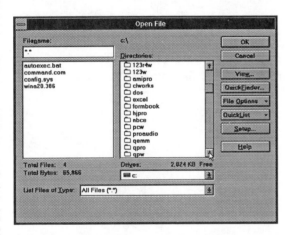

◀ Click and hold the down arrow on the lower right corner of the *Directories* box until you see the directory formbook.

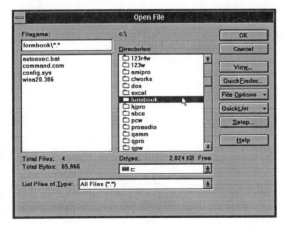

◀ Double click on formbook.

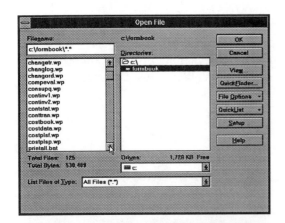

◀ Notice that all the forms you installed with a .WP file type appear in the *Filename* box at the left of the screen. To scroll down the list of file names, click and hold the mouse cursor on the down arrow at the lower right corner of the *Filename* box. See the mouse cursor in the illustration. Form names are listed in alphabetical order.

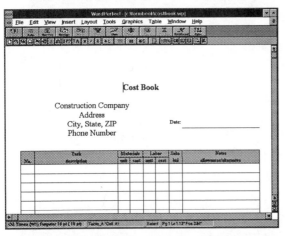

◀ Double click on the name of the form you want to use.

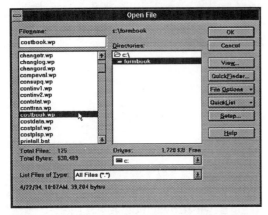

◀ The form is converted to WordPerfect 6.0 for Windows format and then displayed on the screen.

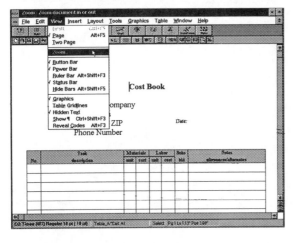

◀ To see a preview of the complete form, click on View. Then click on Zoom.

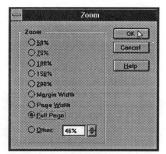

◀ Click on Full Page and OK.

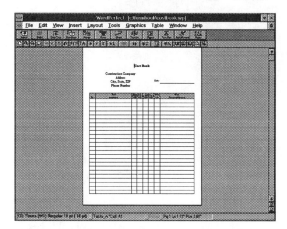

◀ WordPerfect 6.0 displays the entire form on your screen.

Changing the Type Style

Construction Forms & Contracts for WordPerfect are in WordPerfect 5.1 for DOS format. WordPerfect 5.1 does not use True Type fonts. Computers that use Windows usually use True Type fonts. Your computer will try to select a type font that's appropriate for the construction forms and contracts. But the font selected depends on the printer you use and type fonts you've installed with Windows. If some headings are too wide for a column or if type spills off the page, it's easy to change to another type style or size: With the construction form displayed on the screen, hold both the Ctrl key and the Shift key down while pressing the End key. That selects the entire document. Then press the F9 key to open the *Font* dialog box.

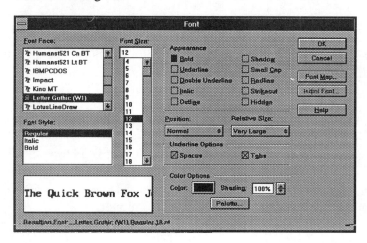

Click and hold the mouse cursor on the up or down arrow on the right side of the *Font Face* box until you see the face you prefer. Times New Roman is usually a good choice. Click on the font face you prefer. Then click on a smaller font size (such as 9 or 10) in the *Font Size* box. Finally, click on OK to confirm your choice.

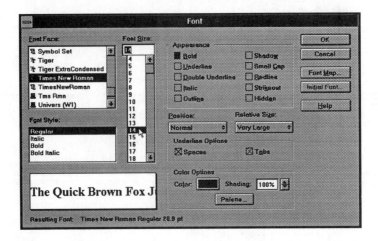

Changing the Margins

Some construction forms may not fit on one page when printed with some printers. If part of a form spills over onto a second page, try resetting the margins: Hold the Ctrl key down while pressing the F8 key. Release both keys and the *Margins* dialog box will open. Click on the up or down arrow on the right side of each of the top, bottom, left and right margin boxes to adjust margins to the minimum your printer can handle. That's about 0.300" (three tenths of an inch) on most laser printers. Then click on OK to confirm your selection.

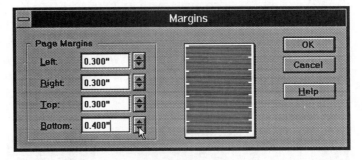

If that doesn't solve the problem, try reducing the form length by deleting a line or reducing the form width by making one column a little narrower.

Saving in WordPerfect 6.0 for Windows

Construction Forms & Contracts are in WordPerfect 5.1 for DOS format. When you open a form with WordPerfect 6.0 for Windows, the form is automatically converted to WordPerfect 6.0 format. Any time you save a form to disk, accept WordPerfect's recommendation that the form be saved in WordPerfect 6.0 format.

Save a Revised Form to a New File Name

When you customize a form by making changes, it's a good idea to save the revised form to a new file name or to a different directory. That prevents accidental overwriting of a customized form if you decide to reinstall forms from the Construction Forms & Contracts disk. To save to a new file name, press the F3 key. That opens the *Save As* dialog box.

Change the name slightly before saving. For example, click in the *Filename* box and change COSTBOOK.WP to COSTBOK1.WP. Then click on OK.

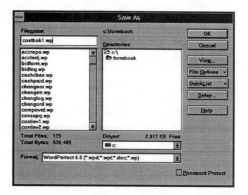

Reinstalling Construction Forms & Contracts

Occasionally you may customize a contract or form and then decide you like the original document better. It's easy to reinstall any single contract or form on the Construction Forms & Contracts disk. See "Selecting Individual Forms for Installation" on page 336.

Install forms from the file ASCII.ZIP on the Construction Forms & Contracts disk. The installation procedure is explained in the section "Installation Instructions" beginning on page 333.

Begin WordStar 2000 and the Opening Menu appears.

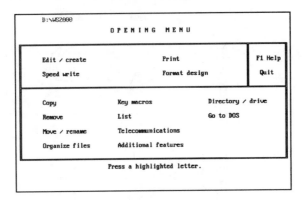

Set Up for Printing ASCII Files

If you've already set up a WordStar 2000 printer definition file (.PDF) to print pure ASCII files with embedded printer codes, you can skip this section. These steps have to be followed only once.

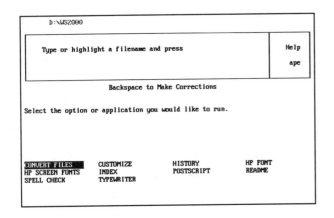

◀ Type the letter A and the *Additional Features* menu appears.

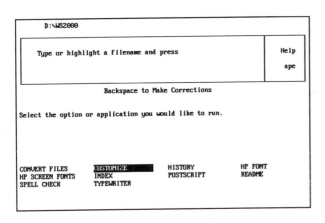

◀ Press the → key once to highlight Customize.

```
For WordStar 2000 to run correctly, a path must be set so the
program knows where to look for its files.  The installation
program can add a path statement to your AUTOEXEC.BAT file now.

If you don't want the installation program to add a path statement
to your AUTOEXEC.BAT file, you'll need to set a path yourself after
you've completed this installation.




Reminder: Re-boot your computer when you've completed the installation.

Do you want a PATH statement added to your AUTOEXEC.BAT file (Y/N)?
```

◀ Press Enter. You are asked if you want to add a path to WordStar 2000 in your AUTOEXEC.BAT file. Type the letter N.

```
                    Main Menu

              Install a printer
              Modify printer settings
              Change editing default settings
              Select a monitor
              Add a feature
              Remove a feature
              Quit and save changes




 Directions:  Move the highlighting to the selection you want
 and press ←┘. Use the ↑ and ↓ keys or type the first few
 letters of the selection to move the highlighting.
Esc = quit
```

◀ The *Main Menu* appears.

```
           Printer Database Selection Menu

             HP lasers and compatibles
             Other laser printers
             Non-laser printers
             Extra database




 Directions:  Move the highlighting to the selection you want
 and press ←┘. Use the ↑ and ↓ keys or type the first few
 letters of the selection to move the highlighting.
Esc = Main Menu
```

◀ Press Enter to select Install a Printer. The *Printer Database Selection Menu* appears.

```
           Printer Database Selection Menu

             HP lasers and compatibles
             Other laser printers
             Non-laser printers
             Extra database




 Directions:  Move the highlighting to the selection you want
 and press ←┘. Use the ↑ and ↓ keys or type the first few
 letters of the selection to move the highlighting.
Esc = Main Menu
```

◀ Press the ↓ or ↑ key to move the highlight to the Non-laser printers option.

```
Please put the printer data disk containing WS2PRM3.PDB
into a drive.

If you are using 5.25" floppy disks, use the disk labelled
        Printer Data 3

OR If you are using 3.5" floppy disks, use the disk labelled
        Advanced Page Preview & Printer Data 3

Please enter the letter of that drive.
```

◀ Press Enter. You are now prompted to insert the Printer Data disk that came with WordStar 2000. Insert that disk in your floppy disk drive, but do not press Enter! Just type the drive letter, such as "C."

```
                Printer Selection Menu  ( 1 of 18 )

 ** ASCII (to disk)             AT&T 455
 ** ASCII (to disk with backspace)  AT&T 470/471/475/476
 ** Backspacing Standard        AT&T 473
 ** Nonbackspacing Standard     =AT&T 478/479
 =Abati LQ-20                    Binder BP120 S (ECS)
 Alps P2000                      Binder BP300 (ECS)
 Amdek (daisywheel models)      =Blue Chip BCD-4015 Handytype 1
 AMT Office Printer (AMT mode)   Brother 2024L (DP mode)
 AMT Office Printer (Diablo mode) Brother 2024L (WP mode)
 =Anadex DP-6500                 Brother HR-10/15/25/35
 Anadex DP-9000/9500            Brother HR-20 ECS
 Anadex WP-6000 (Diablo mode)   Brother M-1109/1509/1709 (Epson)

 Printers are listed in alphabetical order by manufacturer.

  Directions:  Move the highlighting to the selection you want
  and press ←┘. Use the ↑ and ↓ keys or type the first few
  letters of the selection to move the highlighting.
 Esc = Main Menu            PgUp/PgDn = move between menus
```

◀ The *Printer Selection Menu* appears. Press Enter.

```
                Printer Selection Menu  ( 1 of 18 )

 ** ASCII (to disk)             AT&T 455
 ** ASCII (to disk with backspace)  AT&T 470/471/475/476
 ** Backspacing Standard        AT&T 473
 ** Nonbackspacing Standard     =AT&T 478/479
 =Abati LQ-20                    Binder BP120 S (ECS)
 Alps P2000                      Binder BP300 (ECS)
 Amdek (daisywheel models)      =Blue Chip BCD-4015 Handytype 1
 AMT Office Printer (AMT mode)   Brother 2024L (DP mode)
 AMT Office Printer (Diablo mode) Brother 2024L (WP mode)
 =Anadex DP-6500                 Brother HR-10/15/25/35
 Anadex DP-9000/9500            Brother HR-20 ECS
 Anadex WP-6000 (Diablo mode)   Brother M-1109/1509/1709 (Epson)

 Printers are listed in alphabetical order by manufacturer.


 You have selected: ** ASCII (to disk)
 Is this correct?  (Y/N)
```

◀ WordStar 2000 will ask for confirmation of your selection. You should have selected ** ASCII (to disk). Type the letter Y if this is correct.

```
                Installed Printer Menu  ( 1 of  1 )

 PRINTER
 Create a new printer file







 The printers you have installed are listed on this menu.

  Directions:  Move the highlighting to the selection you want
  and press ←┘. Use the ↑ and ↓ keys or type the first few
  letters of the selection to move the highlighting.
 Esc = Main Menu            PgUp/PgDn = move between menus
```

◀ The *Installed Printer Menu* appears.

```
                Installed Printer Menu  ( 1 of  1 )

 PRINTER
 Create a new printer file







 The printers you have installed are listed on this menu.

  Directions:  Move the highlighting to the selection you want
  and press ←┘. Use the ↑ and ↓ keys or type the first few
  letters of the selection to move the highlighting.
 Esc = Main Menu            PgUp/PgDn = move between menus
```

◀ Press the ↓ or ↑ key to move the highlight to the "Create a new printer file" option.

```
                Create a new printer description file

Printer you have selected:  ** ASCII (to disk).

WordStar 2000 keeps information about your printer in a file
called a "printer description file."  You need to name the
printer description file for the printer you just selected.

If you have only one printer, you can name this file PRINTER.
If you have more than one printer, type a descriptive filename
(up to eight characters) for the printer you just selected.  (For
example, DIABL620).



   Directions:  Press ↵ to name your file PRINTER.  If you want
   a different name, type the name then press ↵
```

◀ Press Enter. The *Create a new printer description file* screen appears.

```
                Create a new printer description file

Printer you have selected:  ** ASCII (to disk).

WordStar 2000 keeps information about your printer in a file
called a "printer description file."  You need to name the
printer description file for the printer you just selected.

If you have only one printer, you can name this file PRINTER.
If you have more than one printer, type a descriptive filename
(up to eight characters) for the printer you just selected.  (For
example, DIABL620).



   Directions:  Press ↵ to name your file PRINTER.  If you want
   a different name, type the name then press ↵ CFORMS
```

◀ Type the name you want to give to this printer file, such as CFORMS. Remember this name and select it when you want to print construction forms and contracts.

```
                Create a new printer description file

Printer you have selected:  ** ASCII (to disk).

WordStar 2000 keeps information about your printer in a file
called a "printer description file."  You need to name the
printer description file for the printer you just selected.

If you have only one printer, you can name this file PRINTER.
If you have more than one printer, type a descriptive filename
(up to eight characters) for the printer you just selected.  (For
example, DIABL620).


 You have selected: CFORMS
 Is this correct?  (Y/N)
```

◀ Press Enter. Confirm the name you typed. Type Y to confirm your choice.

```
                        Character Table Selection

A character translation table is used to map onscreen characters
to printed characters.  For example, the onscreen character "ç"
is created by combining "C" and ",".  Some printers have more
than one table that you can choose or modify.

Do you want to choose or modify a character translation table (Y/N)?






   Directions:  Type Y to change your current table.
                Type N to skip.
```

◀ The *Character Table Selection* screen appears. Type the letter N.

```
                    Main Menu
             Install a printer
             Modify printer settings
             Change editing default settings
             Select a monitor
             Add a feature
             Remove a feature
             Quit and save changes



 Directions:  Move the highlighting to the selection you want
 and press ←┘. Use the ↑ and ↓ keys or type the first few
 letters of the selection to move the highlighting.
 Esc = quit
```

◀ The *Main Menu* appears.

```
                    Main Menu

             Install a printer
             Modify printer settings
             Change editing default settings
             Select a monitor
             Add a feature
             Remove a feature
             Quit and save changes



 Directions:  Move the highlighting to the selection you want
 and press ←┘. Use the ↑ and ↓ keys or type the first few
 letters of the selection to move the highlighting.
 Esc = quit
```

◀ Press the ↓ or ↑ key to move the highlight to Quit and save changes.

Press Enter to return to the *Opening Menu*.

Loading Forms with WordStar 2000

```
 D:\WS2000                    Disk Space: 18538496
              C H O O S E   A   N A M E

 Type or highlight a filename and press ←┘.      F1 Help

 To locate a filename you've forgotten, press ^L.  Escape

             Backspace to Make Corrections

 Document to edit or create?



 2000.BAT       CUSTOM\        DOCUMENT\      FORMATS\
 GRAPHICS\      PREVIEW\       PRINTER\       README.TXT
 TRAINING\      WS2.CFG        WS2000.TBL     WS2HELP.LIB
 WS2HELP.USR    WS2PRN1.PDB    WSAPPS.CFG
```

◀ At the *Opening Menu*, type the letter E. The *Choose a Name* menu appears and prompts you for a path and file name to open.

```
 D:\WS2000                    Disk Space: 18407424
              C H O O S E   A   N A M E

 Type or highlight a filename and press ←┘.      F1 Help

 To locate a filename you've forgotten, press ^L.  Escape

             Backspace to Make Corrections

 Document to edit or create? C:\FORMBOOK



 2000.BAT       CUSTOM\        DOCUMENT\      FORMATS\
 GRAPHICS\      PREVIEW\       PRINTER\       README.TXT
 TRAINING\      WS2.CFG        WS2000.TBL     WS2HELP.LIB
 WS2HELP.USR    WS2PRN1.PDB    WSAPPS.CFG
```

◀ Type the drive letter, a colon, a backslash and the name of the directory, such as C:\FORM-BOOK.

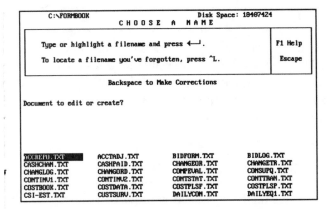

```
C:\FORMBOOK                        Disk Space: 18407424
                    C H O O S E   A   N A M E
┌─────────────────────────────────────────────────┬─────────┐
│ Type or highlight a filename and press ←─┘.       │ F1 Help │
│                                                   │         │
│ To locate a filename you've forgotten, press ^L.  │ Escape  │
└─────────────────────────────────────────────────┴─────────┘
                  Backspace to Make Corrections

Document to edit or create?



ACCREPO.TXT       ACCTADJ.TXT      BIDFORM.TXT      BIDLOG.TXT
CASHCHAN.TXT      CASHPAID.TXT     CHANGEOR.TXT     CHANGETR.TXT
CHANGLOG.TXT      CHANGORD.TXT     COMPEVAL.TXT     CONSUPQ.TXT
CONTINU1.TXT      CONTINU2.TXT     CONTSTAT.TXT     CONTTRAN.TXT
COSTBOOK.TXT      COSTDATA.TXT     COSTPLSF.TXT     COSTPLSP.TXT
CSI-EST.TXT       CUSTSURV.TXT     DAILYCON.TXT     DAILYEQ1.TXT
```

◄ Press Enter. Notice that all the forms you installed with a .TXT file type appear in the Files box. Press the ←,↑,→ or ↓ key until the highlight is on the name of the form you want to open. See the file names toward the bottom of your screen. Form names are listed in alphabetical order.

```
C:\FORMBOOK                        Disk Space: 18407424
                    C H O O S E   A   N A M E
┌─────────────────────────────────────────────────┬─────────┐
│ Type or highlight a filename and press ←─┘.       │ F1 Help │
│                                                   │         │
│ To locate a filename you've forgotten, press ^L.  │ Escape  │
└─────────────────────────────────────────────────┴─────────┘
                  Backspace to Make Corrections

Document to edit or create?



ACCREPO.TXT       ACCTADJ.TXT      BIDFORM.TXT      BIDLOG.TXT
CASHCHAN.TXT      CASHPAID.TXT     CHANGEOR.TXT     CHANGETR.TXT
CHANGLOG.TXT      CHANGORD.TXT     COMPEVAL.TXT     CONSUPQ.TXT
CONTINU1.TXT      CONTINU2.TXT     CONTSTAT.TXT     CONTTRAN.TXT
COSTBOOK.TXT      COSTDATA.TXT     COSTPLSF.TXT     COSTPLSP.TXT
CSI-EST.TXT       CUSTSURV.TXT     DAILYCON.TXT     DAILYEQ1.TXT
```

◄ When the form name you prefer is highlighted, press Enter.

```
      COSTBOOK.TXT  Noformt Ln   1 Col 1          Insert Horiz
├──────▼──1───────▼──2───────▼──3───────▼───────▼─5───────▼──6──▼──7──▼
+%-12345X@PJL
@PJL DEFAULT LPARM : PCL SYMSET = PC8
@PJL DEFAULT LPARM : PCL PITCH = 10.00
+%-12345X+(s4099T+&l00+&l6D
                              COST BOOK
    Construction Company
        Address
     City, State, ZIP
     Phone Number                      Date: _____

┌─────┬────────────┬──────────┬──────────┬──────┬──────────────────────┐
│     │            │ Materials│  Labor   │ Subs │        Notes         │
│     │    Task    ├────┬─────┼────┬─────┼──────┼──────────────────────┤
│ No. │ description│Unit│Cost │Unit│Cost │ bid  │ Allowances/alternatives│
├─────┼────────────┼────┼─────┼────┼─────┼──────┼──────────────────────┤
│     │            │    │     │    │     │      │                      │
├─────┼────────────┼────┼─────┼────┼─────┼──────┼──────────────────────┤
│     │            │    │     │    │     │      │                      │
├─────┼────────────┼────┼─────┼────┼─────┼──────┼──────────────────────┤
│     │            │    │     │    │     │      │                      │
└─────┴────────────┴────┴─────┴────┴─────┴──────┴──────────────────────┘
```

◄ WordStar 2000 loads the form and displays it on your screen.

If you selected either a laser (H-P compatible) or dot matrix (Epson compatible) printer when installing the forms, the top four lines of all forms will be printer control codes. These codes are instructions to your printer and will not appear in the printed forms. Printer codes select:

☑ Printing in either portrait (upright) or landscape (sideways) style, and

☑ Line spacing, symbol set, typeface and pitch.

The instruction manual for your printer has more information on control codes for your printer. As long as you use the same printer, the control codes on your forms should not be changed. Many dot matrix printers will not be able to print in landscape style.

Printing Forms with WordStar 2000

When printing forms, WordStar 2000 will ask if you want to "Print using standard defaults? (Y/N/Esc)." Type the letter N. WordStar 2000 will then ask how you want the forms printed. Press Enter in response to all questions except the question, "Obey page formatting commands? (Y/N)." Type the letter N in response to that question. That instructs your printer to obey the printer formatting commands (rather than print them).

Changing Forms in WordStar 2000

You can change letters and numbers (text) anywhere on the construction forms by typing over. First, be sure you're in overtype mode (not insert mode). If you see the word Insert at the top of your screen, press the Ins key once. That should switch to overtype mode. You'll see the word Over at the top of the screen. Note that typing over any vertical or horizontal line will remove that line.

Drawing Lines with WordStar 2000

There may be times when you need to change the location of vertical or horizontal lines on a form or even add new lines. Your keyboard doesn't show any keys that will make lines and boxes. But it's possible to make lines and boxes using the extended ASCII character set. With a construction form open on your screen, try this:

Press the ←,↑,→ or ↓ key to move the cursor to where you want to start drawing the upper left corner of a box. Press the Num Lock key to turn Num Lock on. Then hold the Alt key down while typing the number 213 on the numeric keypad at the right of you keyboard. Release the Alt key and you'll see an upper left box corner. Use the same procedure to create any symbol shown in the ASCII Conversion Chart on page 374.

Save a Revised Form to a New File Name

When you customize a form by making changes, it's a good idea to save the revised form to a new file name or to a different directory. That prevents accidental overwriting of a customized form if you decide to reinstall forms from the Construction Forms & Contracts disk.

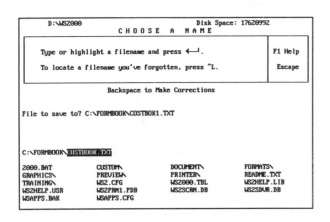

To save a file to a new name, press and hold the Ctrl key while you type the letter Q. Then type the letter N. The *Choose a Name* menu appears.

To save a form to the new name COSTBOK1, for example, type C:\FORMBOOK\COSTBOK1.TXT.

Then press Enter. WordStar 2000 saves your form to the new file name.

The Contractor's Computer Bulletin Board System (BBS)

Several editing programs mentioned in this manual are available at no charge on the Contractor's BBS. This BBS has many other programs of particular interest to professionals in the construction industry. To use Contractor's BBS, you'll need a computer running Windows with 600 K free on a hard drive, a modem and a connection to a phone line. There's no charge for using most of the information on this bulletin board. The pages that follow explain how to connect with the Contractor's BBS (usually called logging on) and how to copy programs from the Contractor's BBS to your computer (usually called downloading).

If You Have a Favorite Communications Program

Just set your modem for 8 data bits, 1 stop bit and no parity. Then have your modem dial 1-319-242-0060. Contractor's BBS supports the following speeds: 1200, 2400, 9600, 14400, 16800, 19200. Skip to the section Using Contractor's BBS on page 423 once your modem has made the connection.

If You've Never Used a Modem Program

Try clicking on the Terminal icon in Program Manager. Terminal is a communications program that was placed in the Accessories group when Windows was installed on your computer. The following instructions assume you are using Terminal, but the same principles apply no matter which communications program you're using. Begin by starting Windows. Open your Accessories group and double click on the Terminal icon, as shown at the left.

If you don't see any error message, skip to "Set the Communication Parameters" on the next page. If there's a conflict between communication ports (COM ports), Windows will ask you to select another port.

You'll see the Terminal-Error message when another program or device is already using the COM port Terminal is trying to use. For example, your mouse may be using COM1 when Terminal tries to use COM1. Fortunately, it's easy to select another COM port. Start by clicking on OK to clear the warning off your screen.

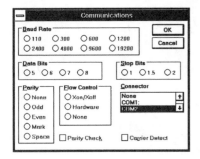

Windows will display the Communications dialog box so you can assign a different COM port to Terminal. Notice the options under Connector at the lower right of the Communications dialog box.

The COM port your modem uses is probably selected with a jumper or switch on the modem itself. Communication programs can't determine which COM port your modem is set for, so you have to help. Either:

1. Reset the modem to the COM port Terminal is trying to use, or

2. Have Terminal try a different COM port.

If You Decide to Reset the Modem . . .

Most modems use COM1 or COM2 and have a dip switch or jumper that changes the COM port. The user's manual for your modem will explain how set the switch or move the jumper to select another COM port.

If You Want Terminal to Try Another COM Port . . .

If you know which COM port your modem is set for, select that COM port in the Connector box. If you don't know which COM port your modem is set for, try each of the four options to see which one works. The COM port Terminal is trying to use will be highlighted in the Connector box. For example, if COM1 is selected, try selecting COM2. If the highlight is on COM2, try COM1. Then click on OK. If you don't see the Terminal - Error warning, you've probably selected the right COM port.

Set the Communications Parameters

Once you've got the correct COM port, set the communications parameters. Click on Settings. Then click on Communications. The correct settings for Contractor's BBS are:

Baud Rate   The speed of your modem

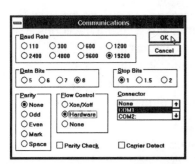

Data Bits   8

Stop Bits   1

Parity   None

Flow Control XON/XOFF for modems slower than 14,400. Set to Hardware for 14,400+

Click on OK when finished making changes. Your cursor should be flashing in the upper left corner of the Terminal window. Type ATZ and press Enter to reset your modem. If your screen displays OK, the modem is working.

If you don't see OK, Terminal is not communicating with your modem. Make sure your modem is turned on. Internal modems (the type installed inside your computer) are always on when your computer is on. But external modems have to be connected to an external power source and turned on.

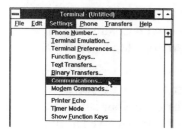

If you still don't see OK, check the COM port again. Click on Settings. Then click on Communications and try a different COM port.

If the modem still isn't working correctly, you may have a conflict with the COM port's interrupt (IRQ) address. The remedy for this problem is beyond the scope of this book. Try calling the tech support number of the manufacturer of your modem.

Dialing Contractor's BBS

If you got the OK message and are using a touch tone line, type:

atdt13192420060

Then press Enter.

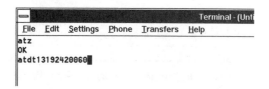

If you normally dial 9 to get an outside line, try dialing:

atdt9,,13192420060

Then press Enter. Each of the two commas provides a one-second delay in the dialing sequence.

If you don't have a touch tone phone line, type:

atdp13192420060

Then press Enter.

After pressing Enter, you'll probably hear the modem dialing (if the volume setting on your modem speaker isn't set too low).

Using Contractor's BBS

When you see CONNECT, you've connected with Contractor's BBS. Press Enter and Excalibur (the communications program Contractor's BBS uses) will request information about the communications protocols available on your computer. The choices are:

XMODEM

1k XMODEM

YMODEM

ZMODEM

ABORT

Press the key that matches the first letter of your protocol (X, 1, Y, Z, or A). The best choice is ZMODEM. If you're using the program Terminal that comes with Windows, you have no choice. Only XMODEM CRC works, so you have to type an X. When you've made the choice, press Enter.

Next, Contractor's BBS will send the Excalibur communications program to the hard disk of your computer. In the future, you'll use Excalibur to connect with Contractor's BBS. Excalibur includes an icon that can be installed on the Windows Program Manager.

Instruct your communications program to receive the Excalibur file and write it to disk. In Terminal, click on Transfer. Then click on Receive Binary. Then type the file name EXCALTRM.EXE. Press Enter. This file requires about 600,000 bytes on your hard disk. Your communications program will probably display a summary of bytes received as the file is downloaded.

Time required to receive this file depends on the modem you're using and the quality of the phone line. At 2400 baud, expect a transfer time of about 45 minutes using YMODEM or ZMODEM protocols. At 14,400 baud, transmission takes about 7 minutes with ZMODEM.

When transmission is complete, end the communications session. In Terminal, click on File. Then click on Exit.

Installing Excalibur

EXCALTRM.EXE has to be installed under Windows. Start Windows and go to the Program Manager. Click on File. Then click on Run.

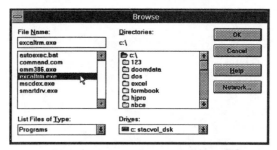

In the Run dialog box, click on Browse.

In the Browse dialog box, locate the file EXCALTRM.EXE. It's probably in the directory where your modem program is installed. If you used Terminal to download the file, you'll probably find EXCALTRM.EXE in the directory C:\WINDOWS.

When you've found the file, double click on EXCALTRM.EXE.

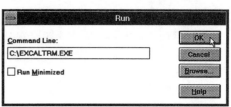

The Browse dialog closes and the Run dialog box reopens. Click on OK.

In the Excalibur Loader dialog box, type the drive letter and path name where you want Excalibur installed. C:\WINDOWS\EXCALIBUR is recommended. Then click on Install.

Next, instruct Excalibur *not* to create a program group by clicking on No. Installation continues until you see the Notice dialog box.

Click on OK and you'll see a READ.ME file with the latest information about Excalibur. Click on File. Then click on Exit to close the READ.ME file.

Creating a New Excalibur Icon

When Excalibur is installed, an icon is created in whatever program group is active on your Program Manager. Go to Program Manager and click on the Excalibur icon. Click on File. Click on Properties. Click on Change Icon and you'll see the Excalibur sword and thunderbolt icon. Click on that icon. Click on OK. Click on OK again and the sword and thunderbolt icon should appear as the Excalibur icon in Program Manager. Double click on that icon to begin Excalibur.

Setting Preferences

The first time you use Excalibur, you'll be reminded to begin by setting preferences. Click on OK. Fill in the blanks in the User Information dialog box. Press Tab to move from box to box. Leave blank any boxes that don't apply. When complete, click on OK.

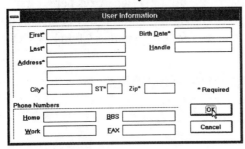

To add Contractor's BBS to the dial directory, click on System. Then click on Dialing Dir...

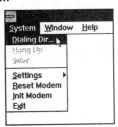

In the Dialing Directory dialog box, click on New Entry.

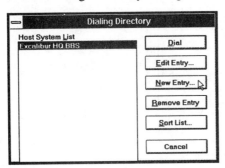

In the Edit Directory Entry dialog box, fill in information needed to call Contractor's BBS. Press Tab to move from box to box. For example, type Contractor's BBS. Press Tab. Type 1-319-242-0060. Press Tab. Press Tab again to skip entering a second phone number. Type your first and last name. Then type the password you want to use when calling Contractor's BBS. This password can be any sequence of letters or numbers, but make it unique – don't use the same password you use on other computer bulletin boards. Enter the password here so you don't have to type the password every time you log on to Contractor's BBS.

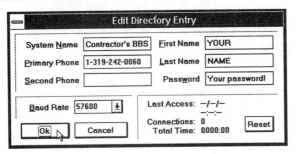

When you're finished making entries in the Edit Directory Entry dialog box, double click on the minus sign at the upper left corner of the box.

Click on System once again. Click on Settings. Then click on Modem to open the Modem Setup and Defaults dialog box. Most of the information in this box will look like Greek to you. But don't worry. You'll use only two boxes here. First, click on the down arrow button to the right of the Comm Port box to display the COM ports available. Click on the COM port your modem is set for, usually either COM1 or COM2. Next, click on Modems.

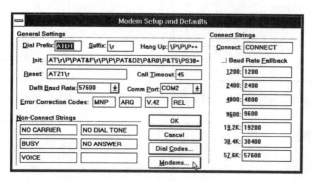

In the Modem Settings dialog box, click on the up or down arrow button to scroll through the list of available modem configurations. Your modem is probably on this list. If not, try one of the Hayes settings. A little experimentation may be needed to find the right modem setting. Then click on OK.

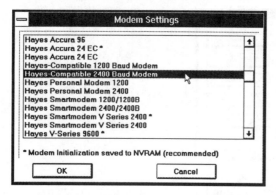

Click on System again. Click on Settings. Then click on Preferences to see the default Upload and Download directories. The Download directory is where you'll find files downloaded from Contractor's BBS. The directory you specify must already exist. If it doesn't exist, create it with File Manager. When finished, click on OK.

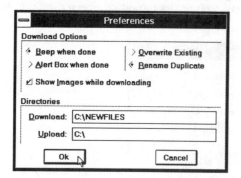

Making Connection with Excalibur

Now, try using Excalibur. If Excalibur isn't running already, click on the Excalibur icon in the Windows Program Manager. Click on the System option. Then click on the Dialing Dir option. In the Dialing Directory dialog box, click on Contractor's BBS. Then click on Dial.

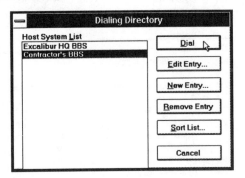

If your settings are correct, your modem should begin dialing. Excalibur will display commands sent to the modem and responses received from the modem.

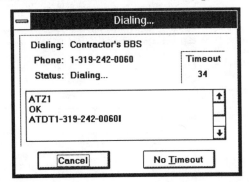

Upon connection, you'll be asked to confirm that you're a new user. Excalibur will display a few rules and ask for your compliance. Indicate that you plan to comply. Then click on the Craftsman button to begin exploring Contractor's BBS. Note that you're welcome to leave messages for other BBS users or ask for assistance. Whether you call to download files, to get the latest revisions, or just to satisfy your curiosity, we hope you can make good use of Contractor's BBS.

Online Assistance (Paging the SysOp)

Unfortunately, the SysOp (System Operator) is rarely available for chatting. If you have a request or comment, leave an E-Mail message for the SysOp. The reply will probably be waiting the next time you log on.

Sound Card Compatibility

If you have a sound card installed in your computer and have installed a Windows sound driver, consider downloading the sound file library EXCALWAV.ZIP to your Windows directory. Install the .WAV (Windows audio files) in your Windows directory. The next time you log onto Contractor's BBS, you'll hear both instructions and comments. Sound files on Contractor's BBS are revised from time to time.

Index

Other Practical References

Basic Engineering for Builders

If you've ever been stumped by an engineering problem on the job, yet wanted to avoid the expense of hiring a qualified engineer, you should have this book. Here you'll find engineering principles explained in non-technical language and practical methods for applying them on the job. With the help of this book you'll be able to understand engineering functions in the plans and how to meet the requirements, how to get permits issued without the help of an engineer, and anticipate requirements for concrete, steel, wood and masonry. See why you sometimes have to hire an engineer and what you can undertake yourself: surveying, concrete, lumber loads and stresses, steel, masonry, plumbing, and HVAC systems. This book is designed to help the builder save money by understanding engineering principles that you can incorporate into the jobs you bid. **400 pages, 8½ x 11, $34.00**

Drafting House Plans

Here you'll find step-by-step instructions for drawing a complete set of home plans for a one-story house, an addition to an existing house, or a remodeling project. This book shows how to visualize spatial relationships, use architectural scales and symbols, sketch preliminary drawings, develop detailed floor plans and exterior elevations, and prepare a final plot plan. It even includes code-approved joist and rafter spans and how to make sure that drawings meet code requirements. **192 pages, 8½ x 11, $27.50**

How to Succeed With Your Own Construction Business

Everything you need to start your own construction business: setting up the paperwork, finding the work, advertising, using contracts, dealing with lenders, estimating, scheduling, finding and keeping good employees, keeping the books, and coping with success. If you're considering starting your own construction business, all the knowledge, tips, and blank forms you need are here. **336 pages, 8½ x 11, $24.25**

Residential Steel Framing Guide

Steel is stronger and lighter than wood — straight walls are guaranteed — steel framing will not wrap, shrink, split, swell, bow, or rot. Here you'll find full page schematics and details that show how steel is connected in just about all residential framing work. You won't find lengthy explanations here on how to run your business, or even how to do the work. What you will find are over 150 easy-to-ready full-page details on how to construct steel-framed floors, roofs, interior and exterior walls, bridging, blocking, and reinforcing for all residential construction. Also includes recommended fasteners and their applications, and fastening schedules for attaching every type of steel framing member to steel as well as wood. **170 pages, 8½ x 11, $38.80**

Managing the Small Construction Business

You can lead a crew of carpenters, but can you run a business? This book lets 50 successful builders tell you how to negotiate contracts, estimate and schedule jobs, keep accurate accounts, and manage relationships with employees, subs, and most of all, customers. You'll find the information you need on: bidding strategies, unit pricing, contract clauses, preconstruction meetings, bookkeeping basics, quality control, computers, overhead & markup, managing subs, scheduling systems, cost-plus contracts, personnel policies, pricing small jobs, insurance repair, and conflict resolution. **243 pages, 8½ x 11, 27.95**

Construction Estimating Reference Data

Provides the 300 most useful manhour tables for practically every item of construction. Labor requirements are listed for sitework, concrete work, masonry, steel, carpentry, thermal and moisture protection, door and windows, finishes, mechanical and electrical. Each section details the work being estimated and gives appropriate crew size and equipment needed. Includes an electronic version of the book on computer disk with a stand-alone *Windows* estimating program FREE on a 3½" disk. **432 pages, 8½ x 11, $39.50**

Roof Framing

Shows how to frame any type of roof in common use today, even if you've never framed a roof before. Includes using a pocket calculator to figure any common, hip, valley, or jack rafter length in seconds. Over 400 illustrations cover every measurement and every cut on each type of roof: gable, hip, Dutch, Tudor, gambrel, shed, gazebo, and more. **480 pages, 5½ x 8½, $22.00**

Builder's Guide to Room Additions

How to tackle problems that are unique to additions, such as requirements for basement conversions, reinforcing ceiling joists for second-story conversions, handling problems in attic conversions, what's required for footings, foundations, and slabs, how to design the best bathroom for the space, and much more. Besides actual construction methods, you'll also find help in designing, planning and estimating your room-addition jobs. **352 pages, 8½ x 11, $27.25**

Rough Framing Carpentry

If you'd like to make good money working outdoors as a framer, this is the book for you. Here you'll find shortcuts to laying out studs; speed cutting blocks, trimmers and plates by eye; quickly building and blocking rake walls; installing ceiling backing, ceiling joists, and truss joists; cutting and assembling hip trusses and California fills; arches and drop ceilings — all with production line procedures that save you time and help you make more money. Over 100 on-the-job photos of how to do it right and what can go wrong. **304 pages, 8½ x 11, $26.50**

Project Survey Forms

Use these forms for walk-throughs with the homeowner so that every item is checked off as being included or excluded in your bid. These forms can save you hours of time and help prevent mistakes and misunderstandings. **100 forms, 11 x 25, $35.00**

Craftsman's Illustrated Dictionary of Construction Terms

Almost everything you could possibly want to know about any word or technique in construction. Hundreds of up-to-date construction terms, materials, drawings and pictures with detailed, illustrated articles describing equipment and methods. Terms and techniques are explained or illustrated in vivid detail. Use this valuable reference to check spelling, find clear, concise definitions of construction terms used on plans and construction documents, or learn about little-known tools, equipment, tests and methods used in the building industry. It's all here. **416 pages, 8½ x 11, $36.00**

Roofing Construction & Estimating

Installation, repair and estimating for nearly every type of roof covering available today in residential and commercial structures: asphalt shingles, roll roofing, wood shingles and shakes, clay tile, slate, metal, built-up, and elastomeric. Covers sheathing and underlayment techniques, as well as secrets for installing leakproof valleys. Many estimating tips help you minimize waste, as well as insure a profit on every job. Troubleshooting techniques help you identify the true source of most leaks. Over 300 large, clear illustrations help you find the answer to just about all your roofing questions. **432 pages, 8½ x 11, $35.00**

CD Estimator

If your computer has *Windows*™ and a CD-ROM drive, CD Estimator puts at your fingertips 85,000 construction costs for new construction, remodeling, renovation & insurance repair, electrical, plumbing, HVAC and painting. You'll also have the National Estimator program — a stand-alone estimating program for *Windows* that *Remodeling* magazine called a "computer wiz." Quarterly cost updates are available at no charge on the Internet. To help you create professional-looking estimates, the disk includes over 40 construction estimating and bidding forms in a format that's perfect for nearly any word processing or spreadsheet program for *Windows*. And to top it off, a 70-minute interactive video teaches you how to use this CD-ROM to estimate construction costs.
CD Estimator is $59.00

National Construction Estimator

Current building costs for residential, commercial, and industrial construction. Estimated prices for every common building material. Manhours, recommended crew, and labor cost for installation. Includes an electronic version of the book on computer disk with a stand-alone *Windows* estimating program FREE on a 3½" disk.
528 pages, 8½ x 11, $37.50. Revised annually

National Repair & Remodeling Estimator

The complete pricing guide for dwelling reconstruction costs. Reliable, specific data you can apply on every repair and remodeling job. Up-to-date material costs and labor figures based on thousands of jobs across the country. Provides recommended crew sizes; average production rates; exact material, equipment, and labor costs; a total unit cost and a total price including overhead and profit. Separate listings for high- and low-volume builders, so prices shown are specific for any size business. Estimating tips specific to repair and remodeling work to make your bids complete, realistic, and profitable. Includes an electronic version of the book on computer disk with a stand-alone *Windows* estimating program FREE on a 3½" disk. **416 pages, 8½ x 11, $38.50. Revised annually**

Building Contractor's Exam Preparation Guide

Passing today's contractor's exams can be a major task. This book shows you how to study, how questions are likely to be worded, and the kinds of choices usually given for answers. Includes sample questions from actual state, county, and city examinations, plus a sample exam to practice on. This book isn't a substitute for the study material that your testing board recommends, but it will help prepare you for the types of questions — and their correct answers — that are likely to appear on the actual exam. Knowing how to answer these questions, as well as what to expect from the exam, can greatly increase your chances of passing.
320 pages, 8½ x 11, $35.00

Unit Price List Forms

Actual unit prices for most areas of remodeling. These forms help you quickly and accurately create a unit price estimate on your jobs.
100 forms, 11 x 17, $35.00

 Craftsman Book Company
6058 Corte del Cedro, P.O. Box 6500
Carlsbad, CA 92018

24 hour order line
1-800-829-8123
Fax (619) 438-0398

Order online
http://www.craftsman-book.com

In A Hurry?
We accept phone orders charged to your
Visa, MasterCard, Discover or American Express

Name _____

Company _____

Address _____

City/State/Zip _____

Total enclosed_____(In California add 7.25% tax)
We pay shipping when your check covers your order in full.

If you prefer, use your
❑Visa ❑MasterCard ❑Discover or ❑American Express

Card#_____

Expiration date_____Initials_____

10-Day Money Back Guarantee

❑34.00 Basic Engineering for Builders
❑27.25 Builder's Guide to Room Additions
❑35.00 Building Contractor's Exam Preparation Guide
❑59.00 CD Estimator
❑39.50 Construction Estimating Reference Data with FREE stand-alone *Windows* estimating program on a 3½" disk.
❑36.00 Craftsman's Illustrated Dictionary of Construction Terms
❑27.50 Drafting House Plans
❑24.25 How to Succeed w/Your Own Construction Business
❑27.95 Managing the Small Construction Business
❑37.50 National Construction Estimator with FREE stand-alone *Windows* estimating program on a 3½" disk
❑38.50 National Repair & Remodeling Estimator with FREE stand-alone *Windows* estimating program on a 3½" disk.
❑35.00 Project Survey Forms
❑38.80 Residential Steel Framing Guide
❑22.00 Roof Framing
❑35.00 Roofing Construction & Estimating
❑26.50 Rough Framing Carpentry
❑35.00 Unit Price Forms
❑39.75 Construction Forms & Contracts with a 3½" disk.
     Add $15.00 if you need ❑Macintosh disks.
❑FREE Full Color Catalog

Tax Deductible: Treasury regulations make these references tax deductible when used in your work. Save the canceled check or charge card statement as your receipt.

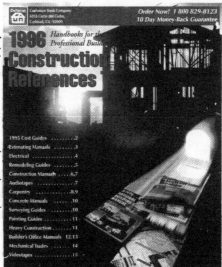

PLEASE
PLACE
STAMP
HERE

Construction Business Computing
PO Box 2050
Richmond, VT 05477